MOTIVES
FOR
METAPHOR

PITTSBURGH SERIES
IN COMPOSITION,
LITERACY, AND
CULTURE

David Bartholomae and
Jean Ferguson Carr, Editors

MOTIVES
FOR
METAPHOR

Literacy, Curriculum Reform,
and the Teaching of English

JAMES E. SEITZ

University of Pittsburgh Press

Published by the University of Pittsburgh Press, Pittsburgh, Pa. 15261
Copyright © 1999, University of Pittsburgh Press
All rights reserved
Manufactured in the United States of America
Printed on acid-free paper
10 9 8 7 6 5 4 3 2 1

A CIP catalog record for this book is available from
the Library of Congress and the British Library.

To the memory of Geoffrey Summerfield

Every true book of criticism may be read
like one of the texts it deals with, as a web
of poetic metaphors.

ITALO CALVINO

CONTENTS

ACKNOWLEDGMENTS

THIS BOOK, like many books, was a long time in the making, and there are numerous people who provided intellectual and emotional sustenance as my project evolved over the years. For their encouragement and perceptive response when I first began to investigate theories of metaphor as a graduate student at New York University, I am indebted to David DeVries, Claire Gleitman, David Hicks, Ron Kasdorf, and James Schiff. These friends made graduate school not merely tolerable but actually enjoyable. I am also grateful to the faculty at Long Island University, Brooklyn, especially Barbara Henning, Seymour Kleinberg, and Deborah Mutnick, whose provocative visions of education gave me much to consider as an impulsive young teacher in a complicated urban environment.

Many of my colleagues in the English Department at the University of Pittsburgh have contributed to my thinking in recent years, particularly Stephen Carr, Nicholas Coles, William E. Coles, Jr., and Mariolina Salvatori, each of whom has offered invaluable guidance and support. Paul Kameen, who responded both generously and incisively to several versions of this book, helped me to recognize that any conception of metaphor implies a conception of literalism—an insight that led me just where (I now believe) I needed to go. My editors, Jean Ferguson Carr and David Bartholomae, deserve thanks for their careful scrutiny and patient accommodation of a book whose final form retained so little of its initial configuration. I also wish to acknowledge Steve Sutherland, Gwen Gorzelski, and Juli Parrish for their care and good cheer in providing research assistance; Kathy Meyer for her expert assistance in preparing the final manuscript; and *College English* for granting permission to draw upon my article, "Roland Barthes, Reading, and Roleplay: Composition's Misguided Rejection of Fragmentary Texts" (vol. 53, November 1991), for the revised and expanded essay that is now chapter 4.

Special thanks to John Twyning, Judith Summerfield, and Steve Parks for their friendship, acumen, and countless hours of edifying dialogue. As for Geoffrey Summerfield, reader and teacher *par excellence*—no words can express my gratitude.

Finally, this book could not have been written without the forbearance and understanding of my wife, Annette, and "my main man," Kieran. They kept me going, through thick and thin.

MOTIVES
FOR
METAPHOR

PROLOGUE

Metaphor and the English Studies Curriculum

THERE IS A POEM by Wallace Stevens that begins:

> You like it under the trees in autumn,
> Because everything is half dead.
> The wind moves like a cripple among the leaves
> And repeats words without meaning.

What strikes me about these lines—and brings me back to them again and again—is the irony, the near contradiction, of the addressee's enjoyment ("You like it . . .") and the objects of that enjoyment: things that are "half dead"; the wind "like a cripple"; the repetition of "words without meaning." What is it that attracts this person—and perhaps the poet is addressing himself—to such symbols of loss? Why the preference for all that is on its way toward absence?

The poem—entitled, interestingly enough, "The Motive for Metaphor"—continues:

> In the same way, you were happy in spring,
> With the half colors of quarter-things,
> The slightly brighter sky, the melting clouds,
> The single bird, the obscure moon—

The season now changed to spring, the word "half" appears here again, along with a number of other qualifiers—"slightly brighter," "melting," "single," "obscure"—that temper the presence of those images poetry has so often associated with replete, effulgent Nature: sky, clouds, bird, moon. As I imagine Harold Bloom might observe, these opening stanzas can be said to recall and revise those of Keats's in "Ode to a Nightingale":

"Darkling I listen: and, for many a time / I have been half in love with easeful Death."[1] But while Keats's poem speaks from within, and thereby attempts to seize, the fleeting present, Stevens's words look to the past, as if he were writing an elegy for a time not simply dying but now fully dead.

Yet the title of Stevens's poem indicates that he is after something else —not just a Modernist's refiguring of Romantic metaphors for Nature, but the very "motive" that leads to metaphor in the first place. It is toward this motive that Stevens moves in the stanzas that bring the poem to a close:

> The obscure moon lighting an obscure world
> Of things that would never be quite expressed,
> Where you yourself were never quite yourself
> And did not want nor have to be,
>
> Desiring the exhilarations of changes:
> The motive for metaphor, shrinking from
> The weight of primary noon,
> The A B C of being,
>
> The rudder temper, the hammer
> Of red and blue, the hard sound—
> Steel against intimation—the sharp flash,
> The vital, arrogant, fatal, dominant X.

In that final series of images—from the "weight of primary noon" to the "sharp flash"—each item would appear to reflect something fully defined, clear, unambiguous: the sun at its peak, the basic elements of life, the vigor of spirit, the contrast of colors, the solidity of sound, the stab of light. Moreover, the last line of the poem—"The vital, arrogant, fatal, dominant X"—brings to a climax this crescendo of metaphors presented as that which metaphor rejects: whatever can be definitively named ("X") and, as a result, directly apprehended. Such naming is "vital" to human understanding, but it is also "arrogant, fatal, dominant": to ascribe names—to resort to literal language—is to participate in what might be called the *fixing* of knowledge. To apprehend is, after all, both to know and to arrest, to halt the elusive movement of the unknown.

If metaphor represents an impulse that opposes sharp definitions, then the early stanzas of the poem take on new meaning. Perhaps the figure addressed "likes it" in autumn and spring because during these seasons nothing remains the same long enough to be named: all is fluid. What this person desires (and here it seems all the more likely that Stevens is referring to the poet) is not so much personal expression but "the exhilarations of changes"—the thrill of transforming everything that is otherwise frozen by its literal definition. Metaphor, from this perspective, serves not to clarify but to blur; its effect is that of an "obscure moon lighting an obscure world." Hence the paradox of taking pleasure in the "half dead": in a culture that demands you to be exhaustively articulated—to be fully present to self and others—there may be considerable solace in a realm where "you yourself were never quite yourself / And did not want nor have to be." Stevens seems to be telling us that this realm is the space opened by metaphor, which intermingles, even dissolves, what literal language would keep apart.

On the other hand, as a colleague pointed out to me in a response to this interpretation of the poem, Stevens may be saying exactly the opposite. If the person addressed, be it self or other, represents someone the poet intends to rebuke, then the entire poem might be read as a critique of metaphor—a plea, as my colleague put it, "for us to please just say what we mean."[2] From this perspective, the problem with metaphor is that it timidly "shrinks" from the importance of making things clear, and from the responsibilities that attend the effort to do so. Stevens would thus appear to be calling not for more metaphor— more evasion —but for a more committed attempt to provide "the sharp flash" of the literal, of words that convey "The A B C of being."

The value of these contrastive readings comes not so much from one or the other as from holding the two of them in productive tension— the very form of tension I hope to sustain throughout this book. Rather than revere metaphor above all other uses of language, I approach it as an ambiguous discursive phenomenon, one whose powers are as problematic as they are impressive. Indeed, the ambiguity that has long surrounded metaphor makes it an especially useful place to begin to reimagine the teaching of English, for metaphor constitutes a subject that neither those who teach literature nor those who teach composition can claim entirely as their own. At least as far back as Aristotle, who gave it attention both in his *Poetics* and in his *Rhetoric,* metaphor has "belonged" to both fields of study and has held uncertain status within each. In the Western rhetorical tradition, metaphor has generally been treated on the one hand as an invaluable aid to expression and on the other hand as a dangerous trope that, because it sometimes strains to bridge expansive gaps between dissimilar things, should be used with extreme caution. And while literary studies has frequently affirmed Aristotle's proclamation that "the greatest thing by far is to be a master of metaphor" (*Poetics* 255), its association with style rather than substance has led metaphor to be viewed just as often as a mere "tool" for the achievement of something else—a literary image or theme or effect. In other words, metaphor has been characterized by both fields as inescapably important and at the same time necessarily subordinate.

As with most contradictions, this one begs further exploration. While most studies of metaphor begin with, and often never get beyond, questions of definition—what *is* a metaphor in the first place? how do we know one when we see one? in what ways does the metaphorical differ from the literal?—this study begins instead with questions of education: What have a wide range of students, particularly those enrolled in courses offered by English departments at American colleges and universities, been taught to think about metaphor? How, and for what purposes, have they been shown to identify metaphors in the texts they are assigned to read? What have they been asked to do with metaphor in their own writing? I begin with such questions because I am seeking not a definitive solution to the philosophical "problem" posed by metaphor but an understanding of how instruction about figurative language contributes, for better or for worse, to the teaching of reading and writing in post-secondary institutions. I am wondering why, for instance, most students in the composition and literature courses I teach at a large state-related university in the Mideast have only the vaguest (if any) notion how to describe a metaphor, or even how to recognize one, though all will admit to having heard the term since junior high school. I am wondering why even the senior English majors I have encountered in various upper-division seminars still imagine metaphor to occur primarily in poetry and assume that it should be avoided, except for decorative flair, in prose. Beyond these observations from my own teaching, I am wondering why, despite over thirty years of unprecedented academic interest in metaphor—in which time an assortment of philosophers, linguists, literary theorists, anthropologists, and cognitive psychologists have produced thousands of articles and dozens of books devoted to the subject[3]—all of this intellectual activity seems to have made little difference in the classroom, where students should supposedly benefit from such "advances" in scholarship. And finally I am wondering how it might affect these students' habits as readers and writers were they to hold a different conception not only of metaphor but also of literalism, which seems equally misunderstood when considered our primary mode of communication.

With these questions in mind, I devote the initial chapters of this book to an investigation of some of the more prevalent approaches taken to metaphor by the two major (and often competing) pedagogical endeavors within departments of English: the teaching of composition and the teaching of literature. While I later discuss these projects in terms of values they might share and ends they might jointly pursue, I have found it necessary to start by presenting them separately in order to consider the unique, albeit related, ways that metaphor has been conceived and taught by those working on either side of a pervasive institutional division. If I look first to composition, this is meant to reflect no more than a temporal priority: I want to begin where students themselves are most likely to begin—that is, with their course in freshman writing. In my opening chapter, then, I turn to the foremost resources to which students have been turned for lessons about metaphor during their first year in college—namely, to textbooks and handbooks designed for composition courses. After examining the remarkable consistency with which these books have long followed Aristotle's demarcation of not only the benefits but also, and more significantly, the perils of this preeminent trope, I discuss the alternative conceptions of metaphor offered by two well-known literary theorists—I. A. Richards and J. Hillis Miller—who share an interest in the teaching of writing and who each proposes a challenge to the Aristotelian view of figurative language. Since part of my concern with such challenges lies in their implications for pedagogical practice, I conclude chapter 1 by considering the attempt to bring revisionist perspectives on metaphor into the composition class, where they are assumed to be of value to students of writing. As it happens, however, when it comes to metaphor, direct pedagogical applications may prove more elusive than those in search of them would wish. I argue that this is one of the crucial paradoxes with which teachers of composition must contend when they contemplate the lessons of figurative language—for how do we "use" what is always in use even when the users don't know they are using it?

Chapter 2 turns from the composition course to the literature course —in particular, to a course I recently taught to a group of upper-division students who planned on becoming high school teachers of English. Part of what I found challenging about this course stemmed from the students' insistence on taking metaphorically any piece of poetry, fiction, or drama they encountered, as if the whole purpose of reading literature were to solve a puzzle put before them by the text: once the "meaning" of its metaphors had been uncovered, the text could be set aside as "read." I argue that such an approach to reading raises serious questions not only about the teaching of literature but also about the teaching of literacy, which can often seem impoverished rather than enriched by the pervasive search for metaphor. On the other hand, as I demonstrate by comparing my students' reading of a poem by Robert Frost with readings of the same poem by a host of literary scholars, the identification of metaphor serves as one of the primary means by which *any* reading composes itself, since it is only by distinguishing between the metaphorical and the literal that readers can decide which parts of a text call for creative interpretation and which can be said to "speak for themselves." Intriguingly, there appear to be few (if any) rules governing the process of making these distinctions, with scholars disagreeing as much on what constitutes a metaphor in a given text as on how to interpret a metaphor once its presence is located. Here, then, lies another paradox for those who would instruct students in metaphor (or, for that matter, in literature): how are we to demonstrate the constraints of an interpretive process whose initial gesture—the attempt to identify where the metaphors are to be "found" in a text—seems constituted by little more than a leap of faith? Indeed, it may well be beside the point to seek the pedagogical means whereby students would learn to "locate" metaphors in the texts they read, given that the interdependence of the metaphorical and the literal prevents us from ever neatly or neutrally dividing one from the other.

In the second part of the book, I turn from "paradox" to "possibility" —that is to say, I attempt to formulate some of the curricular possibilities teachers of English might pursue in the face of the paradoxes they can recognize but cannot escape. (For the paradoxes of metaphor must be incorporated into the curriculum, not left behind or shut away in the hope that they will somehow disappear.) My first suggestion, discussed in chapter 3, emerges from a reconception of metaphor that begins by sharply distinguishing it from simile. Rather than saying that metaphor and simile are two of a kind, I contend that while simile is a trope of comparison, metaphor is a trope of *equivalence*. Metaphor does not, as even the most reductive handbooks notice, say that this is *like* that; it says that this *is* that. For almost every commentator on the subject, this assertion of equivalence means that the comparison made by metaphor is implied—whereas for me it means that metaphor is not making a comparison in the first place. By *equating* one thing with another, metaphor performs at once the most radical and the most common of rhetorical gestures, one that completely overlooks "keeping things in their proper places." Readers of metaphor are thus asked not simply to discern resemblances between this and that; they are asked to enter a fictional world in which the distinction between this and that no longer obtains. Given that such a move could be either enabling (by breaking down an order that we normally take for granted) or debilitating (by leading people to forget differences that should not be forgotten), I confront the ideological ambiguity of metaphor by proposing that teachers and students investigate what I call the "dialogic metaphor"— that is, the metaphor that manages to retain rather than erase difference in the course of making its equivalence. Or, better stated, teachers and students can *read* metaphor dialogically by keeping difference in mind even as they acknowledge equivalence; instead of merely identifying with the fiction conjured by the metaphor, they can resist the pull of identification in order to extend their "conversation" with the metaphor they have been asked to believe.

Given that works of fiction can themselves be conceived as elaborated metaphors, the pedagogical implications that follow from my concept of the dialogic metaphor concern not only the reading of individual tropes but the reading of whole texts as well. The most resonant fictions, like the most resonant metaphors, are those that paradoxically encourage and yet prevent complete identification with the worlds they evoke. This observation suggests that the recent drive evident in curricular revision toward the inclusion of texts with which students from various backgrounds can "identify" has, in addition to providing necessary attention to issues of diversity, conveniently disregarded crucial problems that attend the act of identification itself. To the extent that identifying with others (be they fictional or actual) requires that these others become a metaphor for oneself, the tendency for perceptions of equivalence to overwhelm perceptions of difference presents a constant challenge to teachers of reading and writing. Metaphor, in other words, offers not the solution to literalism—nor to literacy—but another set of problems. Indeed, it may be that what we need in the English studies curriculum is not simply more texts that speak to different groups of students but more texts that call the process of "speaking to" into question, while at the same time recognizing both its value and its inevitability.

One such text, as I argue in chapter 4, is the text that assumes fragmentary form. In many respects, the fragment could be said to suffer from the same curricular contradictions that accompany metaphor, for students are expected to study and celebrate the fragmentary in certain literary works, and yet nevertheless to avoid the fragmentary altogether in their own work. The fragment, in student writing, represents not a rhetorical maneuver but an error, a sign of illiteracy: most writing assignments, whether in the composition or the literature class, direct students toward the production of unity. In contrast to this practice, I maintain that in order both to broaden and to deepen students' experience with literacy (and not just with literature), teachers of English should ask students to write fragmentary as well as unified texts, each of which can help illuminate, and neither of which exists independent of, the other. Here I return to Roland Barthes, a currently out-of-fashion critic whose many experiments with and deep appreciation of the unpredictable powers of fragmentation demonstrate why teachers of English should reconsider their preoccupation with unity in student writing. Barthes's commitment to the fragment leads him to ideological as well as aesthetic questions, and in his nuanced consideration of "the pleasure of the text" we may find good reason to reject the prevalent notion that teachers must choose between a political and a hedonistic relationship to literature. For Barthes, an exploration of the pleasures of reading and writing is not an abandonment of political concerns but a consequence of them.

Finally, this attention to questions of textual politics and pleasure leads me, in chapter 5, to examine a type of writing assignment that, outside of creative writing classes, has held only a marginal place in the English studies curriculum—namely, the assignment that asks students to write not as themselves but in the guise of another. Often called "role-play" in those few textbooks that make limited use of it, the kind of writing this assignment invites challenges the notion that teachers should encourage students to express "what they really believe" or "how they really feel." Rather than seeking the divulgence of their literal selves (an approach that presumes subjectivity is not only hidden but also stable), role-play assignments urge students to metaphorically invent themselves through the texts they write—and thus to investigate the ways in which they not only compose but are also composed *by* language and its social negotiations. Role-play, in other words, allows students to participate in the making of fictive personae, which in turn helps to illustrate the constructed quality of all discourses, including those that purport to reveal no more than "the facts." As a result of their experiments with alternative roles, students can come to see that every text they write contains a "narrator" of one sort or another, even those that most assiduously attempt to locate themselves in the language of objectivity—an insight that can direct students toward more perceptive reading in addition to more flexible writing.

But as in the case of metaphor itself, assignments based on what might be called the "metaphorization" of the writer bring ideological problems as well as pedagogical promise. While writing in the guise of another may seem rather harmless (or perhaps even frivolous) at first glance, the moment we ask *who* this "other" might be we begin to confront ethical issues that call for extensive and uneasy deliberation. Should students be taught to imagine that they can "become" anyone at all—regardless of race, gender, class, age, experience—simply by writing *as if* that person were themselves? What differences do such equivalences potentially conceal? What colonizations do such appropriations potentially enact? Though students may increase their stylistic fluidity through "taking on" other identities, they may also ignore what they still need to learn, and what they can never fully learn, about those different from themselves. My response to this dilemma is to recommend not that role-play assignments be abandoned as ideologically suspect but that they be redesigned in ways that require students to critique as well as to "inhabit" textual roles—to investigate the values upon which various roles depend and the forms of social interaction they attempt to promote. I argue that students in composition and literature courses should compose not simply "fictions" but *metafictions*—texts in which narrators intrude upon their own stories to comment upon the rhetorical strategies that give (or deny) those stories persuasive power. Turning to a course wherein I asked first-year students to produce a metafictional novella by the end of the semester, I explore the possibilities for teaching literacy—by which I mean teaching an attention to the desires, resonances, and implications of particular acts of language—through a writing project ordinarily reserved for students seeking careers as fiction writers. Playing as it does along the borders of the metaphorical and the literal, metafiction constitutes not simply a chic postmodern game for celebratory or critical review, but a literate *practice* that presents new opportunities, as well as new difficulties, for the English studies curriculum.

It is in just such practices—practices that offer fresh challenges for teachers and students alike—that a revitalized approach to metaphor, literacy, and the teaching of English might be found.

Whatever can be said for or against the arguments described above, it seems reasonable to ask whether the entity I cite in my subtitle—namely, "the teaching of English"—can still be regarded as a cohesive or even coherent endeavor. Just what do I mean by "English" at a time when there seems less and less agreement among teachers themselves about not only the purpose and value of study in the field but also what should count as study to begin with? Is it really even possible to address teachers of English with the expectation that a sizeable number of them hold something in common?

Obviously, I hope that it does remain possible to do so, though I think that the opportunity may soon dissolve if the institutional divisions that have marked the profession since its inception in the late nineteenth century continue to solidify—as I believe they are, despite many well-intentioned pleas for integration over the past two decades. Particularly in the larger universities, departments of English often appear to have split into factional clans that demonstrate little desire to learn from or (at times) even to speak to one another, and the result can be a veritable battleground on which each special interest group vies for whatever forms of institutional power will best ensure its own survival. While descriptions of this internal strife have often focused on the antagonism between teachers of composition and teachers of literature, to imagine the struggle as merely two-sided is to ignore, as David Bartholomae has observed, the frequent presence of those who identify primarily with creative writing, critical theory, cultural studies, women's studies, gay and lesbian studies, film and media studies, or Africana, Latino/Latina, and other ethnic studies—not to mention the serious divisions at work among teachers and scholars "inside" each of these various groups themselves.[4] In short, the political landscape of today's English departments is both complex and intimidating, to the point that attempting to address the teachers within them as a single group is to flirt with potential disaster.

Nevertheless, I believe there may remain at least this one point of convergence: virtually every teacher of college English today, regardless of his or her area of specialization, has surely heard—and is likely to have expressed, if only to nearby colleagues—complaints about the difficulties a high percentage of students display with reading and writing. No doubt complaints of this kind are as old as, or even older than, the discipline itself; yet it can still be instructive to consider the wide range of positions from which they are currently issued. While the outspoken lamentations of cultural conservatives like E. D. Hirsch, Dinesh D'Souza, and William Bennett garner a disproportionate share of public attention, and the nostalgic remedies they propose have been vigorously denounced by those on the academic Left, such figures are hardly alone, at any point on the political spectrum, in their disappointment with students' abilities as readers and writers. Conceptions of literacy do indeed differ in radical and telling ways, and the proclamation of a "crisis" in literacy, as Richard Ohmann and others have done much to illustrate, may well serve as a means to troubling ends in capitalist society[5]—but the sight of English teachers arguing that the majority of their students read and write to their satisfaction is among the rarest of phenomena either in print or at professional gatherings. If there is one thing still shared by those who work in the many corners of English studies, it may be the perception that most students arrive at and proceed through college unprepared to read and write as they should.

Given this pervasive discontent with student performance, discussions of pedagogy generally begin with some version of the question: "What is to be done?" And the answers, however dissimilar, are often perceptive, original, and ambitious. Writing-across-the-curriculum programs, for example, are bringing new approaches to the teaching of writing (which in many respects includes the teaching of reading) to disciplines throughout the academy, including the social and natural sciences. Such programs offer possibilities for reimagining not only the function of writing in the college curriculum but also the range and diversity of those responsible for writing instruction. Contrary to the notion that a single discipline should see to it that students learn to write competently, many schools are now exploring ways in which each discipline can participate in teaching students how to understand as readers, and how to employ as writers, the unique characteristics of its own discourse. A number of English departments, moreover, are beginning to forge extensive connections with community literacy projects, as well as with elementary and secondary school teachers, in order to contribute to and be informed by those with whom college teachers may have more in common than is usually presumed. Thus, from the perspective of faculty commitment to "do something" about the troubles students exhibit with reading and writing, the present would seem in some respects—despite budget cuts and hiring freezes—to be a time of energy and promise.

Yet the emphasis on solutions can have the effect of obscuring the nature of the problem, as teachers are well aware when students express their desire to be told the exact methods by which they can improve their work. With regard to writing, some student will invariably ask: "What should I do so that I write a better paper the next time?" "If I expand on this and cut back on that," another will speculate, "will I end up with a better grade?" Or, in the ubiquitous and more general version of such questions, a student will politely (or not so politely) inquire: "For this assignment, just what is it that you *want?*" Part of what makes these questions so challenging—and at times so annoying, as many a teacher has confessed—are the problematic assumptions that inform them. In asking for the precise steps by which they can create a piece of impressive prose, students seem to ignore or to hold only the slightest awareness of the intricately complex and elusive nature of writing, which never results as text exactly what we imagine it will become before we begin to write. Indeed, what we imagine in advance is usually not very exact in the first place. As so many professional writers, literary theorists, and composition scholars have observed, writing can often be a thoroughly unpredictable, nonlinear, vicarious process perhaps best described as trial-and-error, however undignified the term. Or to alter the metaphor: much of what we learn about writing we learn through the course of the journey itself, not by constructing foolproof road maps that will invariably take us to our destination.

Which is not to suggest that all forms of planning are futile when it comes to writing, nor that teachers have nothing of value to give their students that can help them to compose or revise with a better conception of the work before them. But what many teachers come to recognize —and what makes teacherly advice about writing at times seem almost beside the point—is that despite the endless stream of how-to books that offer strategies for writing everything from screenplays to memoirs, along with countless textbooks that propose various methods for writing in school, the troublesome truth about writing is that instructions for success become more inadequate as the writer's textual objectives become more sophisticated. By the time students reach college (and much earlier than this, I would argue), their teachers simply cannot say to them, without willfully overlooking the lessons that writing repeatedly conveys: Do this, or do that, and your writing will improve. Even if a particular teacher attempts to stabilize the highly unstable notion of "improvement" by qualifying it as improvement *according to her,* to counsel students with specific proposals for change almost never leads to the results envisioned, if only because teacherly suggestions are bound to be carried out in any number of unforeseen ways, some of which have the effect of making a poor piece of writing look all the poorer. "Support your claims with evidence," for instance, can lead to essays so peppered with "examples" that their arguments hardly make an appearance. "Clarify your position and eliminate unnecessary digressions"—to evoke another well-known recommendation—can result in writing so spare that teachers are forced to contradict themselves, turning now to the virtues of "expansion" and "elaboration."

Instructions for effective reading are no less fraught with struggle. Though teachers from all realms of the English department tend to devote a large part of their pedagogical energies to matters of textual analysis, many attest to their frustration with the apparent incapacity of students to read with care even after attentive reading has been repeatedly modeled and discussed in class. Somehow all the work poured into interpretive practices in the classroom only rarely seems to carry over into interpretive practices at home, to the extent that one of the most familiar complaints among faculty not just in the English department but across the university concerns students' troubles with reading "college-level" texts. Again and again, teachers are shaken to discover that what would seem the most fundamental of all competencies possessed by good readers—their ability to summarize the events of a narrative or to discern the gist of an argument—are not to be found among an alarming percentage of their students. How, these teachers ask, can they address issues of real complexity before their students have managed simply to recognize the fact that a narrator is being ironic or that an author is contending against (rather than for) a particular point of view? More importantly, how are they to help their students read more perceptively the next time around? What can be said in class to make a difference? "Now you *really* need to pay attention with this next text . . ."?

My point is not that the problem lies with our students, who are all too often wrongly characterized as obtuse or negligent or unknowledgeable. To the contrary, my contention is that the unrelenting difficulties that confront not only teachers of English but teachers throughout the university stem not primarily from low levels of student performance but from *the discourses through which the acts of writing and reading are generally understood and taught*—especially those discourses that begin from the notion that these acts consist of certain "basic" practices to be learned before more complex endeavors can be undertaken. As our efforts to help students improve their skill in producing an argument or in summarizing the contents of a text reveal, teaching the supposedly "elementary" habits of writing and reading turns out to be not so elementary after all: indeed, it turns out to be remarkably challenging. Even so "simple" a matter as indicating how students might improve the papers they've written or identify the plot of a short story they've read leads us into much murkier waters than we anticipate when we imagine such things as mere stepping-stones on the path to higher ground. Moreover, wise procedures for confronting such ostensibly crude predicaments are in desperately short supply—not because teachers or students have failed to commit themselves to such work but because the very idea that certain components of writing and reading can or should be established as a "base" for more intricate textual activities forecloses pedagogical strategies that might provide altogether different prospects. If first things must always come first, then the last things may never come at all—or only in compromised form.

Now it could certainly be claimed that the conception of literate practices I am describing here has already come in for considerable critique over the past two decades by any number of scholars across composition and literary studies—scholars who have demonstrated both the surprising complexity of student writing presumed to be "basic" and the intractable ambiguities found in the most "ordinary" acts of reading.[6] But as influential as these challenges to developmentalist assumptions have been, I think it nevertheless imperative to observe that the curricula found in most departments of English continue to support a developmental model, which serves not simply as a way of thinking on the part of certain teachers but as the governing structure that organizes the study of writing and reading in today's colleges and universities. Composition studies' war on skills-based instruction may be over twenty years old, but composition courses still remain at the entrance to the curriculum, where they are conceived as primarily suitable for—and designed to meet the needs of—first-year students who lack "preparation" for courses they will encounter further on in their education. Similarly, though critical theorists of various stripes have long commented upon the nuanced and multiple forces that shape any act of reading, the introductory literature course that follows freshman composition continues by and large to be designed as a "prerequisite" to courses that supposedly engage in more serious and strenuous forms of interpretation. Indeed, even when sophisticated matters of theory are presented to students in either of these courses (as they often have been in recent years), such an approach tends to be justified with the notion that students who are given a "foundation" in theoretical issues will do better work once they reach the upper levels of the curriculum.

In this book, I explore the possibilities that emerge when the presumably rudimentary features of literate behavior are reconceived as beyond our reach—that is to say, beyond the capacity of any writer or reader (not just that of students) to bring under secure control. If writing and reading are, as numerous scholars have insisted for the past quarter-century, tenuous, uncertain, indebted acts of imagination, then they are tenuous, uncertain, and indebted through and through: there is no solid ground upon which to stand, not even in the early stages of one's work with presumably "accessible" texts. I say this not in order to reaffirm an overworn poststructuralist credo but to recognize the need for taking our own insights about writing and reading with the seriousness they deserve. It makes little sense to assert that interpretive activity belongs to a tangled personal, social, and cultural web we have hardly begun to understand, and yet to approach the teaching of writing and reading as if they can be "acquired" through the sequenced indulgence in a set of discrete and preliminary practices, one after the other. While almost nobody would still claim that college students should begin with reading and writing sentences, then move to paragraphs, until finally they are introduced to whole texts, there are many who still imagine that students in the first years of study in an English department should be given the "tools" for performing the more complicated tasks they will encounter once they reach upper-division courses. As a result, the teaching of upper-division courses carries a kind of prestige not associated with the teaching of lower-division courses, which any number of teachers surely teach only because they have to. And yet the performance of upper-division students as readers and writers is often no more "advanced" than that of students two, three, or four years behind them. As Keith Hjortshoj has observed of writing in particular: "All experienced writers, including scholars in every field, know that the process of writing remains challenging, complex, and unpredictable—usually messy and frustrating—throughout one's career. . . . Why do we continue to pretend that college freshmen have the most trouble with writing?" (499)

Hjortshoj's question might lead us to wonder what it would mean were the curriculum based not on the assumption that acts of writing and reading come into our possession once and for all, but on the recognition that these acts are endlessly negotiated and discovered anew. What if freshman and sophomore courses were not constructed to "lay the groundwork" for the courses that follow? What if so-called "introductory" courses did not set out to *introduce* anything at all? How might "advanced" undergraduate and graduate courses in English departments be redesigned so as to make virtue of (rather than lament) the necessary attention that must continually be given to supposedly elementary literate practices, such as shaping an argument or composing a summary? In what ways might these practices be connected with those commonly deemed more complicated and demanding? And how might an appreciation of the persistent and irresolvable difficulties inherent in all writing and reading, no matter the "level"—a metaphor we might decide to relinquish altogether—help to reconstitute the relationships between the various and divisive factions to which faculty in English studies currently assign themselves?

These are some of the questions I address in the chapters to come—questions I have found pressing not only as I have observed the entrenched antagonisms that characterize English as a discipline but also as I have attempted to teach the students, be they first-year undergraduates or final-year Ph.D. candidates, I encounter in my own courses. Coupled with an education "in" literature yet a dissertation regarded as "belonging" to composition, my teaching has granted me an insider's —while simultaneously an outsider's—view of both sides of this institutional division, one that I find, as many others have found, generally does both teachers and students more intellectual harm than good. I normally teach four courses per academic year, two of which are designated by the department in which I teach and by the campus course directory as "literature" courses (one introductory and one advanced or graduate level), while the other two are designated as "composition" courses (one freshman and one advanced). I also receive two courses of release time from the department's "three-three" teaching load for research, writing, and administrative or committee work. In other words, my teaching situation is not simply comfortable; it is in many ways ideal, in that I have the privilege of teaching students at various points in their academic careers and from various sites within the departmental curriculum, while at the same time being granted time for other pursuits.

While my liberties as a teacher (particularly as a teacher at least nominally identified with composition) are certainly atypical in the world beyond the major research university, I nevertheless find the courses I teach a useful point of reference for the purposes of this book precisely because of the ways they demonstrate that formidable problems with student reading and writing confront teachers from one end of the English studies curriculum to the other—even those teachers whose jobs are considered enviable. I do not mean to claim that things are everywhere the same—for they most assuredly are not—but I do wish to indicate how misguided it can be to imagine, at a prestigious institution or anywhere else, that the "fundamentals" of reading and writing should be well under control by the end of the freshman year, or by the beginning of the junior year, or, at the very latest, by the time a student graduates from college. Such a vision of the curriculum leads to confusion, dismay, and self-doubt on the part of both teacher and student, who might work together much more productively were they to hold a different understanding of literacy and its ever-present challenges.

My proposal for change, then, begins from the hope that teachers of English might yet find a way to work together toward an alternative approach to the teaching of reading and writing—an approach that a revised conception of metaphor can help us to articulate. What I do not wish to disregard, however, is my impression that the consensus I seek seems now, in the late 1990s, much less likely to be attained than it did a mere ten years ago. Compared to the 1980s, when numerous scholars from "literature" as from "composition" regularly made claims for a vision of English studies dependent upon a thoroughgoing integration of reading and writing, the current decade has witnessed far less attention to the means by which the pervasive barriers between these fields might be eradicated.[7] The annual conventions of both the Modern Language

Association and the Conference on College Composition and Communication, for example, have appeared content of late to give token nods of recognition to "the teaching of writing" (on the part of the former) and to "the teaching of literature" (on the part of the latter)—but a handful of such panels in convention programs composed of hundreds of others only serves to emphasize the apparent absence of shared concern between these organizations. Moreover, as a growing number of graduate programs in composition define themselves through curricula quite distinct from those in literature, the connections between members of these fields may become much more difficult to discern than they were when virtually everyone "in" composition had begun his or her work "in" literature. All of which goes to say that no matter how insightful those theories that have formulated meaningful connections between the teaching of composition and the teaching of literature, theory alone— even when imagined as holding implications for "practice" in individual classrooms—has not been up to the task of establishing an institutional structure in which teachers from both realms could work productively *with* one another rather than in semidetached and hierarchically related spheres.

Yet strangely enough, at the same time that it looks as if composition and literary studies have in many respects continued to move their separate ways, they may now have more pressing reasons for working together than members of either field seem to recognize. The current budgetary crisis in higher education shows no signs of coming to a close, and it is likely that pressures will continue to build on the English department, as on all departments in the humanities, to account in more specific terms for the value of its work with students. Should this supposition prove true, the "high" versus "low" curricular distinction (with literary studies mostly above and composition studies mostly below) examined so perceptively by Susan Miller in *Textual Carnivals* may well haunt departments of English with a vengeance—particularly those departments that have invested heavily in the "high." After all, if administrations, state legislatures, corporations, parents, and students themselves come to demand (as many already do) that a college education primarily provide the "basic skills" imagined necessary for employment, then teaching positions in the upper end of the curriculum will be those deemed most expendable (as some English departments have already discovered).[8] But while this turn of events may initially appear to work in favor of teachers of composition and at the expense of teachers of literature, it will be equally dire for the former, since their association with the "low"—that is, with what anyone can supposedly teach—will enable institutions to fill more and more of these positions with part-time and adjunct faculty. Composition has "risen" enough in recent years that a good many of its programs are now directed by specialists who have emerged from graduate programs in the field—but it would be a grave miscalculation to expect the surge in composition hires to continue much longer, especially if the discipline remains at the entrance to the curriculum, where its "preparatory" function suggests to the rest of the academy a lack of complexity. There are few inside or outside the English department likely to protest, particularly in a time of intense competition for resources, the notion that composition can be taught just as well by a second-tier faculty.

Unfortunately, it is students, not just faculty, who suffer when the teaching of reading and writing are approached as an obligation to be "taken care of" in the first year or two of a postsecondary education. For not only do students *not* put their troubles with writing and reading behind them (since they can do so no more than anyone else can), but those teachers who think that students should "overcome" such difficulties thus find their encounters with student work largely disillusioning or at least disappointing affairs, wherein expectations are seldom fulfilled and advice seems seldom heard. If those of us working in the broad field of English are to reimagine the structure and function of our discipline and the relationships we cultivate with the students who help to compose it, then it may be useful to discuss the possibility of a curriculum, not just a theory, in which writing and reading are valued precisely because of the ways they place their own procedures into doubt. To design such a curriculum—one in which literate practices are conceived as dialogical rather than hierarchical, cyclical rather than progressive—in the face of current political pressures to do the opposite will require more than a little ingenuity and courage. But to miss the opportunity now may be to lose it altogether in the years to come.

one

PARADOX

I

ABERRANT FIGURES

Composition and the "Teaching" of Metaphor

> "The way towards a solution . . . is not by a lucky
> choice of a right answer to the many very difficult
> questions that arise about metaphor. It is rather by a
> more discerning understanding of the reasons which
> make these questions themselves so difficult."
>
> I. A. Richards, *Interpretation in Teaching*

I HAVE OFTEN been struck—particularly during the past academic year, while the English department in which I teach has been engaged in discussions of curricular reform—by the reiterated wish on the part of faculty members that students who enter upper-division courses be able "to know a metaphor when they see one." While other descriptions of student aptitude (an ability to read "closely"; to demonstrate "historical awareness"; to write "cogently"; and so on) have brought to these discussions their more frequent and familiar refrains, it has been intriguing to observe how often, both in public and private conversations, various enumerations of a teacherly desire concerning metaphor have appeared: "If my students could *simply* identify a figure of speech . . ."; "If I could know that *at least* my students have been told what a metaphor is . . ."; "If these students *just* had a sense of the difference between the metaphorical and the literal . . . ," and so on. Though the aura of fashion that surrounded new theories of metaphor in English studies ten or fifteen years ago has all but evaporated from the journals and conferences where it once was evident, the hope that students might be taught to discern figurative from literal language still seems conspicuously present whenever the members of this department have recently attempted to define the essential elements of an introductory curriculum. *If* students could

recognize the presence of metaphor—so goes the wishful conditional—
then they might be capable of meeting the more challenging tasks they
encounter in advanced courses during the later part of their college education.

What interests me about this desire (which I, no less than others,
sometimes share) is its reflection of the conflicted position metaphor
has long held within English studies. On the one hand, by suggesting
that the recognition of metaphor is crucial to learning what the discipline has to offer, we affirm the high praise accorded metaphor from
classical times to the present day. On the other hand, by envisioning such
recognition as a habitual skill to be mastered before further progress can
take place, we align metaphor with "basic" proficiencies that are supposedly acquired once and for all, the earlier the better. As with other practices imagined to be the responsibility of the introductory curriculum
—composing an argument, say, or tracing the plot of a narrative—the
capacity to identify metaphorical uses of language becomes a lower-
order building block upon which higher-order activities can eventually
be constructed. Teachers tend to long for students who *already* know
about metaphor, since the actual teaching of something so elementary
seems a burden that most would rather not carry. And who can blame
them? When the recognition of metaphor is regarded as the equivalent
of learning to play scales on the piano, then there are few who do not
prefer to teach students the more intriguing and entertaining pursuits
that come *after* the scales have been practiced. (Though even this metaphor overlooks the fact that many accomplished pianists continue to
play scales throughout their careers.)

The teaching of composition is often seen in a similar light. Indeed,
its very place at the entrance to the college curriculum has ensured
that composition would be regarded as "preparatory" work within the
academy—a place for students to be tested for their "competence" or
"proficiency" as writers, socialized into the proper discursive habits of
the academy, and introduced to issues they will study in more "depth"
in later courses.[1] As with instruction about metaphor, writing instruction has been widely perceived as foundational (and therefore to be valued) yet also as preliminary (and therefore to be shunned): though

someone has to do it, most academics would prefer it to be someone else. Now there is no doubt that composition has made perceptible headway during the past three decades in establishing itself as a scholarly discipline and in gaining institutional support for its undertakings; but it remains to be seen whether the curricular changes evident in recent years—such as writing-across-the-curriculum programs and writing as an "emphasis" available to English majors—will be sufficient to overcome the separate-yet-*un*equal institutional and professional position composition continues to occupy in relation to literary studies and other disciplines. Though the study of writing has witnessed some striking changes in the second half of the twentieth century, the extent to which these changes will challenge the division between "introductory" and "advanced" work in the college curriculum (or even the English studies curriculum, for that matter) is far from clear.

In this chapter, I examine the ways in which a reductive view of metaphor has contributed to and currently helps to sustain a reductive view of composition, both "inside" and "outside" the field. Beginning with a survey of how composition textbooks have defined metaphor and its rhetorical function over the past two centuries, I demonstrate the threat that metaphor has posed to the teaching of writing, a cultural and institutional project whose primary concern (or at least whose ostensible intention) has been to grant students sure-handed *control* over discourse—as if such control were anyone's to give, or even to acquire. While textbooks are often criticized for their simplification of theoretical complexities, careful scrutiny of their representations of metaphor nevertheless offers a telling glimpse of the contradictory attitudes toward language that students have been expected to adopt before they advance to the study of literature and/or other subjects. From here I move to a consideration of two conceptions of metaphor that challenge the long-dominant Aristotelian perspective, and I conclude the chapter with a glance at some admirable yet problematic attempts to bring a revisionist perspective on metaphor to the composition class. Faced with this effort to incorporate new theories of metaphor into classroom practice, we are returned to an ancient and troublesome set of questions: Can metaphor be "taught"? If so, by what means? If not, then what might it still have to teach? I argue that the answers to such questions may matter more to the future of composition than the field has been inclined to assume.

Conceptions of Metaphor in Composition Textbooks

As Robert Connors observes in his recent book, *Composition-Rhetoric*, the place of figurative language—and thus the place of metaphor—in rhetorical theory was already in decline by the end of the eighteenth century. Both George Campbell and Hugh Blair, whose influence on the teaching of writing in the United States would prove considerable, give a certain attention to figures of speech in their discussions of style, but figurative language could hardly be described as an area of central concern for either of these rhetoricians. Rather than emphasizing the long list of tropes and schemes so dear to the rhetorics that precede them, Campbell's *Philosophy of Rhetoric* (1776) stresses general qualities of style such as "perspicuity," "vivacity," and "elegance," while Blair's *Lectures on Rhetoric and Belles Lettres* (1783) pointedly suggests that figurative language holds much less importance than is commonly thought:

> The great place which the doctrine of tropes and figures has occupied in systems of rhetoric . . . has often led persons to imagine, that, if their composition was well bespangled with a number of these ornaments of speech, it wanted no other beauty; whence has arisen much stiffness and affectation. For it is, in truth, the sentiment or passion, which underlies the figured expression, that gives it any merit. No figures will render a cold or an empty composition interesting; whereas, if a sentiment be sublime or pathetic, it can support itself perfectly well, without any borrowed assistance. (277)

Coming as it does in the early pages of a lecture entitled "Figurative Language," this passage would seem to question the need for rhetoricians to provide lectures on such matters in the first place, given their thoroughly subordinate significance. On the other hand, it may be—as I hope to demonstrate—that comments of this kind remain necessary precisely because of the ways in which they serve to keep a figure like metaphor where it supposedly belongs.

We catch a glimpse of the ensuing demise of figurative language in college writing instruction simply by looking at the location figures of speech are assigned and the amount of space they are apportioned in the array of composition textbooks that emerges over the next two hundred years.[2] Initially, the figures retain a fairly sizeable sphere when textbook authors address the subject of style. Heavily indebted to Blair, who despite his reservations dedicates several lectures to issues of figurative language, composition textbooks from the first half of the nineteenth century are sure to include at least a chapter on the elucidation of a select group of figures. Samuel Newman, for instance, devotes one of the five chapters in his *Practical System of Rhetoric* (1827) to an explication of eight figures (simile, metaphor, allusion, metonymy, synecdoche, personification, apostrophe, and hyperbole), each of which he delineates and exemplifies at some length. Likewise, in the fourth chapter of his *Grammar of Rhetoric and Polite Literature* (1831), Alexander Jamieson discusses a somewhat more extensive set of figures (listed here as in his table of contents): metaphor, comparisons or similes, personification, allegory, apostrophe, hyperbole, climax, antithesis, interrogation, repetition, exclamation, irony, wit. Chapters with a similar inventory can be found in textbooks published during the middle years of the century as well, from George Quackenbos's *Advanced Course in Composition and Rhetoric* (1854) (sixteen figures) and Mary Harper's *Practical Composition* (1870) (eight figures) to Alexander Bain's *English Composition and Rhetoric* (1866) (sixteen figures) and A. D. Hepburn's *Manual of English Rhetoric* (1875) (nineteen figures). Even as late as John Genung's *Practical Elements of Rhetoric* (1886), we still encounter a full chapter, prominently situated in an opening unit on style, given to the examination of fourteen figures of speech.[3] My point is not, as I explain below, that these are *perceptive* treatments of figurative language; indeed, Albert Kitzhaber has provocatively remarked that "as a guide to actual composition, most of this material [on figures] was completely useless" (175). But I think it important to observe that through much of the nineteenth century figurative language still holds a rather visible, if waning, position in the teaching of writing—a position it has yet to regain over one hundred years later.

As Connors indicates, composition textbooks published during the final years of the nineteenth century responded to the growing importance of vernacular writing instruction by seeking "low-level rules and exercises" that could have immediate application in the classroom (266). But the theories of style passed down from Campbell and Blair were, as Connors puts it, "relatively resistant to textbook practicalization, at least in their original forms. They could not be easily simplified except by sterile reductions to taxonomic headings . . . nor could they be easily applied in exercises" (266). Connors goes on to note that with the dissipation of the taxonomic approach to style, instruction in figures of speech also "slipped away" (268).[4] It is not that the figures were no longer to be found in textbooks; rather, they were "simplified, reduced, knitted into other discussions" (268)—as is plainly evident when we scan any number of textbooks from the turn of the century. In his *Beginnings of Composition and Rhetoric* (1902), Adams Sherman Hill includes but a handful of pages on figurative language, which appears not as a primary factor in discursive style on the whole but as the last of several decisions a writer might make in choosing "words and phrases" (402–04). That same year, Rose Kavana and Arthur Bailey, whose *Composition and Rhetoric Based on Literary Models* reflects the growing presence of the four modes of discourse, briefly examine metaphor (with no mention of other figures) in a chapter on "description." Alongside "enunciation," metaphor is given one paragraph of attention in a subsection whose marginality can be discerned from its name: "Other Devices for Giving Vividness to Detail" (161). Indeed, it wasn't much longer before Alphonso Newcomer and Samuel Seward would decide, in their *Rhetoric in Practice* (1908), to remove the figures from their location in a specific chapter and consign them to the appendix, where they could serve a solely referential function—or be conveniently ignored.

Part of what proves interesting about the composition textbooks that follow (including those currently in use in the 1990s) is the steadfast, if seemingly insignificant, place that discussions of figurative language manage to retain over the years. Given their near total lack of presence in twentieth-century composition pedagogy, the figures might be expected simply to vanish from textbooks altogether. But they do not. More specifically, even when the other figures are eliminated, metaphor remains. While many of the anthologies or "readers" now popular in composition courses make no mention of metaphor, I have yet to find a "rhetoric" (as those textbooks that provide explicit instruction in writing are called by their publishers) that does not grant some space for the discussion of metaphor. Similarly, metaphor continues to receive notice, however briefly, from virtually every composition handbook on the market.[5]

The question, then, is why this is the case: why has metaphor held a position in textualizations of writing instruction that is simultaneously infirm yet resolute, diminished yet undefeated? In order to address this question, we must look not merely at *where* metaphor appears in composition textbooks but at *how* these textbooks represent metaphor in those places where they pay it heed. And it is here that we encounter a remarkable consistency, for in one volume after another, from the early-nineteenth-century productions that predate the modern university to the late-twentieth-century enterprises that reflect the emergence of composition as a professional field of study, textbook authors tend to approach metaphor in two basic steps. The first step is to describe the virtues of metaphor as a figure of speech, which are commonly identified as its ability to clarify concepts and its capacity to stimulate the reader's imagination. Yet no sooner have these virtues been named than a second step follows the first—whereupon all discussion of the assets of metaphor is curtailed (and in many cases overwhelmed) by the presentation of its flaws. This is not to say that the terms employed to articulate the possibilities and limits of metaphor always and everywhere remain the same, nor that the emphasis never shifts. But what proves difficult to ignore is the striking regularity with which the values attributed to metaphor are quickly subsumed by anxiety over its defects. Indeed, metaphor is the *only* figure that receives such treatment, for none of the other figures commonly defined in composition textbooks—simile, synecdoche, metonymy, and so on—are discussed, as is metaphor, in terms of their shortcomings and dangers.

Blair's *Lectures,* as always, makes for a towering example. In his lecture on metaphor, Blair comes early on to his praise for metaphor above the other figures: "Of all the Figures of Speech, none comes so near to painting as Metaphor. Its peculiar effect is to give light and strength to description; to make intellectual ideas, in some sort, visible to the eye, by giving them color, and substance, and sensible qualities" (297). The clarity granted by metaphor, in other words, is that which derives from the picture it creates by means of verbal expression: through metaphor, the invisible becomes corporeal—and hence discernible. But having just begun to state his admiration for the ways in which metaphor brings the ineffable into view, Blair turns, in the next sentence, to the potential problems that metaphor presents its user: "In order to produce this effect, however, a delicate hand is required; for, by a little inaccuracy, we are in hazard of introducing confusion, in place of promoting Perspicuity. Several rules, therefore, are necessary to be given for the proper management of metaphors" (297). After digressing in order to describe what he considers "a very beautiful metaphor" in the work of Lord Bolingbroke (197–98), Blair goes on to discuss for several pages a total of seven rules that comprise the "proper management" of metaphorical expressions, which must be: (1) "suited to the nature of the subject . . . neither too many, nor too gay, nor too elevated for it" (300); (2) not of the sort that "raise in the mind disagreeable, mean, vulgar, or dirty ideas" (302); and (3) founded on a resemblance that is "clear and perspicuous, not far-fetched, nor difficult to discover" (303). Moreover, we should never (4) "jumble metaphorical and plain language together" (305); (5) "make two different metaphors meet on one object" (308); (6) produce metaphors that are "heaped on one another" (311); or (7) extend metaphors "too far," whereby "we tire the reader . . . and we render our discourse obscure" (313). Given that Blair never returns to his remarks on the value of metaphor after he has exemplified the many ways in which metaphor can go wrong (rather, he drops the subject and turns to a discussion of allegory), his lecture in certain respects seems more a sally *against* metaphor than a recommendation on its behalf.

The pervasive influence of Blair's lecture on metaphor is evident in the many nineteenth-century textbooks that take it as their model, either by quoting it directly or paraphrasing it in related terms,[6] so that almost a century after the *Lectures* first appeared we still find striking similarities. Listen, for instance, as John S. Hart describes the virtues of metaphor in his *Manual of Composition and Rhetoric* (1870): "Metaphor, indeed, of all the figures, comes nearest to painting, enabling us to clothe at will the most abstract ideas with life, form, color, and motion" (155). As with Blair, the emphasis here is on the visibility granted by metaphor; and, as with Blair, the adulation quickly comes to a stop. After providing a few examples of the difference between metaphor and simile, Hart moves immediately to a longer discussion of the "rules" for these figures—five rules that all have their precursors in Blair's longer list of seven: "Rule 1. The metaphorical and the literal should not be mixed in the same sentence" (156); "Rule 2. Two different metaphors should not be used in the same sentence and in reference to the same subject" (157); "Rule 3. Metaphors on the same subject should not be crowded together in rapid succession" (158); and so on. Once again, if the first of two standard steps in textbook commentary on metaphor is to offer approval so abbreviated that it barely has the chance to register, then the second is to offer a somber, and usually more elaborate, warning whose message can hardly be missed: *metaphor is dangerous*. To use a metaphor, in other words, is to risk breaking one or more of several strictures that can expose one to ridicule.[7] (Hart, like Blair, gives a good deal of space to displaying and critiquing the poor metaphors of famous writers such as Shakespeare and Pope.)

Though their treatment of metaphor is considerably condensed when compared to that of their predecessors, twentieth-century composition textbooks generally follow the same pattern of praise and blame, right up to contemporary times. Tellingly, even the praise tends to represent metaphor as a subsidiary rather than a fundamental element of language. In a later edition of James McCrimmon's long-popular *Writing with a Purpose* (7th ed., 1980), for example, the discussion of metaphor and other figures of speech appears in a small, buried section of the book entitled "Imagery." For McCrimmon, "imagery" serves to create "good diction," which he describes as "the choice of words that best allows you to communicate your meaning to your readers" (153). Figurative language, as a form of imagery, would thus seem to be at least potentially significant to a piece of writing. Yet in this conception of language, one in which "meaning" somehow preexists the "choice of words" we use to "communicate," metaphor becomes at once both useful and ancillary—an occasional, by no means essential, resource. Metaphor apparently assists meaning by providing images, but these images have no role in producing meaning itself; they only facilitate its transfer to others. Moreover, as McCrimmon goes on to explain at the close of his chapter, the writer must always be on the alert for "ineffective imagery":

> You have seen that an effective figure of speech can lend concreteness to writing. But a figure that is trite, far-fetched, or confused is worse than useless, since it calls unfavorable attention to itself and distracts the reader. *Mixed metaphors*—metaphors that try to combine two or more images in a single figure—are especially ineffective. (178)

After providing an example of a metaphor that woefully combines its conflicting images, McCrimmon makes sure that his point has gotten through: "The lesson to be learned from the mixed metaphor given above is that a poor figure of speech is worse than none at all" (178). Better to stay away from metaphor entirely than produce one that breaks the rules.

This preoccupation with the metaphor gone astray is all the more prominent in present-day reference "handbooks" (now commonly six- or seven-hundred pages long) to which instruction about figurative language has largely been consigned. Consider *The Holt Handbook* (3rd ed., 1992), which, after explaining the value of metaphor in a single statement—"Because of their economy of expression, [metaphors] can convey ideas with considerable power" (Kirszner and Mandell 314)—includes an entire section devoted to "Avoiding Ineffective Figures of Speech." Here students are urged to refrain from "dead metaphors or similes"; "mixed metaphors"; and, last but not least, "strained metaphors"—those that compare "two things that do not have enough in common to justify the comparison" (317). Similarly, *The St. Martin's Handbook* (3rd ed., 1995), having given one sentence each to simile and metaphor, soon thereafter turns to a full page on the subject of "Clichés and mixed metaphors," wherein students are warned that "*ineffective* figures of speech can create the *wrong* impression by boring, irritating, or unintentionally amusing readers" (Lunsford and Connors 427). The authors' emphasis of the terms *ineffective* and *wrong* underscores how definitively metaphors can go awry, to the extent of completely reversing the effect a writer hopes to attain. All the more caught up in this distress over error-prone figures, *The Simon and Schuster Handbook for Writers* (4th ed.,

1996) cannot even offer its two-line definition of metaphor without parenthetically interrupting to offer these words of advice: "(Be alert to avoid the error of a mixed metaphor, explained in the text)" (Troyka 403). Intriguingly, none of the other figures defined (analogy, irony, overstatement, personification, simile, and understatement) come accompanied with such a warning, and we shortly discover "in the text" that one of the two paragraphs offered in this concise section on "Using figurative language" concerns itself entirely with the problem of mixed metaphors. "Avoid confusing your reader," students are told, "by combining two or more images that do not blend well" (403).

Finally, the most recent edition (at this writing) of *The Little, Brown Handbook* (7th ed., 1998) follows up its brief definitions of simile, metaphor, personification, and hyperbole with the following paragraph:

> To be successful, figurative language must be fresh and unstrained, calling attention not to itself but to the writer's meaning. If readers reject your language as trite or overblown, they may reject your message. One kind of figurative language gone wrong is the *mixed metaphor,* in which the writer combines two or more incompatible figures. Since metaphors often generate visual images in the reader's mind, a mixed metaphor can be laughable. (Fowler and Aaron 471)

"Trite," "overblown," "wrong," "incompatible," "laughable"—that's quite a list of reasons to keep away from metaphor altogether.

While part of what I wish to indicate here is that students can hardly be encouraged to engage in figurative language when the risks are given greater emphasis than the benefits, it seems equally important to observe those contradictions that reside in the very definitions of the "ineffective" metaphors students are told to avoid. When we peruse the list of dead metaphors the *Holt* cites as examples ("beyond a shadow of a doubt"; "green with envy"; "off the beaten path"; "smooth sailing"; and so forth), it is far from clear that any of these items forms what the authors call a "meaningless expression that evokes no particular visual image" (316). To the contrary, such expressions continue to be uttered so frequently precisely because people find them meaningful, and we need only pause to take them literally—as is the case with most metaphors—in order for them to evoke a quite particular image. Similarly, the only mixed metaphor offered by the *Holt* ("Management extended an olive branch in an attempt to break some of the ice between the company and the striking workers") does not necessarily, as this handbook suggests, "leave readers wondering what [the writer] is trying to say" (317) —for if the readers referred to can comprehend each of the individual metaphors (and there is no suggestion made that they cannot), then this sentence would seem to be perfectly intelligible. Indeed, the instructor's edition of the *Holt* includes in the margin Shakespeare's oft-quoted mixed metaphor "to take arms against a sea of troubles"—which the authors introduce only by commenting that "the mixed metaphor does, on occasion, trap the greatest of us" (317). Whereupon we can only ask: if the most memorable speech in the English language includes a mixed metaphor among its most forceful lines, what is it that continues to motivate the ubiquitous condemnations of metaphor mixing?[8]

Even those few (and mostly out-of-print) handbooks that refrain from prohibiting mixed metaphor as a matter of course—such as Kenneth Rothwell's *Questions of Rhetoric and Usage* (1971)—cannot quite figure out how to allow students to experiment with something that at least potentially forms a threat to literal paraphrase. Rothwell, who defines mixed metaphor as "an illogical yoking together of two unrelated images," subsequently goes on to admit: "The truth of the matter is, however, that many writers of genius, including William Shakespeare and Charles Dickens, have mixed metaphors shamelessly" (181). After quoting a marvelous description of Mr. Gradgrind from Dickens's *Hard Times,* Rothwell observes that in a single sentence the author likens the schoolmaster's head to "a clearing surrounded by a forest, the crust of a plum-pie, and a warehouse for hard facts" (181)—thereby triumphantly mixing his metaphors in just the way that Gradgrind would find horrifying. Yet upon tentatively informing students that they may mix metaphors "under certain circumstances," Rothwell immediately returns to safer ground by reminding students that mixed metaphors "will always stand out conspicuously in a passage of objective, analytical prose"; and surely his concluding words give students little reason to attempt to be unconventional: "If you do mix, then be sure you know when and why you are doing so. Never mix metaphors in excess under any circumstances, and always be prepared for attacks from the literal minded"

(181). As Rothwell's own language suggests—note that Dickens "shamelessly" mixes metaphors while students must arm themselves against "attacks"—the stakes are imagined to be not only rhetorical but fervidly moral as well.

Perhaps most revealing, however, are the warnings from handbooks about "strained metaphors"—figures that, according to the authors of the *Holt,* compare two things "that do not have enough in common to justify the comparison." Worry over this transgression can be traced as far back as Aristotle's *Rhetoric,* where admiration for the "clearness, charm, and distinction" provided by metaphor is immediately followed by these words of caution: "Metaphors, like epithets, must be fitting, which means that they must fairly correspond to the thing signified: failing this, their inappropriateness will be conspicuous: the want of harmony between two things is emphasized by their being placed side by side" (168–69). In other words, since the "things" metaphor compares are supposedly arranged in their proper places *before* language refers to them, they should derive from proximate rather than distant realms of origin; otherwise, metaphors that stretch to bridge expansive gaps will create a disturbing countereffect, exposing not the correspondence of the things compared but the "want of harmony" between them. This combination of spatial and judgmental metaphors for describing metaphor itself, whose elements are imagined as either appropriately adjacent or inappropriately far apart, continues to appear throughout the history of instruction in figurative language, from antiquity to the present day. While it might not seem that surprising to find the anonymous author of the *Rhetorica ad Herennium,* the influential Roman textbook that followed Aristotle's *Rhetoric* by some three hundred years, still asserting that "a metaphor ought to be restrained" in order to avoid taking "an indiscriminate, reckless, and precipitate leap to an unlike thing" (345), the persistence of this conception of metaphor is rather extraordinary when we encounter it in a much later and entirely different context—say, for instance, in Samuel Johnson's well-known essay on the metaphysical poets of the seventeenth century. For Johnson, the great fault of the metaphysical poets lies in their metaphors, by which "the most heterogeneous ideas are yoked by violence together" (*Lives* 20). Here, in what is arguably one of Johnson's most famous lines, writers—in this case, experienced writers, not just student writers—continue to be scolded for creating metaphors that connect "ideas" that are considered too remote for such contact. The lesson, it would appear, is that only through cautious judgment and moderation can the writer prevent metaphor from disrupting the harmonious relationship between language and pre-existent reality.

But what these critics of the strained metaphor invariably overlook is the fact that they define even the "acceptable" form of metaphor as an aberration—and subsequently expect it to behave with modesty and subservience. For Aristotle, "Metaphor consists in giving the thing a name *that belongs to something else*" (*Poetics* 251). The *Rhetorica ad Herennium* asserts that "metaphor occurs when a word *applying to one thing is transferred* to another" (343). And in his *Dictionary*, Johnson defines metaphor as "The application of a word to an use to which, in its original import, *it cannot be put.*" I have emphasized the language of violation in each of these definitions in order to highlight their recognition that metaphor ignores the ordinary rules governing the ascription of names; rather than keeping names and things in their proper places, it brings them together in unusual discursive combinations. Metaphor thus presents something of a quandary for the rationalist depictions of communication upon which writing instruction has long relied, since it confronts such depictions with a pervasive feature of language that challenges the proprietary boundaries which rationalism seeks to keep in place. Hence the contradiction that inheres in any attempt to "teach" metaphor (whatever that might mean) and at the same time produce well-mannered student writers—writers who make connections only between things that are already perceived as relatively homogeneous.[9] For how does one obey decorum with a figure whose very nature is to do otherwise? As we have seen, composition textbooks generally respond to this predicament by briefly acknowledging the creative power of metaphor, and then by compiling a (sometimes extensive) list of its "dangers," which are often detailed with supposedly pertinent illustrations. *The Holt Handbook,* for instance, contributes this sample of a strained metaphor—"The plane was a fragment of candy falling through the sky"—of which they ask rhetorically: "In what sense is a plane comparable to a piece of candy?" (317). Claiming that an "effective" metaphor requires "a strong basis of comparison," the authors then provide this revision: "The plane was a wounded bird falling through the sky" (317).

There is much to notice in this example of pedagogical correction, including the possibility that the purportedly mistaken sentence offers a more thoughtful metaphor than its corrected counterpart. For the authors of the *Holt,* the trouble with the former is that a fragment of candy has nothing in common with a falling airplane: the gap between them is so wide that a metaphor cannot cross it without excessive strain. The latter sentence, on the other hand, has selected an object (the wounded bird) that readily compares with the plane, since both of them are known to fly: here the gap is small enough to be bridged with ease. Yet it could also be said that *because* the "distance" between planes and birds is so short, the second metaphor comes off as the more banal— while the first metaphor, by choosing an object that initially appears to share little with an airplane, potentially provides a fresh and stimulating connection. (Perhaps the plane in question is being viewed by a young child, for whom its descent has no more significance than that of a fragment of candy falling to the ground. Or by a military establishment that has thousands of other shiny planes to play with.) Taken out of context, neither sentence can be judged as definitively as the authors of the *Holt* would wish; but my point is that opposition to the so-called "strained" metaphor seems ultimately to represent opposition to the risks that attend an active discursive imagination. Simply put, metaphor *must* strain if it is to produce new relationships and not merely describe those that are already taken for granted. Though most composition textbooks are willing to admit that metaphor forms an important means by which language stretches its resources, they remain intent on curtailing the kinds of metaphors that serve this very purpose.

A memorable piece of advice from the *Holt* illustrates how even an attempt to encourage the use of figures cannot refrain from mentioning its potential pitfalls: "Although you should not overuse figurative language, do not be afraid to use it when you think it will help you to communicate with a reader" (313). The sentence begins with a warning, then asks that students "not be afraid" of what they have just been told carries a danger. Yet the point at which figurative language becomes "overused"—or when and how it might aid communication—is left unexplored. As in so many other textbooks, this sort of invitation doesn't sound too inviting.

Before I move to other resources wherein discussions of metaphor and student writing occur, I want to briefly note one last way in which composition textbooks attempt to keep metaphor held, so to speak, under lock and key. Thus far, I have focused on the values and hazards these textbooks ascribe to metaphor, not on the ways in which they define metaphor in relation to other figures of speech. But here, too, we find a conspicuous uniformity among textbooks that otherwise display any number of differences in theory, pedagogy, and institutional origins: from the learned philosophical ruminations found in Blair's *Lectures* to the stale assortment of functional strategies compiled by the latest "guide" to writing, the prevailing definition of metaphor remains almost identical.

Metaphor, writes Blair in 1783, "is a figure founded entirely on the resemblance which one object bears to another. Hence, it is much allied to Simile or Comparison; and is indeed no other than a comparison, expressed in an abridged form" (295). That is to say, a metaphor consists of an implied comparison that varies from simile only in its omission of the terms—usually "like" or "as"—through which resemblance is explicitly signaled. With striking homogeneity across the years, composition textbooks reiterate this conception of metaphor for their student (and teacher) readers:

(1827)
[With metaphor] the resemblance, instead of being distinctly stated, is implied. (Newman 73)

(1852)
The Simile or Comparison may be considered as differing in form only from a Metaphor; the resemblance being in that case *stated,* which in the Metaphor is implied. (Whately 196)

(1869)
1. A Simile is an express comparison. 2. A Metaphor is an implied comparison. (Kerl 231)

(1875)
The metaphor is a trope founded upon resemblance. . . . It is often called an abridged simile. It agrees with it in being founded upon resemblance, but differs from it in structure. (Hepburn 98)

(1889)
The Metaphor and the Simile both contain a comparison, but in the latter the resemblance between the things compared is formally expressed, while in the former it is only implied. (Williams 175)

(1909)
Much more commonly we describe by figures springing from likeness. . . . Such comparisons are called *similes*. Comparisons which, instead of being thus fully stated by *like* or *as,* are merely implied, are called *metaphors*. (Baldwin 150)

(1927)
A metaphor implies or states a comparison between two persons or objects unlike, without the use of any special words to indicate the comparison. Thus, the omission of *like* or *as* from a simile usually leaves a metaphor, and, conversely, the insertion of those words in a metaphor produces a simile. (Canby and Opdycke 662)

(1936)
The simile is an expressed likeness or comparison between two ideas. . . . The metaphor is an implied comparison. . . . The only difference between these two figures of speech is the expression of likeness in the simile and the implication of it in the metaphor. (Ramey 64–65)

(1951)
A simile states that one thing is like another. In a *metaphor* the comparison is abbreviated still further; a metaphor states or implies that one thing is, or has the attributes of, another. (Bradford and Moritz 177)

(1969)
A simile is a compressed but still explicit comparison, introduced by *like* or *as.* . . . A metaphor is an implied comparison, using one thing as the equivalent of another. . . . (Guth 78)

(1975)
A metaphor is a comparison embodied in a word or phrase without the addition of *like* or *as.* (Barzun 136)

(1988)
Like a simile, a metaphor is also a comparison. The difference is that a simile compares things explicitly; it literally says that X is *like* Y. A metaphor compares things implicitly. (Kane 218)

(1997)
A *simile* directly expresses a similarity by using the word *like* or *as* to announce the comparison. . . . A *metaphor,* on the other hand, is an implicit comparison by which one thing is described as though it were the other. (Axelrod and Cooper 498)

And so on. Note that in each case metaphor gets defined by way of simile or comparison. More specifically, metaphor and simile are both presented as *versions* of comparison: what simile compares explicitly, metaphor compares implicitly. Simile thus becomes equivalent to comparison "properly speaking," while metaphor appears as an offshoot of sorts, a comparison in disguise. We must begin with simile (so goes the thinking) in order to understand the kind of service performed by metaphor, which, given its refusal to call things by their own names, might otherwise remain mysterious. In composition textbooks, simile becomes metaphor unmasked—an equation that conveniently enables textbook authors to continually rehash the same old story about these figures, one in which simile is unproblematic, while metaphor, because it sometimes falls dead, overstrains, or mixes its elements, must be used with special care and discretion.

But what if we were to question, rather than accept, the textbook presumption that metaphor is no more than an abbreviated simile? Though Paul Ricoeur takes the conventional view that "simile explicitly displays the moment of resemblance that operates implicitly in metaphor" (27), he also observes that for Aristotle, simile is a species of metaphor, not the other way around; it is Cicero and Quintilian who reverse Aristotle's priorities and describe metaphor as a condensed simile (*Rule* 24–25). The authors of a vast array of composition textbooks over the past two centuries apparently subscribe to the Roman, not the Aristotelian, position on this matter, given that they so unwaveringly define metaphor as a shortened version of simile. While this may initially seem a matter of minor importance, it helps to explain how textbooks have managed to reduce metaphor to an incidental figure of speech of little consequence; for if metaphor is but a compressed simile, then nothing more need be said (nothing, that is, except those warnings about metaphors that leap out of control). Similes compare explicitly, metaphors compare implicitly—end of discussion. If, on the other hand, simile serves as a particular form of metaphor, then metaphor becomes the larger field, one with a potentially wide range of possibilities beyond those created by identifying the similarity between one thing and another. From this perspective, the indication of resemblance may be *one* of the functions of metaphor, but not the only one.[10]

Within the marginal space to which they consign figures of speech, composition textbooks manage to keep metaphor contained, separated from those sites where its penchant for disruption might raise questions about the very possibility of teaching anyone "how to write" to begin with. My contention is that composition textbooks have so closely tied definitions of metaphor to definitions of simile in order to elude the problems that metaphor brings to the theories of language these textbooks endorse—theories in which language functions primarily as an instrument for prescribing (and proscribing) the movements of meaning. Recognizing that metaphor lifts its terms from their familiar contexts so that they might be read in light of novel, even alien, surroundings, textbook authors seem aware—as their admonitions about this figure demonstrate—that metaphor in large part relinquishes the management of meaning that writing instruction generally hopes to confer. Metaphor, in other words, represents language at its most vulnerable moment, not only because it stimulates multiple, unpredictable readings but more importantly because it risks the obfuscation that can result from calling *this* by the name of *that*. In the next section, I turn to the work of two literary theorists, both of whom exhibit considerable interest in the teaching of writing, in order to examine the implications that such a conception of metaphor might hold for the field of composition.

Refiguring the Figure

As many have observed, scholarly study of metaphor appears to enter a new era with the publication of I. A. Richards's *The Philosophy of Rhetoric* in 1936. Richards devotes the last two chapters of this book to metaphor, and from the moment he turns his attention to the subject, he makes clear his desire to challenge the long dominant notion that metaphor serves as something striking or unusual—a departure from the normal modes of discursive exchange. For Richards, "metaphor is the omnipresent principle of language. . . . We cannot get through three sentences of ordinary discourse without it" (92). Not even a discourse as rigorous as philosophy can elude the grasp of metaphor, however certain it may be that it has succeeded in doing so: "As [philosophy] grows more abstract we think increasingly by means of metaphors that we profess *not* to be relying on. The metaphors we are avoiding steer our thought as much as those we accept" (92).

Contrary, then, to the assumptions of classical rhetoric, Richards argues that metaphor requires no deviation from ordinary forms of speech. In his view, it is erroneous to regard metaphor as an ornamental device —"a sort of happy extra trick with words"—given that metaphor is nothing less than the "constitutive form" of language itself (92). Richards's definition of metaphor, moreover, is an attempt to reimagine the relationship between its constituent parts: "In the simplest formulation, when we use metaphor we have two thoughts of different things active together and supported by a single word, or phrase, whose meaning is a resultant of their interaction" (93). The key word is the last, for through his suggestion that the two parts of a metaphor "interact" with one another, Richards offers an alternative to the conventional conception of metaphor as a figurative term that simply stands in for some literal equivalent. According to Richards, the use of metaphor is not a mere substitution but a complex combination of what he calls "tenor" and "vehicle" (96), each of which represents one of the "two thoughts" brought into play by metaphor. While it can be argued that these terms preserve the very understanding of metaphor that he wishes to replace (since "vehicle" would appear to correspond to the metaphorical utterance and "tenor" to its literal paraphrase), Richards insists that the vehicle alone cannot create a metaphor. Rather than separating the language/ vehicle of metaphor from its meaning/tenor, Richards claims that "the co-presence of vehicle and tenor results in a meaning . . . which is not attainable without their interaction" (100). In other words, metaphor works by *combining* its two elements, not by substituting one for the other.

If "interaction" seems a vague description of the process, this may be by design. Throughout his discussion of metaphor, Richards stresses the importance of contextual parameters that shape the relationship between tenor and vehicle, and it is this emphasis on the variable conditions for communication that leads to his rejection of resemblance as the foundation of metaphorical meaning. As we have seen, composition textbooks are remarkably unified in their representation of metaphor as an implied comparison. But for Richards, a generic depiction of metaphor as a figure that illustrates similarity fails to respect the wide range of alternatives: "Once we begin 'to examine attentively' interactions which do not work through *resemblances* between tenor and vehicle, but depend on other relations between them including *disparities,* some of our most prevalent, over-simple, ruling assumptions about metaphors as comparisons are soon exposed" (107–08). This is a crucial, original observation. Through his recognition that individual metaphors project a variety of tenor-vehicle relationships, Richards begins to suggest a conception of metaphor based as much on difference as on resemblance. Tenor and vehicle refer, after all, to two distinct ideas or things —and the possibility that metaphors are not necessarily eager to cover over their differences seems well worth further investigation. While Richards rejects the endeavor by surrealists such as André Breton to create metaphors whose elements are combined simply *because* they clash, he carefully demonstrates how attention to "disparities" can be of significance to readers who might otherwise recognize only half of the potential meanings in a particular metaphor. When Hamlet, for example, asks "What should such fellows as I do crawling between heaven and earth?," the force of the metaphor, Richards notes, "comes not only from whatever resemblances to vermin it brings in but at least equally from the differences that resist and control the influences of their resemblances. The implication there is that man should not so crawl. . . .

In general, there are very few metaphors in which disparities between tenor and vehicle are not as much operative as the similarities" (127).

In addition to rejecting standard depictions of resemblance in metaphor, Richards resists the widespread doctrine that metaphor helps us to "see" or "visualize" the intangible. Though composition textbooks commonly praise metaphor for converting the "abstract" (which is apparently beyond comprehension) into the "concrete" (which all can supposedly understand at a glance), for Richards such a notion is "patently false" (129); and he specifically takes issue with T. E. Hulme's contention that poetry "make[s] you continuously see a physical thing, to prevent you gliding through an abstract process" (qtd. in Richards 128). Referring again to Hamlet, this time to his lines as the play draws to a close—"If thou didst ever hold me in thy heart / Absent thee from felicity awhile / And in this harsh world draw thy breath in pain / To tell my story"— Richards comments: "You *see* nothing while reading that, and the words certainly do not work by making you see anything. . . . The language of the greatest poetry is frequently abstract in the extreme and its aim is precisely to send us 'gliding through an abstract process'" (129). Ultimately, for Richards, the problem lies not so much with theorists like Hulme (who may well have meant to use "see" metaphorically) as with the classroom, where "the patient toil of scores of teachers is going on every day . . . into the effort to make children (and adults) visualize where visualization is a mere distraction and of no service" (130). What students need to recognize is not that "the image fills in the meaning of the word" but that "it is the word which brings in the meaning which the image and its original perception lack" (131).

The view expressed here—that discourse constructs meaning independently of, and more powerfully than, the senses—may seem but a step away from poststructuralist conceptions of language whose ascendance *The Philosophy of Rhetoric* predates by some thirty years. Yet in the closing pages of his book, Richards turns away from the radical conclusion toward which he has appeared to be moving, in favor of a more conservative vision of our ability to gain control over discord.[11] Arguing that words form the "completion" of what the "intuitions of sensation" begin, he asserts: "[Words] are the occasion and means of that growth which is the mind's endless endeavor to order itself. That is why we have language" (131). And two pages later, with the same kind of categorical firmness: "Words are not a medium in which to copy life. Their true work is to restore life itself to order" (133). While I have no wish to dispute that language can provide a sense of order and harmony, Richards seems here to forget what he has recognized so perceptively earlier on—namely, the potential of language, and of metaphor in particular, to create dissonance and anomaly as well as consonance and design. By the end of his final chapter, tellingly entitled "The Command of Metaphor," we find Richards hoping not only that "a patient persistence with the problems of Rhetoric may . . . throw light upon and suggest a remedial discipline for deeper and more grievous disorders" (136), but also that the study of "the small and local errors in our everyday misunderstandings with language" will eventually teach us "how these large scale disasters may be avoided" (136–37). Again, the problem is not that the study of rhetoric cannot shed light on deeper "disorders" within society but that, in his quest for a "command" of metaphor, Richards overlooks the potential value of "misunderstandings," which point not simply to the presence of "errors" but more importantly to a social world constituted by irreducible differences. When Richards calls in his opening chapter for rhetoric to be approached as "a study of misunderstanding and its remedies" (3), he fails to realize that certain misunderstandings can only be remedied through the elimination of the very "disparities" he goes on to locate in metaphor.

Be that as it may, Richards's conception of metaphor establishes a generous space for much of the study of this subject that follows, and his view of rhetoric as a product of the imagination has inspired contemporary composition scholars such as Ann Berthoff to reconceive the teaching of writing as an inevitably philosophical rather than merely technical endeavor.[12] In his next book, *Interpretation in Teaching* (1938), Richards directly addresses questions concerning writing instruction, and he even suggests that professional journals reserve space for the "critical discussion" of pedagogical problems encountered in actual classroom practice (75). Furthermore, a good portion of this book is devoted to commenting on samples of student writing from his own courses, particularly those in which students were asked to respond to the use of metaphor in specific texts. For Richards, ways of writing about metaphor reflect ways of reading metaphor, and a collection of student papers thus becomes the occasion for observing the many means by which readers and writers compose meaning from words:

> The varieties of interpretation which a well-chosen passage can elicit do sometimes astonishingly repeat in miniature the characteristics of vanished literary epochs. They are, I suggest, if carefully examined, capable of presenting a fascinating synopsis of intellectual history—not less interesting for being more compassable. As a word or a grammatical form may contain the germ of a whole philosophy, so certain ways of reading carry implicitly with them a characteristic outlook or culture. . . . On these grounds alone, [presenting student papers in class] would be capable of some justification as a part of general education aside from the help which it may give to the development of linguistic ability. (72–73)

However modestly, Richards is attempting to provide not only a warrant for attending to student work in the classroom but also an alternative vision of English studies, one in which the interpretation of student texts and the interpretation of literary texts would be brought together in order to observe what he has earlier called "how language works and fails" (5). It is a vision that might remind us of the proposals put forward almost a half-century later—by Terry Eagleton, Jonathan Culler, and Steven Mailloux, among others—to integrate the study of reading and writing under the banner of Rhetoric.[13]

While I will offer my own proposal for curricular integration later in this book, I want here to look in more detail at the recommendations of one of those figures—J. Hillis Miller—who has regularly called for departments of English to grant equal value to the teaching of writing and the teaching of reading. I choose Miller for three reasons: first, his effort to locate a meeting place for composition and literary studies explicitly depends, as does Richards's, on a theory of metaphor; second, his theory of metaphor, derived in large part from the work of Jacques Derrida and Paul de Man, reflects the very conception of rhetoric toward which Richards moves but ultimately turns away; and third, his appreciation of composition as a discipline is relatively unusual among literary scholars of his stature. Accordingly, Miller's discussion of metaphor in the context of his suggestions for curricular reform may help to illuminate why the hope placed in new theories of metaphor in the 1980s, along with the desire repeatedly expressed during those years for an amalgamation of composition and literary studies, now seem on the decline in the 1990s. Like Miller, I believe that metaphor lies at the heart of the conceptual and pedagogical problems that confront the study of language—and so the question becomes why the attention given to metaphor by deconstruction and other poststructuralist theories has had so little effect on the structure of the English department curriculum, which still in large part divides courses in composition from courses in literature.

In his essay "Composition and Decomposition: Deconstruction and the Teaching of Writing," Miller argues that "reading is itself a kind of writing" and that "writing is a trope for the act of reading" (41). Consequently, the teaching of reading and the teaching of writing are thoroughly interdependent endeavors, to the extent that "any artificial detachment of one from the other will be a disaster for both disciplines" (42). Going on to assert that it is metaphor that "gets the writer or reader from here to there in his argument" (47), Miller contends that a recognition of the ubiquity of metaphor is crucial to instruction in reading and writing, and he writes with dismay of a small survey he has performed on representations of metaphor in current composition textbooks. With the exception of a single textbook (which failed to mention metaphor at all), each of the well-known textbooks that Miller investigated were marred by "a system of mistaken assumptions," from "the idea that metaphor is a detachable part of language, something supplemental, adventitious, or external to a given argument" to "the idea that metaphor may be defined by opposition to some presumed literal language, whether 'concrete' or 'conceptual'" (53). For Miller, metaphors serve not as an option the writer occasionally decides to employ but rather as "the universal medium in which the writer—novice, intermediate, and advanced—must learn to swim. . . . The 'dream' into which we are all born is figurative language itself" (54). While he admits that most teachers of writing probably hold such a view of metaphor yet believe it to be "impossible, impractical, or ineffective to try to teach this to beginning college students" (54–55), Miller maintains that to do otherwise is to ignore the ways in which deconstruction—particularly through its dissolution of the barrier dividing metaphorical from literal discourse —might contribute to pedagogical practice.

In a related essay entitled "The Two Rhetorics: George Eliot's Bestiary," Miller draws more explicitly on the claims of Paul de Man in order to discuss the implications that a revised conception of metaphor holds for rhetoric in general. As those familiar with his book *Allegories of Reading* are aware, de Man displays a strikingly anticlassical approach to rhetoric, which he considers the *un*doing of its own persuasive art. Rhetoric, according to de Man, inevitably subverts the position it simultaneously attempts to establish, and thereby defeats the very project it promotes. In Miller's words,

> The claim of "deconstruction" . . . is that language is figurative through and through, all the way down to the bottom, so to speak, and that rhetoric in the sense of tropes inhibits or prevents both the mastery or plain sense of texts, which is promised by grammar, and the mastery of reasoning, which is promised by logic. . . . If this is the case (and it is), rhetoric is not so much the imperial queen of the trivium and of basic studies in the humanities generally, as it is the odd man out, the jack of spades or the wild card, who suspends the game or at any rate causes much trouble in playing it. ("Two Rhetorics" 113)

As opposed to Richards's belief that rhetoric offers our best hope in the attempt to locate "remedies" for misunderstanding, the view presented here is that rhetoric, because of its metaphorical dimension, *creates* misunderstanding rather than repairs it. In other words, since metaphors seek to bridge gaps between different discursive realms, they must be interpreted and not just decoded—which means that they necessarily disrupt the easy movement from grammar to reference on which clarity of meaning relies. In a line often quoted by his commentators (including Miller), de Man remarks: "Rhetoric radically suspends logic and opens up vertiginous possibilities of referential aberration" (10).

Now as I see it there is much to recommend the accounts of metaphor and its relationship to rhetoric provided by deconstructionists like Miller and de Man, not the least of which lies in the challenge they pose for the teaching of writing. If rhetoric, via metaphor, takes apart as much as it puts together, then composition courses might be expected to radically reconfigure their typical goals for student texts, which are so often pushed in the direction of seamless coherence.[14] Yet strangely enough, Miller seems at a loss when it comes to imagining the practices through which teachers of writing might apply the lessons learned from his reconception of metaphor: "What a 'deconstructive' textbook of freshman writing would be like I am not sure, though it would certainly have more and different material on figurative language" ("Composition" 55). While Miller goes on to argue that such a textbook needs to be written, he can only say what it should *not* include by way of faulty assumptions about metaphor and discursive unity; how students might be taken in new directions is nowhere to be found. Indeed, for all the wisdom these essays offer about metaphor, there is little sense of what to do with this wisdom now that we have it before us: literary theory has apparently come to the rescue of composition, but the specific form of its salvation has yet to articulated.

Not that every piece of scholarship should provide surefire solutions to pedagogical problems. My point is that Miller, like many other recent scholars who find metaphor a ubiquitous and inescapable agent of discourse, stops short of all but the vaguest suggestions for change not because he lacks interest in change but because it is far from certain just what sort of change such a perspective on metaphor should bring to the teaching of English.[15] For Richards, metaphor remains useful because it reveals those places where "misunderstanding" begins—and thus provides an opportunity to get students back on the right interpretive track. But for Miller, de Man, and a whole generation of scholars for whom misreading is the very nature of reading itself, it remains unclear just what should be done with metaphor that would lead to significant revision of the curriculum. In what ways, for instance, might an awareness of metaphor effect students' performance as writers and not just as readers? Would consciousness of the presence of metaphor in so-called "nonliterary" discourses as well as poetry and fiction lead students to approach their own writing with more creativity and experimental verve? Should students attempt to include *more* metaphors in their texts than they ordinarily do?

In the next section, I examine how certain composition scholars have attempted to address these questions. As I hope to demonstrate, pedagogical endeavors to promote explicit awareness of the difference between figurative and literal language ironically reveal nothing so much as the irrelevance of such awareness when it comes to helping students steer metaphor to their advantage as writers—for oddly enough, metaphor seems to resist the efforts of those who would control its appearance and effect, be it in their own writing or in the writing of others. Paradoxically, what may prove most instructive about metaphor is the extent to which it refuses instruction.

Metaphor and the Student Text

One of the more intriguing features of Aristotle's commentary on figurative language lies in his insistence that instruction about metaphor —even as he himself provides such instruction—is fruitless. In the *Rhetoric,* he bluntly declares that metaphor is "not a thing whose use can be taught by one man to another" (168); and in the *Poetics* he goes even further, asserting that a mastery of metaphor is "the one thing that cannot be learnt from others" (255). For Aristotle, not only are good creators of metaphor born rather than made, metaphor is the *only* feature of writing that a teacher cannot teach.

While a good many composition textbooks over the past two hundred years have seemed to place more hope than Aristotle does in the possibility of teaching students the use of metaphor, it is interesting to observe how limited (and limiting) are the practical "exercises" concerning metaphor that these textbooks have imagined to be productive for the students who engage in them. In nineteenth-century textbooks, one of the more prevalent exercises in chapters on figures of speech simply provides a series of incomplete sentences and asks students to fill the empty spaces with metaphors; how this practice is supposed to carry over into the students' own writing is anyone's guess. "Fill up the blanks with the metaphorical words needed to complete the sense," instructs an exercise in James Robert Boyd's *Elements of Rhetoric and Literary Criticism* (1844)—whereupon students are provided sentences like the following: "In Rome eloquence was a ——— of late growth and short duration" (85). The possibility here that a term like *late growth* might already constitute a metaphor is left unnoticed.[16] Another popular exercise, one still found in composition handbooks on the current market, requires students to identify the metaphors (and sometimes other figures of speech) in a list of already completed sentences. "Consulting section 21c," students are told in the *Simon and Schuster Handbook for Writers* (4th ed., 1996), "identify each figure of speech. Also revise any mixed metaphors" (Troyka 404). What follows are sentences such as "If I eat one more bite of that chocolate cake, I'll explode"—which the instructor's edition of this handbook informs us is an example of overstatement, not metaphor. Why the sentence cannot be considered both figures at once is not pursued, and the implications this exercise holds for student texts themselves goes unspoken. As in most other exercises of this sort, metaphor becomes a word or phrase that we can occasionally pick out of the crowd—a sporadic rather than fundamental feature of language.[17]

But by far the most widespread method by which composition textbooks offer practice with metaphor lies in exercises that ask students to "convert" supposedly literal sentences into their figurative equivalents and/or supposedly figurative sentences into their literal equivalents. While the catalogue of textbooks that includes such exercises is a long one,[18] a version of them can be found in contemporary textbooks such as *The Holt Handbook,* which provides the following instructions for one of the exercises in its section on figurative language:

> Rewrite the following sentences, adding one of the figures of speech discussed above to each sentence to make the ideas more vivid and exciting. Identify each figure of speech you use, and be sure to use each of the five figures of speech at least once.
>
> Example: The room was cool and still.
>
> The room was cool and still like the inside of a cathedral. (simile) (Kirszner and Mandell 318)

Students are then offered a series of brief and mundane sentences—"The December morning was bright and cloudy"; "House cats can be very lazy"—whose "ideas" they are to make "more vivid and exciting" by "adding" a figure of speech. This notion, frequently reiterated in composition textbooks, that metaphor supplements an otherwise literal discourse illustrates how wedded such textbooks remain to the long-standing view of figures as mere decorations for the true substance of language. The very structure of this assignment, in which the literal sentence is to be draped with figurative attire, directs students to think of figuration as that which comes *after* the essential core of one's discourse has already been established.

Yet even those textbook authors who abjure trivial exercises and recognize figurative language as serving more than a decorative function have trouble identifying what good it does to "teach" figures of speech. Edward P. J. Corbett, for instance, whose well-known *Classical Rhetoric for the Modern Student* (3rd ed., 1990) devotes an unusually extensive section to a discussion of the figures, explains that the study of some forty tropes and schemes he goes on to define can provide an awareness that students may lack: "If nothing else, you should become aware, through this exposure, that your language has more figurative resources than you were conscious of. And you may discover that you have been using many of the figures of speech all your life" (425). As the phrase "if nothing else" suggests, Corbett seems uncertain whether "exposure" to the figures he includes does anything other than name the things that students already do with language. Admitting shortly thereafter that knowing the names of various rhetorical figures is not a prerequisite for their use, Corbett attempts to salvage his introductory remarks on the subject by suggesting that "if we make a conscious effort to learn the figures of speech, it is likely that we will resort to them more often" (426). But it remains unclear exactly how an awareness of the figures and their definitions would lead students to employ them more frequently. Given that composition scholars have long rejected the notion that writers need conscious knowledge of grammatical terminology in order to construct grammatical sentences, it seems equally problematic to hold that conscious knowledge of figurative terminology will make much difference in the use of figures. Though Corbett later contends that "in acquiring any skill, we must at first do consciously what experts do automatically" (458), he overlooks the fact that students *already* use figures "automatically": if figuration is a "skill," then it is one that students "acquire" long before they enter college, for writing of any kind would not be possible without it. No writer need *decide* to create a figure in order for one to appear ("I think I'll use chiasmus here—or perhaps asyndeton"); rather, rhetorical fluency is such that various figurative movements, whether conscious or unconscious, shape the writer's responses to textual and contextual demands during the act of writing itself.[19]

But clearly composition studies cannot be equated with textbooks alone, and there are a number of composition scholars who have attempted to incorporate recent theories of metaphor into their approach to the teaching of writing.[20] One of these scholars is Donald McQuade, who offers one of the more thoughtful accounts of the role of metaphor in student writing in his essay "Metaphor, Thinking, and the Composing Process." While a good deal of the attention given to metaphor by those in composition has focused on what Linda Peterson calls "the early stages of composing"—when metaphor supposedly holds "generative possibilities" for writers who need help in discovering what they wish to say (429)—McQuade contends that metaphor can assist writers in revising their prose even after they have already produced one or more drafts. Drawing on the work of Paul Ricoeur, McQuade describes metaphor as a recomposition of reality: "Metaphor assimilates what previously seemed incompatible. In this sense, it is more appropriate to state that metaphor creates the likeness rather than that metaphor simply gives verbal form to some preexistent similarity" (225). As the mention of "likeness" suggests, McQuade's view is one that retains the classical notion of metaphor as a trope of resemblance, while at the same time contending that metaphor *creates* resemblances rather than merely discerns their *a priori* presence in the external world.[21] Metaphor thus depends upon creative imagination to push through the differences between things in order to assert—and thereby bring into being —their similarities. Like Richards, McQuade argues that it is not only language but also thinking itself that is drenched in metaphor, and he endorses Ricoeur's claim that "the figure of speech we call 'metaphor' allows us a glance at the general procedure by which we produce concepts" (qtd. in McQuade 225).

Turning to the potential applications of Ricoeur's views in the composition class, McQuade begins by observing that metaphor can be "extremely valuable in pointing out directions for thinking at the outset of writing" (226). A student might compile, for instance, a list of metaphors associated with her subject and then choose one upon which to base her essay. By approaching her subject through that which it resembles, this student "will have discovered the pleasures of working with controlling metaphor, a resourceful feature of rhetoric that has remained neglected for far too long in writing courses" (227). But in addition to this aid to invention, McQuade goes on to note that "metaphor is also a very useful form of redescription" and can thus serve as "an invaluable aid to revision":

> Suppose, for example, that a student has completed a first draft on Poe's influence on the development of the American short story. In revising the draft, the student might decide that Poe's theory can be described metaphorically as a plant. The terms that gravitate around this metaphor ("seeds," "planted," "fertile," "off-shoot," "fruition," etc.) could help the student reexamine both the substance of what has been said and the design for saying it. (227)

While the process by which students "might decide" upon their metaphors remains vague, McQuade brings to light the fact that metaphor can assist students not merely in the early stages of composing but also after they have produced a text, when they may need to reconsider their initial perspective on the subject at hand. In this sense, metaphor would seem to make invention part of the entire composing process rather than a "stage" that exists only at the beginning.

On the other hand, the student in McQuade's example would presumably be using metaphor not just in her revision but in her first draft as well, long before she arrives at the metaphor of the plant. To mention only her conscious choice of metaphor in the revised draft fails to take into account the pervasive and often unconscious presence of figuration in any piece of writing, however rough or preparatory. Taking seriously Ricoeur's equation of metaphor with "the general procedure by which we produce concepts" means that we must eventually ask how students can put into "use," as if it were a tool on the shelf, that which enables them to think anything whatsoever in the first place, whether or not they are aware of its existence. While it is surely important to recognize that students can use new metaphors to see in new ways, it is also imperative not to overlook the ways in which students are used *by* metaphors that inevitably structure their discourse even when they have not the slightest idea what a metaphor is. If metaphor truly holds the power that Ricoeur ascribes to it, then what McQuade calls the "controlling metaphor" is not just a metaphor we control but a metaphor that controls *us*.

But it is just this reversal that composition scholarship on metaphor has found so difficult to address. Since the aim of bringing metaphor into the classroom is shaped by the larger aim of teaching students to master through conscious control the movements of their discourse, the scholar who argues for more attention to metaphor seems bound to retreat—however unwillingly or unwittingly—to a classical conception of figurative language, one in which metaphors are produced or eliminated on demand. In McQuade's essay, the passage that best reveals this about-face occurs in his concluding section, wherein he offers fellow composition teachers a summary of the reasons why they should invite their students to attend to metaphor:

> Metaphor can play a critical role throughout the entire process of composition. It can stimulate, screen, and direct writers' preliminary thinking, help guide their selection of material, control their particular emphasis, and, in general, furnish them with a uniform frame of reference within which individual observations, ideas, and snippets of information about a subject can be enhanced and consolidated. . . . In sum, metaphor can not only actualize but stabilize the nascent meaning of a composition" (228).

Despite the many advantages that McQuade here sees in metaphor, his remarks nonetheless reveal the point at which even the most informed attempts to introduce new theories of metaphor to the curriculum are constrained by reductive theories of writing and of student writing in particular. For as long as the "stabilization" of meaning remains the aim of instruction in writing, metaphor can never be more than a technique for ensuring that student discourse conveniently *holds still* for the teacher. Indeed, such an objective may indicate why McQuade has turned to Ricoeur, whose approach to metaphor stresses what he calls the "new congruence" that emerges from this trope's initial "impertinence." As Ricoeur remarks in "The Metaphorical Process as Cognition, Imagination, and Feeling," "The metaphor is not the enigma but the solution to the enigma" (144). From this perspective, it is metaphor's ability to overcome the disruptive presence of dissimilarity—that is, to use dissimilarity in service of similarity—that signals its genius and achievement. Difference, in other words, is valued only to the extent that it eventually produces harmonious resemblance.

Ultimately, however, McQuade's attempt to discover pedagogical value in an alternative conception of metaphor suggests not so much the inadequacy of Ricoeur's theory (problematic as this theory seems to be) as the possibility that metaphor may prove less directly "teachable" than teachers of writing might hope. Recognizing that metaphor is best seen as integral rather than supplemental to all forms of language, McQuade claims that "we ought to encourage our students to remember that [metaphor] is much more than a cosmetic device; it is a powerful mental act that underlies all discourse and pervades all rhetorical structures and strategies" (225). But what remains uncertain is how this act of remembering the importance of metaphor necessarily grants any more control over the production of discourse than awareness that we require oxygen to live grants control over the functioning of our lungs. To pursue this analogy a bit further: we can learn to slow down our breathing for purposes of relaxation, to hold our breath while underwater, to hyperventilate in order to induce dizziness, and so on—but inevitably we return to breathing as a matter of course when attention moves elsewhere. Similarly, writers may attempt to control their use of metaphor and other figures, and they may even succeed for a short while in remaining "conscious" of their figurative creations—but eventually they turn their eyes in other directions, if only because endless preoccupation with the metaphorical dimension of language, as with any form of excessive self-consciousness, inhibits not only fluency but also the satisfactions that come with making meaning. Yet when writers attend to something else, metaphor, like the lungs, continues to breathe on, absorbing and reconfiguring the discourses with which it works.

None of which is meant to suggest that the best policy for teachers of writing would be to ignore metaphor altogether—quite the contrary. But rather than attempting to fit a revised perspective on metaphor into the conventional goals of writing instruction, the field of composition might do better to establish a different set of goals altogether, goals that a reconception of metaphor can help to articulate. In what ways, for instance, might the teaching of writing be transformed were what Ricoeur calls the "impertinence" of metaphor recognized as a revelation of the impertinence of writing itself? How might composition give as much pedagogical emphasis to the dissonance created by writing as it currently gives to consonance, and what would be the effect of such a change? Regardless of various shifts in pedagogy and subject matter over the years, composition instruction has remained intent on teaching students to produce some version of *nonfiction prose,* be it labeled exposition, argument, academic discourse, personal narrative, or epistemic rhetoric[22]—which in turn means that literalism (or the metaphor whose *congruence,* to use Ricouer's term, overcomes its impertinence) prevails. The most misguided institutional distinction, in other words, may be less that which separates composition from literary studies than that which separates composition from creative writing—as is highly evident in the recent series of debates in the pages of *College English* over the place of "imaginative literature" in the composition course.[23] By refraining (except as the occasional departure) from inviting students to *write* and not just read such literature, the field of composition continues to reject the aberrations of metaphor, which challenge the idea that discourses should be kept in their proper places. Yet composition is itself an aberrant figure among academic disciplines, and it might therefore make the embrace of metaphor a part of its resistance to the literalist tendencies of the academy at large.

I look further in part 2 at the possibilities both for composition and the English department as a whole were divisions between the teaching of metaphorical and literal discourses eliminated from the curriculum. While the *idea* of dissolving such barriers has often been advanced, more extensive consideration must be given to just exactly how a revised curriculum might function and what professional and institutional consequences might follow. But I turn first, in the next chapter, to still another paradox in the "teaching" of metaphor—namely, the ways in which the search for metaphor can hinder, rather than help, readers of literary texts.

2

HIGHER LEARNING

Reading (for) Metaphor in the Literature Class

> "All metaphor breaks down somewhere. That is the beauty of it. It is touch and go with metaphor, and until you have lived with it long enough you don't know when it is going. You don't know how much you can get out of it and when it will cease to yield."
>
> Robert Frost, "Education by Poetry:
> A Meditative Monologue"

LIKE MANY OTHERS, I have long thought that introductory courses, be they in composition or in literature, present the most formidable challenge for teachers of college English. But lately I am not so sure. While "freshman composition" and "sophomore literature," as they are often termed, both remain a special kind of pedagogical project, it may be that all the focus on so-called "preparatory" courses has led discussions of curricular reform to neglect the complex demands of teaching upper-division courses, wherein students are supposedly more astute, informed, and motivated. After all, the very distinction between introductory and advanced courses presumes that the primary difficulties in teaching exist (and must be confronted) early on—for once students have reached an "advanced" level of performance, what is left to impede the spirited teacher's ability to teach? If you can't effectively teach a group of senior English majors—so goes the logic—you have only yourself to blame.

There are at least two unfortunate consequences that follow this set of assumptions. The first is that the vast majority of teachers (and students) imagine that the most interesting academic work occurs the farther away from introductory courses they move, since the "higher" they proceed in the curriculum, the greater the amount of knowledge and skill they can suppose has been previously absorbed by student and teacher alike. Introductory courses thus become "requirements" that most students either can't wait to complete or see fit to postpone to the bitter end, and that most teachers either hope to avoid or attempt to teach with as much selfless zeal as they can muster. But the second consequence is equally problematic: teachers are often disappointed to find that "advanced" students are neither as knowledgeable nor as skilled as they are presumed to be, and that the experience of teaching upper-division courses can therefore seem more troubling than satisfying. In a senior seminar, for instance, students are expected to know already "how to read" and "how to write"—a supposition that can leave teachers dismayed to find that their students still struggle with both.

I write not as one who stands above such difficulties but as one who has experienced them virtually every time I have taught an upper-division course in literature over the last thirteen years. Indeed, my point of departure for this chapter stems from a course I taught in the spring of 1997—a course entitled "Literature for Adolescents," which is regularly offered by our English department but which I was teaching for the first time. As anticipated, the course was composed almost entirely of juniors and seniors who planned on becoming high school English teachers, and many of these students were in the process of applying to postbaccalaureate education programs in order to earn their state certification for teaching in the public schools. They were bright, energetic, committed, and eager to contribute to class discussion. In other words, they were what is sometimes called a "teacher's dream"—students who are already motivated to learn, in no need of further entreaties to convince them that a course holds significance for their own lives.

And yet I was immediately (and naively, it now seems in hindsight) surprised to find that these students, who were but a year from entering classrooms as teachers themselves, had barely begun—despite their intelligence, high grades, and advanced standing—to consider not only *how* they might approach the teaching of literature with their own students but more importantly *why* literature should even be taught in the first place. ("Literature," incidentally, here meant fiction, poetry, and drama—a generic definition I began with, and later in the semester challenged, since this is the definition usually adopted by the high school curriculum.) What good would it do their students, I kept asking these teachers-to-be in the early weeks of the course, to read, and to write about, novels, poems, and plays in their English classes? What was the purpose of it all, beyond racking up another credit toward a high school degree? Even if, as several students suggested in class discussion, those who learned to enjoy reading literature as adolescents were more likely to keep reading literature as adults, what was the point of reading literature at any age? Though they were ready and willing to reply to my queries with either of two familiar views—(1) that the *content* of literature reveals a deeper reality than other forms of discourse; or (2) that the *language* of literature displays a higher aesthetic sensibility than other forms of discourse—the students in this course generally admitted, when pushed to explore these matters a bit further, that they held very little sense of how to support their claims, other than to resort to clichés about truth, universality, and beauty. Indeed, as they gradually lost their assurance that literature was a superior discourse (or lost confidence in their ability to explain its superiority in any detail), students began to wonder aloud whether there *were* good reasons for teaching novels, poems, and plays in high school after all. Couldn't I, a few of them ventured to ask, just tell them the answer I was looking for?

While I initially presumed that these prospective teachers were not working hard enough to imagine alternatives to standard answers about the value of literature, I eventually came to believe that the problem was much more intractable, and that it was thoroughly entangled with issues that are central to, yet at the same time misconceived by, the English studies curriculum—namely, issues of metaphor. In this chapter, I return to a specific class meeting in which metaphor, left unmentioned in prior weeks, was suddenly and enthusiastically cited by a group of students as their guide to reading the text I had assigned them to discuss that evening. The central difficulty that arose in the teacher-student quarrel that ensued, and that I go on to raise again here, concerns how we can tell in the first place which lines of a text should be read metaphorically and which should be read literally—and, once we decide, just how we should go about doing one or the other. After discussing a classificatory scheme that offers some assistance in identifying various kinds of metaphor, I then consider an interpretation advanced by two highly accomplished scholars in response to the same text that gave students such trouble during the class in question. What this scholarly interpretation illuminates, I believe, is the inevitable *risk* that accompanies the reading of metaphor, no matter how "closely" one has read. Moreover, as I go on to demonstrate by examining some samples of student writing produced in my course, supposedly "literal" discourse provokes at least as much interpretive difficulty as its metaphorical counterpart—an observation that could bring a new conception of, and a new set of challenges to, the teaching of English.

A Pedagogical Dilemma

Having spent the first month of "Literature for Adolescents" on prose fiction (whose sentences students seemed certain should be immediately converted into "ideas" and "themes"), I had decided, now that the course was turning to poetry (whose lines I feared might suffer a similar fate), to assign only a small sample of the better-known poems of Robert Frost for our two-and-a-half-hour class that night. Poetry, after all, was bound to intensify these students' reactions when confronted with "literature," which they apparently envisioned as a bastion of seriousness that could only be overcome through scaling the walls of its impenetrable words, behind which lay its secrets. Though I knew that Frost was likely to be considered a "simple" poet, one whose "message" in a given poem is relatively easy to discern, I nevertheless had hope that careful discussion of his work might help students to see how texts deemed "accessible" can prove far more challenging—and rewarding, precisely because of their challenge—than they initially appear. These four poems by Frost ("Mending Wall," "After Apple-Picking," "Birches," and "Two Tramps in Mud Time") seemed perfectly suited to contest the reductive practices that had characterized students' reading habits in the course thus far, as well as to get them thinking about how, if and when they themselves taught Frost to high school students at some future date, they might approach his poetry with respect for its nuance and subtlety.

When class began, I divided the students into eight small groups and arranged responsibilities so that two groups were working on each of the poems. I then distributed a brief study guide that asked them to approach the poem their group had been assigned as if it were a short story rather than a poem—taking care to discuss things like plot, character, and narrative tone. I also asked that, in addition to noting the narrator's attitudes toward the events he depicts, students comment on Frost-the-implied-author's implicit evaluation of these attitudes.[1] My objective was in part to point toward the intersections between poetry and fictional narrative and thereby to connect this part of the course with what had come before; but more importantly it was to insist that students focus on the supposedly trivial matter of *what is happening* in a poem before they leapt to the supposedly more substantive issue of *what it means*. Furthermore, I anticipated that students might equate the speaker of a poem with its author—a problem that tends to be far less prevalent when working with prose fiction—and I thought that my study guide, by generating a gap between Frost and his various narrators, might lead to conversation about the presence of irony and rebuke in poems that are often taken at first glance as straightforward confession or disclosure. While these goals may sound rather modest for an upper-division college literature course, especially for one in which a good number of the students were English majors, that evening's class offered further evidence of how mistaken it is to imagine such concerns can be set aside once they have been addressed in prior courses. Indeed, it may well be that, when it comes to literature, virtually nothing is too "elementary" to consider—precisely because literature continually renegotiates its own elements.

So much for the best laid lesson plans: once we reconvened and the first two groups of students began to report on their half hour's work, it was clear that something had gone awry. Though both of the groups assigned to investigate "Mending Wall" had done their best to follow my directions on the study guide, their fidelity to the parameters I had designed seemed to disable as much as to enable their discussion of the poem. They had identified a "plot" involving two neighbors and a wall; they had recognized that the narrator's attitudes toward his neighbor are skeptical and judgmental; and they had even seen that this narrator need not be Frost—yet establishing these features of the poem had apparently left them with little sense of purpose as readers. As I listened to group members offer flat and unexploratory replies to the questions on the study guide, I saw that I had succeeded only in sending them on a search for material they were fully able to find but did not yet know how to use. After locating the items I had specified, their reading came to a halt, as if they had been taken down a dead-end street.

Then we turned to "After Apple-Picking," and something unexpected occurred. Here is the poem:

My long two-pointed ladder's sticking through a tree
Toward heaven still,
And there's a barrel that I didn't fill
Beside it, and there may be two or three
Apples I didn't pick upon some bough.
But I am done with apple-picking now.
Essence of winter sleep is on the night,
The scent of apples: I am drowsing off.
I cannot rub the strangeness from my sight
I got from looking through a pane of glass
I skimmed this morning from the drinking trough
And held against the world of hoary grass.
It melted, and I let it fall and break.
But I was well
Upon my way to sleep before it fell,
And I could tell
What form my dreaming was about to take.
Magnified apples appear and disappear,
Stem end and blossom end,
And every fleck of russet showing clear.
My instep arch not only keeps the ache,
It keeps the pressure of a ladder-round.
I feel the ladder sway as the boughs bend.
And I keep hearing from the cellar bin
The rumbling sound
Of load on load of apples coming in.
For I have had too much
Of apple-picking: I am overtired
Of the great harvest I myself desired.
There were ten thousand thousand fruit to touch,

Cherish in hand, lift down, and not let fall.
For all
That struck the earth,
No matter if not bruised or spiked with stubble,
Went surely to the cider-apple heap
As of no worth.
One can see what will trouble
This sleep of mine, whatever sleep it is.
Were he not gone,
The woodchuck could say whether it's like his
Long sleep, as I describe its coming on,
Or just some human sleep.

After the first group assigned this poem gave still another plodding account of their observations, members of the next group announced that they had found my study guide "boring" and that they had therefore decided to hold their discussion without it. This group was clearly excited about what they had discovered, and they went on to share their reading of the poem, a reading that—disconcertingly, from my point of view—went something like this: The narrator of "After Apple-Picking" is about to die (as the reference to "heaven" suggests), and as he looks back over his life, he sees that there were some good times ("ten thousand thousand fruit to touch") and some bad times (those apples "bruised and spiked with stubble"). Though he has begun to have discomforting visions of death, he finds himself by and large content that his time for eternal rest has arrived. After all, he is an old man now, "overtired" from all the work he has done, work that he continues to picture in his mind's eye as he awaits the "Long sleep" of death. Ultimately, the students in this group agreed, Frost's poem suggests that life has its ups and downs, but that when death finally makes its move, we can still manage to find peace and acceptance. Going on to explain further why she thought this approach to the poem was more interesting than that which my study guide appeared to promote, one member of the group remarked: "I mean, you can't read the poem as if he's *literally* talking about apple-picking, can you? If you do, then there's nothing to get from it. To read a poem you have to read for *metaphor*."

Whereupon I found myself on the horns of a rather excruciating dilemma—for how was I to tell a class full of juniors and seniors, most of whom wished to become teachers themselves, that we should *not* read poetry (and not read literature in general) for metaphor? Is not literature, and poetry in particular, *the* metaphorical discourse—the set of texts wherein one finds the most and best of metaphor? Yet at the same time I knew that the reading this group had produced was precisely the form of interpretation I had sought to discourage with my study guide. It was the reading heard over and over, often from the most schooled and diligent students, who after years of study in English courses have learned that "reading for metaphor" means to peel back, as if literature itself were an apple, the outer layers of the text in order to discover its inner core, where the "hidden meaning" supposedly lies. From this perspective, literature, like metaphor, is language that "means one thing but says another," and the endeavor of the reader is to replace the former with the latter. Though it remains unclear why writers would engage in such elaborate displays of deception (and why readers should be bothered with translating what could presumably be stated much more plainly and transparently from the outset), innumerable students of literature continue to approach literary texts as the group in my class approached Frost's poem—with an agenda defined by the aims of paraphrase. Once these students had discovered an apparent solution to the enigma that the metaphors in "After Apple-Picking" put before them, they assumed that their task was done. For that is what the reading of literature had become for them: a *task,* one in which the central imperative was to convert the metaphorical overlay of the text into an account of its literal underside. In other words, they not only took what Max Black has called the "substitution view" of metaphor, in which metaphors merely substitute for literal equivalents ("Metaphor" 279), they also took a substitutive view of literature, whereby language stands in, and must ultimately be set aside, for what it means. The satisfaction that some students appeared to take in having unveiled what they considered the literal truth of Frost's poem seemed the ephemeral satisfaction that comes with solving a crossword puzzle or a riddle—words to be left behind once conquered.

While paraphrase surely plays a part in any interpretive activity, "reading for metaphor" as it was practiced by these students would appear to endorse an extremely limited engagement with literature and consequently—for the two are closely related—a disturbingly impoverished form of literacy. The latter problem became all the more evident when I asked those in the group that had interpreted "After Apple-Picking" how they came to the conclusion that the narrator is content to die. One member observed that all the bad apples, those "bruised or spiked with stubble," had gone to "the cider-apple heap" and were therefore no longer any bother to the narrator. Whereupon I read aloud, with emphasis:

> For *all*
> That struck the earth,
> *No matter* if not bruised or spiked with stubble,
> Went surely to the cider-apple heap
> *As of* no worth.

Did these lines really support the group's reading? No one was willing to argue one way or another. Then another member of the group opined that their reading was justified by the next few lines of the poem, which tell us that the "trouble" in the speaker's sleep was "gone." Whereupon I read aloud, with emphasis:

> One can see what *will trouble*
> This sleep of mine, whatever sleep it is.
> Were *he* not gone,
> *The woodchuck* could say whether . . .

Did these lines suggest that the speaker's sleep (or death) will be untroubled? There was a bit of murmuring, but nobody replied: members of the group, enthused only a few minutes earlier, were beginning to turn sullen. Though I went on to explain what I was attempting to demonstrate—that the poem is plenty complicated on the so-called "literal" level, never mind the metaphorical—the group seemed more wounded than enlightened by my response to their work.

I suppose that from their point of view I was behaving like an English teacher—picking away at their interpretations, seizing upon "little things" like verb tenses and pronouns, reading passages aloud in order to undermine their own perception of the poem. I was the master with the key to literature—perhaps all the more so because I refused to propose a reading of the poem myself. But whatever the cause of these students' increasingly timid replies to my inquiries, I don't think the lesson is that teachers should take a less interrogative stance than I did here. While I did become more sensitive in the weeks that followed to students' need for a different approach to challenging their work, the pedagogical problem I am describing is not one that can be resolved by an astute teacher any more than the interpretive problem posed by Frost's poem can be resolved by an astute reader. Indeed, part of what I am attempting to illustrate through this narrative of the classroom is that upper-division students of English are bound to feel themselves sorely abused when they discover that what the curriculum has promised them —"advanced" proficiency as readers—it has not only failed to deliver but *cannot* deliver, precisely because reading never escapes the most "elementary" practices. As Christopher Ricks has said of metaphor, we might also say of reading in general: "The rudiments are immediately the impassable impediments" (182). Presuming that they had demonstrated their interpretive prowess by leaping ahead to an explanation of the poem's metaphors, the students in my class were understandably disappointed to have me respond by questioning their facility with what they considered the most "basic" component of the text—its literalisms. By returning them to a literal reading of the poem, I rejected their eager attempt to display the very form of interpretation that they believed their standing as advanced students (and as prospective teachers) had licensed.

Ultimately, then, the difficulties we all encountered that evening concerned not only the psychology of teacher-student relations but also the contradictions of metaphor, a figure so frequently touted as literature's greatest ally but one that can appear, in classes like that which I've described, to be literature's greatest enemy. I won't bother to rehearse, nor do I wish to deny, all the well-worn clichés regarding the essential contribution that metaphor makes to literary texts and to poetry in particular —but what I do want to indicate is the trouble that "reading for metaphor" can nevertheless cause student readers, who are often so busy looking for figurative meanings that they entirely pass over the *literal* meanings on which poems equally depend. The group of students who proclaim "After Apple-Picking" to be about a man's impending death have not so much misread the poem as they have failed to make contact with the language it places before them—a language whose subtle intricacies and modulations offer the attentive reader far more than an answer to the "puzzle" posed by its metaphors. For while these students might certainly have found, if given the time, sufficient evidence to defend their interpretation of the poem, mounting such a defense would not necessarily put them any closer to an appreciation, or a critique, of what Frost's writing does with language as it moves from line to line. It may be the remarkable difficulty of *this* project—one that would ask not simply what literary texts mean to readers but first and foremost *what they do to words*—that keeps both teachers and students locked into reading *for* metaphor (reading in search of metaphors and on metaphor's behalf) rather than reading metaphor itself as a dynamic, and not always harmless, force of language.

Indeed, one of the questions raised by the discussion that occurred in my class is how any reader, whether teacher or student, is to identify metaphor in the first place. By what means do we know, when reading a text, where to draw the line between the metaphorical and the literal? How do we recognize the different shapes and masks that metaphors are prone to assume? And what methods guide our interpretation of metaphors once we have located their whereabouts?

In Search of the Literal

In "Four Forms of Metaphor," published by *College English* almost thirty years ago, Laurence Perrine proposes what he calls "a new way of looking at and classifying metaphors," one that he thinks "may be pedagogically useful" when it comes to the reading of poetry (125). As Perrine indicates, metaphors are often categorized by identifying their part of speech—so that we have noun metaphors, verb metaphors, adjective metaphors, and so on. But Perrine advances a different approach altogether, and the implications of his alternative scheme are more significant than Perrine himself—or almost anyone else—seems to have realized.[2]

Though he begins with a conventional definition of metaphor ("a comparison between essentially unlike things"), Perrine quickly departs from precedent by naming the two parts of a metaphor the "literal term" and the "figurative term" (125), which respectively correspond to I. A. Richards's "tenor" and "vehicle." To take a simple example: in the metaphorical statement "The speech was sunlight," "speech" would serve, in Perrine's account, as the literal term, and "sunlight" as the figurative term. While such nomenclature may initially sound confusing—for metaphors are usually presumed to oppose rather than include literalism —the advantage of these names is that they remind us of the abiding intersections between the literal and the metaphorical, even within "metaphor" itself. Moreover, Perrine goes on to classify metaphors on the basis of whether their literal and/or figurative terms are stated in the text or merely implied. This results in four different kinds of metaphor (which I include with examples supplied by Perrine):

Form 1: Both the literal and figurative terms are stated.

"All the world's a stage,
And all the men and women merely players."
—Shakespeare, *As You Like It*

Form 2: The literal term is stated, and the figurative term implied.

"Pride, like that of the morn,
When the headlong light is loose.
—W. B. Yeats, *The Tower*

Form 3: The figurative term is stated, and the literal implied.

"Night's candles are burnt out."
—Shakespeare: *Romeo and Juliet*

Form 4: Both the literal and figurative terms are implied.

"Let us eat and drink, for tomorrow we shall die."
—Isaiah xxii, 13

While I will concern myself primarily with what Perrine calls the Form 3 metaphor, there are two important points to be made about this classification in general. The first is that, as Perrine indicates in passing, textbooks designed for courses in composition or literature are so concerned with Form 1 metaphors that they completely ignore the others —and the same is also true of most theoretical discussions of metaphor.[3]

This convenient oversight allows such discussions to begin with the presumption that readers have both terms of the metaphor before their eyes and need only to recognize their similarities. But Perrine illustrates—and this is the second point that should be observed—how one, or even both, terms of a metaphor may be implied rather than stated, thereby leaving readers with considerably more work to perform if they are to comprehend the metaphor. Indeed, it is not the relatively manageable job of discerning similarities but rather *this* interpretive labor—in which we attempt to discern the "absent" part of the metaphor—that poses the most significant challenge for readers of poetry, which often represses either the literal or the figurative term.

But let us look more closely at the Form 3 metaphor, wherein only the figurative term appears outright, leaving the literal term to be inferred. This, I believe, is the situation we encounter in Frost's "After Apple-Picking," which contains not a single metaphor of the A=B (Form 1) variety. As Perrine observes with his example from *Romeo and Juliet* ("Night's candles are burnt out"), there is nothing in this line that signals its metaphorical status, since Romeo may simply be referring to *real* candles (rather than to the stars) that have burnt out now that morning is about to arrive. Consequently: "We must depend upon a larger context for the clues that indicate a metaphorical reading" (128)—such as the speech in which Romeo's line occurs, where we find that he is looking at the sky. But things get considerably more complicated if a metaphor of this kind is extended throughout the entire poem, so that, as Perrine puts it, "there is no surrounding context to refer to, and understanding of the whole poem depends upon recognition of the metaphor" (134).[4] In Frost's poem, for instance, we are never signaled to read any of the lines metaphorically (with two exceptions: the phrase "pane of glass," by which the speaker describes the ice he lifts from the drinking trough; and the reference to a woodchuck that could "say" what form of sleep the narrator of the poem is about to experience). Certainly it is possible to take the events of the speaker's narrative literally from start to finish—in which case the poem becomes the story of a man who is describing his mental and physical exhaustion after picking apples for days on end. Perrine points out that in his own teaching experience, students often overlook the metaphorical structure of certain poems by Emily Dickinson, who is fond of suppressing the literal terms in her metaphors. Yet while Perrine seems primarily concerned with ensuring that students recognize metaphors *as* metaphors, my concern in teaching a poet like Frost (or any poet, for that matter) is just the opposite: students of literature—particularly "advanced" students—can be so quick to jump to a metaphorical reading that they never give the literal a chance. To their eyes, "After Apple-Picking" simply *cannot* be about what it claims to be about because poetry is meant to be read as metaphor.

Of course, the decision to read a poem or part of a poem metaphorically is just one of the many difficulties before us. As Perrine comments: "Once a passage has been diagnosed as metaphorical, there still remains the problem of determining what two things are being compared" (136). For the students in my class, the apple-picking in Frost's poem was being compared to life, the apples to experiences, fatigue to old age, and sleep to death. But since each of the "literal terms" (life, experiences, old age, and death) that in part constitute these metaphors do not appear in the text of the poem, the question becomes how such interpretations can be legitimated—or, indeed, how *any* metaphorical interpretation can be legitimated—when half of the metaphor is nowhere to be found. Taking these considerations one step further, we would have to wonder whether "After Apple-Picking" is a poem filled with metaphors whose literal terms have been suppressed, or whether it is a poem whose literal terms, not belonging to any metaphors to begin with, are exposed for all to see. For how are we to know?

Perrine concludes his essay by noting that his method of classification "presents a simple conceptual framework for teaching metaphor and for clarifying the ways in which metaphor works" (138). He contends, moreover, that "possession of this conceptual scheme may cut down on a few misreadings," since students who are aware that metaphor assumes four distinct forms will have a better sense of what to expect when reading literature (138). To be sure, I can see how it might have been useful for the students in my own class to know what kind of metaphors (again: if they *are* metaphors) they were attempting to comprehend in Frost's poem, and to understand the difference between metaphors whose terms of comparison are both present and metaphors whose terms are only partially in view. But at the same time, I don't think that conceiving of Perrine's taxonomy as a tip for student readers does it justice—for the crucial insight this approach makes available is not simply that there are various forms of metaphor, but that the interpretation of metaphor often demands a radical dependence on what is *not* on the page. In part this means that metaphors produce "gaps" which destabilize the act of reading; but more significantly it means that, except in the case of metaphors that explicitly state both of their terms, the very decision to *call* a word or series of words a metaphor may reveal more about our strategies as readers than about the texts we read.

Metaphors, in other words, are not simply "encountered" in works of literature. Rather, they are *conjured*—to conjure a metaphor myself—in the course of producing a particular interpretation of a text.[5] The question thus becomes how such conjurings are presented in written accounts of reading (by professional critics as well as students), where creative practice is all too often disguised as mere discovery.

Doing Things with Metaphor

As is so often the case, when I think back on why the students in my course were unable to do much with the questions I had given them about Frost's poems, it becomes clear that neither the students nor the questions were to blame. Rather, the outcome derived from a mismatch of assumptions about the purpose of my questions. As the teacher, I wanted to construct a study guide that would keep students focused on the language of each poem before they jumped into a quest for "hidden meanings"; but for them, such a quest was precisely what they assumed they were to enact in an English class devoted to the interpretation of poetry. Consequently, it was possible (even probable, as it turns out) that students would find themselves "getting nowhere" by doing exactly what I had asked of them. The first three groups proceeded to do just that: they answered my questions about plot, narrative tone, and authorial distance—and the result was a series of bland literalisms that completely ignored the metaphorical implications of the poems.

And then came the departure, when one group of students decided to reject my questions and chose to interpret "After Apple-Picking" the best way they knew how—as a set of metaphors that suggests far more than what "appears" on the page. But while such an approach to poetry certainly has its merits, it can also, as I attempted to demonstrate in class, create more problems than it solves, especially when it comes at the expense of words that cry out more for *explor*ation than *explan*ation. What, after all, are we to make of the "strangeness" the speaker in Frost's poem cannot rub from sight since looking through a sheet of ice that morning? What sort of vision was it that, though he let it "fall and break," still pursues him? Toward what form of "sleep" was he "well upon [his] way" even before the ice slipped from his hand? And what of the "Magnified apples" that "appear and disappear" without end, or of the "ache" he retains from "the pressure of a ladder-round"? The students' quick gloss on the metaphorical meaning of the poem took no heed of these nor numerous other questions raised by even a mildly curious perusal of its literalisms—and their interpretation thus betrayed the very language to which they imagined they were faithful. Even had these students presented a more scrupulous reading of the poem's metaphors, the question that would nevertheless remain concerns what it means to produce a "scrupulous" reading of metaphor in the first place: how can we tell when a metaphor is a metaphor? How are we signaled—*if* we are signaled—that Frost's poem is about more, as one student insisted, than *just* picking apples? And how do we move from what Perrine calls the "figurative term" of the metaphor (be it the apples or the ladder or the sleep) to its "literal term," whatever that might be?

In order to illustrate just how perplexing these questions can become, I want to examine the reading of "After Apple-Picking" offered by Cleanth Brooks and Robert Penn Warren in their pioneering (and still in print) textbook, *Understanding Poetry*. I turn to this textbook for two reasons—first, because it *is* a textbook, one that has served as perhaps this century's most influential model for how poems should be read. While any piece of literary criticism can be approached as an effort to instruct its audience, the analyses of particular poems in Brooks and Warren's textbook are specifically intended for college undergraduates, and in this sense they propose methods by which the reading of poetry *might* be taught in post-secondary institutions. Moreover, Brooks and

Warren exhibit a strikingly astute theory of metaphor, one that recognizes not only the resemblances metaphors create but also their dependence upon differences—so that in no sense do they serve as "straw men" whose approach to metaphor can be easily debunked.[6] My second reason for turning to Brooks and Warren stems from the fact that their interpretation of "After Apple-Picking" in the third edition of *Understanding Poetry* (1960) explicitly foregrounds their decisions about which lines to read metaphorically and which to read literally as we move through the poem.[7] By investigating how these decisions are made, I hope to illustrate not only the difficulty of knowing how to choose from one line to the next, but also the fact that Brooks and Warren's choices, however appealing, take liberties with the poem much like the liberties taken by the students in my class, who looked *past* rather than *at* the words on the page. My question, ultimately, is this: If "reading for metaphor" inevitably requires a leap of faith—an act of inference that cannot be fully substantiated by the text—then how are teachers of English to pass along their "discipline" (by which I mean both the academic enterprise they represent and the interpretive restraint they presumably display) as readers to their students?

Brooks and Warren begin their discussion of "After Apple-Picking" by noting that, even if taken as no more than "a realistic account of apple-picking in New England," the poem still "yields a great deal" (363). The literal reading, that is to say, is already one that rewards the attentive reader, so much so that Brooks and Warren speculate: "The student may well feel that there is little to be gained by going beyond that reading" (363).[8] Though this was not the case with the students in my class last spring, the discrepancy may only indicate the extent to which today's students have been educated in the very methods Brooks and Warren were attempting to promote some forty years ago with this textbook. As I have suggested, current students ("advanced" English majors in particular) are likely to "go beyond" the literal interpretation before they have even identified what it is. Be that as it may, Brooks and Warren hope to help students move from an appreciation of the poem's description of apple-picking and its aftermath to a recognition of the "symbolic overtones" generated by this description (363). Where do these overtones begin to make their appearance? According to Brooks and Warren, the "sign-post" that asks for something other than a literal interpretation comes with the word "essence" in the seventh line—a word that they recognize may simply refer to "a characteristic odor," yet that they believe "hints at something more fundamental" (364):

> My long two-pointed ladder's sticking through a tree
> Toward heaven still,
> And there's a barrel that I didn't fill
> Beside it, and there may be two or three
> Apples I didn't pick upon some bough.
> But I am done with apple-picking now.
> Essence of winter sleep is on the night,
> The scent of apples: I am drowsing off.

While it is reasonable, Brooks and Warren observe, to read the first six lines as a straightforward description of the scene, "essence" is a term whose philosophical connotations suggest possibilities for meaning in addition to the literal and thus require the reader "to consider nonrealistic readings" (364). From this moment on, they contend, the poem is asking to be read metaphorically.[9]

But it is also interesting to observe all that could conceivably call for nonliteral interpretation in the first six lines of the poem—those lines that Brooks and Warren have been content to read as mere description. To begin with, the word "heaven" in line two might surely suggest more than mere sky, and its presence could lead us to wonder about the significance of apple-picking, which possesses, after all, an extensive history of figurative resonance. Indeed, perhaps the most prominent scholarly debate surrounding this poem concerns how to interpret its biblical allusions—with some critics, such as Dorothy Hall, contending that the apple-picker is "a latter-day Adam" who "symbolically perpetuates the Genesis legacy of mankind's first act of disobedience" (4), while others, such as Walton Beacham, argue that though the poem may *seem* to be about "Christian fate, redemption, and the virtuous life," Frost is actually "more concerned with earthly existence" (1177). Either view might ask us to read "Essence of winter sleep"—as my students did— with even greater metaphoric force than do Brooks and Warren, who proceed rather gingerly in their reference to the "philosophical weighting" in this line, instead of perceiving it to foreshadow death (364). Though I do not wish to declare that we *should* equate the setting for this poem with the most famous garden in literature, I think it important to emphasize that we *could*—or at least that we could *begin* to read in this way until later lines in the poem lead us to read otherwise. Once we start to "read for metaphor," there is little to stop us from finding metaphors everywhere we look.

And that's not all. Not only is the act of locating metaphors a loosely designed affair, but the act of interpreting the metaphors we locate seems a process all the more haphazard. When, for instance, Brooks and Warren go on to examine the speaker's dream in "After Apple-Picking," they argue that the dream, even though it "seems to be a bad dream, a nightmare of the day's labor," supports their general contention that the poem presents a "contrast . . . between the actual and the ideal" (365). Of course we might wonder how they can claim that such a dream, with its oversized apples and aching feet and rumbling cellar, represents the realm of the "ideal." But Brooks and Warren do so by reading each of these metaphors as bearing positive connotations equal in measure to the negative: for them, the "Magnified apples" in the dream simply magnify the practical good that apples bring as food (366); the speaker's instep arch may ache from standing too long on the ladder, but Brooks and Warren speculate that at least the swaying of the ladder was surely pleasurable (366–67); and if the rumbling of apples from the cellar troubles the speaker's sleep, it also, in Brooks and Warren's view, represents the end of his labor, which they see as "a loving labor, not a labor simply for practical reward" (367). In other words, once they determine what might be called their macro-reading of the poem as a set of contrasts between the actual and the ideal, their micro-readings of individual metaphors can be made to fall in line.

The same can be said of numerous interpretations of this poem offered by other scholars, who likewise find it possible to match its metaphors to the larger motifs that direct their reading. Thus it is that William Byshe Stein, for whom the poem expresses "Frost's skepticism about the Christian myth of eternal salvation" (301), reads the magnified apples as a metaphor for "the unchanging message of nature," which continues on its way "with or without the instrumentality of man"

(303). Noting the pleasure that the speaker has apparently received from picking apples, Stein discerns that "Frost is ridiculing the shame that the Bible attaches to the carnal pleasures of Adam and Eve" (304); and he goes on to argue that at the end of the poem, when Frost muses on death, "he sums up the attitude towards all the casuistry inspired by the myth of the fall of man in the euphemism, 'just some human sleep'— that is, endless oblivion" (305). On the other hand, for Robert Fleissner, who claims that "the apple-picker . . . envisions himself as sinful humanity incapable of being permanently rid of the effects of primal sin simply through its own efforts" (171), the metaphors that Stein reads one way should be taken in precisely the opposite direction. In Fleissner's view, the speaker's desire indicates that "he has fallen archly for the temptation of *cupiditas*" (170); the fallen apples on their way to the cider-apple heap parallel "the sinner . . . slated for perdition" (171); and the "human sleep" of the final line represents that which the speaker hopes not merely to achieve but to transcend (173). Here we see how the very "same" metaphors can be presented as support for strikingly adverse readings of the poem—but more importantly, we see that neither reading can resort to anything in the poem to dispute the other, for both rely upon initial assumptions grounded far beyond the metaphors these readings claim to explicate.

Consider as well the creative readings of "the world of hoary grass" above which the speaker in Frost's poem holds the ice he has lifted from the drinking trough. For Judith Oster, this image serves as a metaphor for the "white hair" of "old age," which leads her to speculate that the frost on the grass may signify Frost the poet, who views himself through the "personal lens" of the ice (239). Following a different line of thought, William Doreski sees "the world of hoary grass" as representative of symbolism and determinate meaning—an approach to language that Frost attempts to oppose with the "unconventional poetics" he glimpses when looking through the ice (40). And then there's Richard Poirier, who observes, pursuing still another path, that the "hoary grass" could either be "real" (frost-covered) or "other-worldly"—"part of a mythic world derived from the Bible and Milton" (*Robert Frost* 297). Each of these scholars reads with careful attention to the language of the poem, both eye and ear attuned to the suggestiveness of rhythm, phrasing, and imagery; and each presents what could be called a "convincing" inter-pretation of the poem as a whole. Yet neither "the world of hoary grass" nor any of the other metaphors in "After Apple-Picking" leads them to-ward conclusions that seem even remotely similar. Like the poem itself, the metaphors within this poem each produce a swirl of possibilities; or perhaps it would be more accurate to say that the possibilities arise not so much from the metaphors themselves as from the reading practices brought to them by the scholars at hand, each of whom carries a dif-ferent form of critical "baggage" to the poem, from biographical infor-mation to poststructuralist theory to intertextual reference.

By no means do I wish to inveigh against any of these responses to the poem, for they all reflect readings whose combination of insight and imagination I admire. But I do wish to point out that the inferential *reach* necessitated by metaphor may well come at the expense of what the text "literally" appears to say or, more tellingly, cannot quite say. It is worth noting, for instance, that while Brooks and Warren insist that the speaker's "dreaming" must be approached as a metaphor (365), the poem does not make clear that the speaker has even *had* a dream, which may, like the sleep he contemplates at the poem's end, be yet to come. A closer look at the verbs that refer to dreaming and sleeping illustrate the ambiguity: first the speaker says "I *am* drowsing off"; but then he tells of a time earlier in the day when he was "well *upon my way* to sleep" and he had a premonition of "What form my dreaming *was about* to take." The dream, then, would appear to have already occurred—but rather than reporting his dream in the past tense, the speaker switches back to the present ("Magnified apples appear and disappear") as he goes on to describe his current predicament at the end of the day. If, like Brooks and Warren, we assume that the dream is not a literal dream but a vision, all of this may simply mean that the speaker continues to ex-perience, even as he speaks, a vision that began several hours before. But then how do we interpret still more references to "sleep" toward the poem's end?

> One can see what will trouble
> This sleep of mine, whatever sleep it is.
> Were he not gone,

> The woodchuck could say whether it's like his
> Long sleep, as I describe its coming on,
> Or just some human sleep.

Is *this* sleep to be taken as a metaphor as well—that is, as the "sleep" that he has already entered during the day—or does it merely point to the literal sleep that the speaker will finally encounter after a long day's work? Brooks and Warren appear to presume the latter, given their emphasis on the contrast between the dreamless sleep of woodchucks and the more significant (and signifying) sleep of humans, who do—literally—dream (386). Yet other critics have read the sleep that the speaker anticipates not as sleep per se but as a sign of something more profound. Jeffrey Meyers, for example, claims that the speaker "needs to regenerate himself, like the hibernating woodchuck, by a long, death-like winter sleep, so he will be ready to re-enter the poet's dream world and achieve another spurt of creativity" (116).

But how are we to know? The speaker's qualifying phrase, "whatever sleep it is," may nudge us in the direction of metaphor—or it may reflect nothing more than the slightly grumpy anticipation of a literal sleep disturbed by the sights and sounds of a tiresome day. Or perhaps the phrase is meant to suggest the very distinction between the literal and the figurative itself, as the speaker wonders whether his sleep tonight will be literal, like that of the woodchuck, or (ironically) just metaphorical, like that of humans, who can both "sleep" and "dream" even when they are awake. Any of these interpretations, however opposed, seems valid. Indeed, there is nothing to stop us from contending, on the one hand, that no sleeping or dreaming whatsoever, either literal or metaphorical, takes place in the poem (since they are only referred to as events that were *about* to happen in the past or the future); or, on the other hand, that almost the entire poem consists of a dream-filled sleep—since from the moment the speaker informs us that he is "drowsing off," all that follows can be read as a dream or a dream within a dream. As Paul de Man indicates in a discussion of Yeats's poem "Among School Children," "it is not necessarily the literal reading which is simpler than the figurative one . . . ; here, the figural reading . . . is perhaps naive, whereas the literal reading leads to greater complication of theme and statement" (*Allegories* 11). While I am not arguing that such is necessarily the case with "After Apple-Picking," I think it revealing to witness just how complex a literal reading can be.

More important, however, is the recognition that neither a literal nor a metaphorical reading ever proceeds in isolation from the other. If, for instance, we interpret the final lines of Frost's poem "literally," there is still no getting away from metaphor, which obtrudes in virtually every line—from the assertion that one can "see" what will "trouble" the speaker's sleep, to the image of a woodchuck that could "say" something about sleep the speaker tells us is "coming on." And since metaphor suggests differences as well as similarities between the discursive realms it identifies, even the so-called "literal" reading depends upon creative acts of association and composition. But it is also the case that a "metaphorical" interpretation of these same lines relies on literalism, for if "sleep" is to be read as a metaphor (be it a metaphor for escape or imagination or death or whatever else), it must also be understood that, according to the literal information provided by the text, it is a sleep that (1) may not yet have arrived, (2) will not go undisturbed, and (3) will be one of two kinds—animal or human. We might conclude, then, that just as literal interpretation begins caught in the instabilities of metaphor, which prompt it to search for the security that comes with definitive meaning, so metaphorical interpretation begins mired in the constraints of the literal, which prompt it to search for the freedom that comes with multiplicity of meaning.

As the students in my class were well aware, literary texts (or at least those who teach them) demand that they "read for metaphor." But what they did not know, and what I did not quite know how to teach, was that they must with equal energy and persistence "read for the literal." The trouble with the metaphorical reading they offered lay not in the extravagance of their claim that the day of apple-picking represented the speaker's life and the impending sleep his death; after all, Brooks and Warren stand on no firmer ground when they convert the speaker's unsettling dream into a representation of the "ideal." Rather, the trouble lay in these students' failure to elaborate and complicate their reading through attention to the literal dimension of the poem's language. It is not, as I initially thought, that they should start with the literal before moving to the metaphorical—but that, wherever they start, the ensuing process of reading should move back and forth between the metaphorical and the literal poles, which can thereby both inform and enlighten one another. As it turns out, Brooks and Warren's interpretation of "After Apple-Picking," whatever we may think of its content, is an excellent example of this kind of reading: after suggesting possibilities for a particular metaphor, they often turn back and ask how it might be read as literal statement, and then turn again to the metaphorical implications, which are enriched by their sense of the literal. Alternately, they accept a line or group of lines at face value—as they do with the opening lines of Frost's poem—then reverse themselves and read in search of the metaphors they have overlooked.[10] *This,* I believe, is what it would finally mean for our students to "read (for) metaphor": they would recognize not only that literature, like all discourse, is awash with words and images that signify something beyond themselves, but, more importantly, that to read intelligently is to move *between* the metaphorical and the literal—that is to say, between the plasticity and the solidity of language, which gives way to but also resists our efforts to make of it whatever we wish.

If the act of reading is in large part constituted by local, value-laden decisions about which words to take metaphorically and which to take literally—decisions that bear the marks of tradition and training—it may be impossible to teach students of literature (or anyone else) how to "know a metaphor when they see one." From this perspective, metaphor becomes not so much a thing to be identified in texts as a strategy to be performed by readers, for whom the metaphorical opens up that which the literal closes down—namely, interpretive speculation, with both the liberties and the hazards that attend it.

After Metaphor-Picking

In one of the final class meetings of "Literature for Adolescents," I again divided students into small groups and asked each group to discuss one of the four essays they had read that week. These essays—by E. B. White, George Orwell, James Baldwin, and Maxine Hong Kingston—all make frequent appearances in textbooks and anthologies designed for high school English courses, where several of the students in my class reported that they had first encountered them.[11] But rather than requesting (as I often had before) that they describe how they would teach the essay their group was assigned to a class of high school students, I told them to prepare to teach the essay to *this* class of their college peers. After they had spent thirty minutes formulating their pedagogical approach to the text, groups would draw straws to see which ones would take turns at the front of the room making presentations and leading discussion with the rest of the class.

For the most part, this was a good idea—one that I feel certain I will use again—for it helped to move us from the kind of conversation we had indulged in each week about *imagined* teaching practices sometime in the distant future, to a conversation about *actual* teaching practices (however problematic the distinction) we had just observed or in which some had just participated. But what I want to draw attention to for my purposes here is the startling phenomenon—or at least one that was startling to me at the time—that not a single student in the class, including those who played the role of the teacher, attempted on any occasion to "read for metaphor" when confronted with these essays. It was as if all the habits and inclinations they had displayed as readers in the eleven weeks prior to this class simply vanished into thin air. Indeed, when I subsequently read their responses to the weekly writing assignment (which had asked that they discuss why they think essays should or should not be included—along with works of fiction, poetry, and drama—among the literature studied in the high school curriculum), I encountered again and again their insistence that essays mean exactly what they say: "Essay writing can discuss topics in an efficient and direct manner . . ."; "Essays are informative . . ."; "The essay is short and easily read . . ."; "[The essay] demonstrates how a clear and concise paper should be written . . ."; "[Students] are drawn into the fact that [in an essay] this is a person relating the events to the reader as they really happened"; "Essays . . . are short, and usually read very quickly"; "Essays get to the point fast"—and so on, ad infinitum. Even the one student who began promisingly by claiming that essays "are one of the most flexible of prose composition forms" had come back to the fold only two lines later: "What all essays do have in common is a logical development of ideas and a careful transition from one idea to another." By the time I had finished reading these papers, it seemed that the student who had best captured the general perspective of his peers was the one who wrote the memorable remark that the essay "has reality on its side."

In the class meeting itself, this perspective gradually became apparent as the first group of students demonstrated their strategy for teaching E. B. White's "Once More to the Lake." Like the groups that struggled several weeks earlier to make something of my questions on Frost's poems, this group struggled to locate pedagogical methods that could spark more than a desultory class discussion. In prior class meetings, the students in this group had often differed from one another in their interpretive approaches to various texts—but on this occasion each member did roughly the same thing when her turn to address the class arrived (in this course, as is all too common in courses composed of prospective primary and secondary school teachers, almost all of the students were female): she chose a passage from White's essay that seemed significant, read it aloud, and asked the class how it contributed to the general message or "point" of the text. While it was clear that the group had hoped this method would stir debate by provoking opposed readings of both the individual passages and the essay as a whole, not even a glimmer of controversy ensued, since it appeared that members of the class were unanimous in perceiving White's essay as no more than the simple portrait of a man who feels nostalgic for a time now gone and who receives an intimation of death in the closing lines. Several students said that they "enjoyed" reading the essay, that White was a wonderfully "descriptive" writer, and so forth—but no one found anything else worth observing in this text that has had such enduring presence in the high school curriculum over the years. Nor did the group that attempted to teach Baldwin's "Stranger in the Village" have any more success engaging the class in exploratory dialogue. Though the discussion was a bit more animated—for a number of students were quite taken by Baldwin's experience as the only person of color in an entire Swiss village—the result was basically the same: consensus that Baldwin's message (about the evils of racism and the need for social change) was perfectly "accessible" and that his text had therefore done its job.

Here, then, was the precise opposite of the problem I confronted in the preceding weeks: rather than depicting (as they had with fiction, poetry, and drama) language as a curtain behind which meaning hides, students now seemed to conceive language as a window through which meaning is plain for all to see.[12] As long as the texts in question were "literary," it had been necessary to locate and uncover metaphor wherever possible; but with our move to the essay, the literal had replaced the metaphorical as the primary mode of communication and interpretation. Though I tried to disrupt this set of assumptions by concluding the class with a discussion of the sometimes dubious distinction between fictive and nonfictive discourse, I knew better than to imagine that this brief exchange made much of an impact. Even when we went on the following week to examine the poetic, fictional, and dramatic elements of so-called "objective" reporting in newspapers and news magazines, students seemed to conclude only that journalism occasionally "borrows" from literature just as literature occasionally borrows from journalism. The key pedagogical question before me—how to help students read expository prose by way of metaphor—I found as perplexing as the question of how to help them read poetry by way of literalism. While I could certainly announce that "reading for metaphor" would henceforth define the object of their endeavors, such a directive might do little more than reify their notion of metaphor as a mere supplement to the fundamental order of literal discourse.

The seriousness of the problem was all the more evident in students' own writing for the course. While it may have been fallacious to assume that, as future teachers, these students would write more reflectively than their peers, I must admit my surprise when, week by week, I read their responses to a series of assignments that asked them to consider how they might teach the material we were reading and discussing once they became teachers themselves. Contrary to my expectations, the writing of most of these juniors and seniors showed no signs of advancement —by any criteria that might be imposed—when compared to the writing of the freshmen I encountered in my composition class earlier in the day. Indeed, the trouble that the students in my upper-division course appeared to confront lay not so much in their failure to propose innovative approaches to teaching (for many were quite imaginative when it came to planning a class) as in their failure to write in ways that did justice to their innovations. If, as Robert Pattison contends, literacy consists of "consciousness of the questions posed by language coupled with mastery of those skills by which a culture at any given moment in its history manifests this consciousness" (5), then I would argue that, while the teaching of English has usually focused on the second of these elements (namely, the mastery of skills), the primary source of students' difficulties as writers can be located in their lack of the first element—"consciousness of the questions posed by language." One of these questions concerns the relationship between metaphorical and literal discourse, neither of which is capable of moving very far in the absence of the other.[13] Without an awareness of the metaphors on which their literalisms relied, the students in my class seemed blind to the ways that their writing fell apart even as they presumed it to be building a solid foundation.

It may help to illustrate the specific problem of literacy I am describing by examining two brief papers written by the same student—a student whose writing I select for two reasons: first, because her work stood neither at the top nor at the bottom of the class but was instead representative of an "average" performance in this course; and second, because this student was a senior English major with an excellent record who was taking her final course before graduating from college. It is students like this one, in other words, who give us a glimpse of the reading and writing practices that not only *can* result but *commonly* result from an education in English studies as it is currently constructed—an education that continues to separate the literal from the metaphorical, the rhetorical from the poetic, and the study of composition from the study of literature. The question that arises here is what price our students pay as a result of such divisions.

The first paper I want to consider was written in response to an assignment that asked students to describe what they would do with one of the poems we had read that week (they were to choose from a group of poems by Whitman or from a group by Dickinson) were they to teach it to a group of tenth graders in a fifty-minute class. In addition to delineating their plans for the class, they were asked to discuss why they believed their approach to poetry would be of value to their students. Here, then, is this student's not-unusual reply:

> If I were to teach a tenth-grade class on Dickinson or Walt Whitman, I would choose "Song of Myself" by Walt Whitman. I would ask my students to concentrate their readings on section 3. I would discuss with the class each line individually. I would try to help my students dissect this section of the poem so that they could gain a deeper understanding of what emotions Whitman was attempting to emulate in the poem. I would help my students understand that this section of the poem is discussing a celebration of life. I would look past the sexual overtones of the poem and focus my classroom discussion on the beauty of the words; of how the words have a natural flow, like the flow of life.
>
> I feel that to teach the poem as a whole would not benefit my students. Tenth graders are not mature enough to fully understand the true meaning of the poem as a whole. By only taking one section of the poem the students can better focus on the words. They will be able to gain an understanding of the poem. Poetry is complex, and I feel that it would be to the benefit of my students if it is taught slowly and thoughtfully.

Now there are any number of problems that most teachers would immediately identify in this text, from its misuse of the term "emulate" and its vague allusion to "the beauty of the words" to its contradictory assessment that tenth-grade students "are not mature enough to fully understand the true meaning of the poem" yet that they will nevertheless "gain an understanding of the poem." Why, we might ask, has the writer selected section 3 of "Song of Myself" and not some other section? What *kind* of attention to each of its lines would bring "a deeper understanding" of the "emotions" in the poem, and how would this understanding come about? Why would the writer ignore the "sexual overtones" in favor of a discussion of the poem's aesthetics? And so on.

While such observations might lead to familiar calls for specificity and consistency, the problem that I wish to indicate in this text is one that does not translate so readily into pedagogical advice. Like the students who failed to recognize the presence of metaphor in the essays by White and Baldwin, this student apparently fails to recognize the presence of metaphor in her own writing—more than likely because she presumes that, as an instance of literal discourse, her text places its meaning directly into the reader's hands. Accordingly, there is no attempt to explain even the relatively overt metaphors that clearly beg further commentary. What does it mean, for instance, to "dissect" a poem or to identify the "natural flow" of poetic discourse? Since these words are treated as if they wore their meanings on their sleeves—perhaps because the student has encountered them in prior English courses—they are left behind as soon as they are inscribed. The possibility that terms like "dissect" or "flow," because of their metaphorical suggestiveness, might call to mind quite different meanings for different readers (even inside the educational contexts in which they tend to appear) does not seem to occur to the writer, who therefore leaves us grasping for sense. It is simply assumed that readers understand what the text is "talking about," for writing has here been approached as if it were a form of speech— that is, a form of communication that need not consider the effect of the writer's absence from the scene.

But even more important, this writer's text evinces no awareness of metaphor in the larger sense—as the means by which language *figures* or gives shape to the "realities" it seems merely to describe. Consequently, any number of declarations can be made without attention to the unspoken assumptions that generate them, from the notion that poetry is "complex," with a "true meaning" that tenth-grade students are not "mature enough" to understand, to the idea that the teaching of poetry must proceed "slowly" and "thoughtfully," with the "focus" of "discussion" on "the beauty of the words." What makes this kind of language particularly insidious (for the writer as well as the reader) is the way in which its terms can seem perfectly normal, sensible, and unobjectionable, especially given that the philosophy of literary education they support remains ensconced in many a high school English course across the country. But the moment we attempt to discern with any specificity just what these terms "figure"—that is to say, just what it is they compose, what world they make intelligible—the text comes across as something close to nonsense, or perhaps as a halting struggle to establish the merest outline of sense. For what does it mean to assert that poetry is "complex"? Complex in comparison to what? What is the difference between a "true" meaning and a meaning? What signals that someone is "mature enough" to understand Whitman's "Song of Myself"? For that matter, what does it mean to "understand" anything at all? Such questions do not matter to this text because it displays no reflexive interest in the figurings, the metaphors, by which it operates.

We get a closer view of what an inattention to metaphor might mean in future high school classrooms by perusing the same student's response to an assignment several weeks later, when the course turned to Arthur Miller's *Death of a Salesman*. This assignment had asked that students compose their own writing assignment for a class of tenth graders reading Miller's play. As with the earlier text, the response that follows, in which this teacher-to-be addresses her imaginary students, was not atypical when placed alongside others I received that week:

> I want you to focus on the relationship between Willy Loman and his son Biff. In the Requim *[sic]*, the family members are discussing Willy's life. It is evident that even though Willy is dead, Biff does not forgive his father for his infidelities towards the family. For your paper topic, I want you to write a paper discussing why you think Biff is unable to forgive his father. A question you could ask yourself is "Does Biff hate his father because he cheated on his mother or because he cheated on Biff?". Think about how before Biff caught his father having an affair, he looked up to him as a hero figure; as the perfect father and husband. Do you think that if Arthur Miller wrote a third act, focusing on a family conversation ten years after Willy's death, do you think that Biff's view on Willy could have changed? Do you think that time could have healed Biff's wounds, or do you feel that Biff would never able *[sic]* to forgive his father? This paper should be no shorter than five pages and no longer than seven. You can incorporate quotes from the play if you feel that they support your claim. This question is objective so there is no correct answer; but make sure you put thought into your paper and back up your ideas.

Once again, I do not think the chief difficulty we encounter here lies in the more obvious imperfections of this text—be they misguided syntax ("For your paper topic I want you to write a paper"), faulty diction ("objective" in place of "subjective"), or warped reference ("This question" after several questions have been asked)—though certainly each of these defects would make it that much more challenging for the tenth-grade student reading the assignment. And while we certainly might question the overall direction of the assignment itself—why limit students to writing about Biff's inability to forgive his father?—it seems beside the point to pick away at the initial attempts of future teachers to determine a subject for their students' writing. Assignments necessarily involve constraints, and even experienced teachers sometimes fail to give students enough room to maneuver.

I would argue that the most pressing problem in this text concerns its complete subordination to the aims of literal discourse. Such a claim has nothing to do with the fact that, aside from its reference to time healing wounds (which is idiomatic in any case), the text contains no overt metaphors. What matters here are not the metaphors the writer has failed to use but the metaphors that are using her—duping her into thinking that her writing has provided her student readers all they need to do their work. From the opening imperative that students "focus" on the relationship between Willy and Biff to the closing admonitions that they "put thought into" their papers and "back up" their ideas, this text refuses to tell its audience what it means even as it purports to be handing them meaning in the most literal language it can muster. That students might wonder just how narrowly their vision must be circumscribed in order to constitute a "focus" on the subject at hand; that writing itself might produce thought as much as thought gets "put into" writing; that to "back up" an idea might require still another idea that likewise requires backing up—each of these possibilities is not so much eluded as erased from view by a prose that refuses to turn around in order to see where its own words have gone. Yet such are the possibilities that attention to the metaphorical dimension of language might offer this writer, for it is through the process of what Michael Shapiro and Marianne Shapiro call the "revivification" of lifeless metaphors that we become alert to the ways that texts have taken shape and might be shaped anew. In their book *Figuration in Verbal Art,* the Shapiros note that a trope that has died of its own success in popular usage (and has thus acquired "lexicalized" status) can later be brought back to life "by substituting a virtual (covert) meaning for the contextually anticipated one" (39). Thus, another way to describe the student texts above would be to say that, by failing to seek out discrepancies of meaning in the terms on which they relied, these texts became little more than discursive graveyards—writing wherein dead metaphors remain dead, buried underground, out of the composer's sight.

This was not a problem that I learned to solve, nor is it one I believe *can* be solved through a specific pedagogical technique. To be sure, teachers might ask their students to hunt for dead metaphors both in their own writing and in the writing of others, whereupon some sort of small lesson might be learned—but this approach would be akin to putting a bandage somewhere near the site of an internal hemorrhage. Though we can name "metaphor" as the source of a fundamental challenge that stands before the teaching of English, the paradox is that we cannot meet this challenge by simply deciding to make metaphor more prominent. We need not an inversion of the literal and the metaphorical, so that one becomes dominant wherever the other usually prevails, but an active recognition of their inescapable interdependence—a recognition that might inform not simply the sensibilities of individual teachers but the very structure of the curriculum. If the students who commit themselves to the study of English are to practice, when they work with their own writing as well as when they work with that of others, what Pattison calls "consciousness of the questions posed by language," then deeper changes will be required than those that departments of English have generally been willing to make, most notably a thorough integration of the study of literature (widely, and wrongly, identified with metaphor) and the study of composition (widely, and wrongly, identified with literalism).

Whether such a union currently appeals to those on either side of this institutional division—for both appear increasingly content with attempting to establish a more equitable, but still separate, presence in the English studies curriculum—it may well prove necessary in order to help students "advance" with literate awareness into occupations like teaching. Literacy, as so many have observed, is multidimensional, and we must continue to seek the curricular means to explore its many dimensions at once.

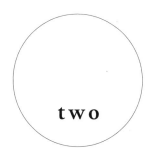

two

POSSIBILITY

3

LITERAL FICTIONS

Equivalence, Difference, and the Dialogic Metaphor

> "In pure identification there would be no strife. Likewise, there would be no strife in absolute separateness, since opponents can join battle only through a mediatory ground that makes their communication possible, thus providing the first condition necessary for their interchange of blows. But put identification and division ambiguously together, so that you cannot know for certain just where one ends and the other begins, and you have the characteristic invitation to rhetoric."
>
> Kenneth Burke, *A Rhetoric of Motives*

ONE OF THE MOST striking features of contemporary theories of metaphor lies in how often these theories refer to the "speaker" and the "hearer" of metaphor—as if figurative language were primarily an oral phenomenon. While it is evident that some theorists, in recognition of the fact that metaphor occurs in texts as well as in speech, prefer terms such as the "producer" and the "recipient," this conflation of speech and writing seems little more than a variant of the same problem. Such is also the case with theorists who alternate their terms, relying here on *speaker/hearer* and there on *reader/writer,* as if it makes no difference which pair they invoke.[1] Yet if we attend, as Susan Miller suggests in her book *Rescuing the Subject,* to the historical and technological divergence of *textual* rhetorical practices from the oral practices studied by classical rhetoricians, we may begin to wonder what possibilities might emerge —not simply for the theory of metaphor but also for the teaching of English—were the difference between metaphors heard and metaphors read treated *as* a difference rather than as a trivial distinction that can easily be ignored. Might not an approach to metaphor based on its reading and writing help to challenge prevailing assumptions about what is involved in reading and writing themselves?

The failure of the "revolution" in recent conceptions of metaphor to have much effect on English department curricula may well stem from the tendency for these conceptions not only to conflate writing with speech (whereupon, as Derrida indicates, the former becomes subordinate to the latter) but also to embed themselves in what Mary Louise Pratt has called, in an essay of the same name, "linguistic utopias"— purportedly ideal speech situations that are nowhere to be found.[2] Like the theories of discourse Pratt's essay critiques, most theories of metaphor work from models of social interaction in which "all participants are engaged in the same game and . . . the game is the same for all players."[3] That is to say, the social differences that mark various forms of real-world discursive exchange are ignored in favor of an imagined "community" of speakers who see eye-to-eye and who presume an identical communicative endeavor. Pratt notes that the linguistic utopias upon which so much scholarly analysis of language relies seem "often to be a fraternity of academics or bureaucrats, or perhaps talking machines speaking either the true-false discourse of science or the language of administrative rationale" (55). As I hope to demonstrate, this remark is especially pertinent when we turn to theories of metaphor, which commonly postulate speakers and listeners whose sole aim is to avoid "falsity" and to capture the "truth." Overlooking what Pratt calls "the relationality of social differentiation" (59), these theories manage to avoid all discussion of how metaphors are mobilized and interpreted in numerous ways and for numerous purposes, depending on the "modes and zones of contact between dominant and dominated groups, between persons of different and multiple identities, [and] speakers of different languages" (60).

The "zone of contact" that most interests me in this chapter is that which occurs between readers and texts—and, subsequently, between (teacher) readers and (student) readers, among whom there are differences aplenty in today's post-secondary institutions. This interest leads me not to an ethnographic study of how teachers and students differ in their responses to metaphor (valuable as such a study could surely be[4]) but to an exploration of the ways in which a conception of metaphor based on the phenomenology of reading might encourage teachers and students alike to attend to "difference" in new and perhaps more daring ways than most curricular revisions of English studies have appeared to sanction. (Multicultural textbooks, for instance, tend to organize their readings by way of "universal" themes—such as Family, Work, Death, etc.—that ultimately deny the significance of the very cultural differences that these textbooks ostensibly reveal.) I believe that metaphor could be crucial to teaching and learning projects concerned with issues of difference not simply because different people interpret metaphors differently but more importantly because metaphor is itself the primary means by which language confronts and negotiates difference. Whatever their incongruities, all definitions of metaphor recognize that what distinguishes this trope from others lies in its blatant attempt to combine terms or things that are otherwise considered incompatible: metaphor brings together that which the literal would keep apart. Paradoxically, this characteristic signals the considerable triumph yet also the inherent flaw of metaphor, which, like multicultural textbooks, displays the capacity both to span critical differences and to neglect them completely.

Or rather, *we* display, in our acts of reading, a proclivity to interpret metaphor for either purpose. Though I at times "metaphorize" metaphor by personifying it, one of my objectives in this chapter is to move from an analysis of what metaphor "does"—on its own, as it were—to an analysis of what readers themselves might do with metaphor. I begin, then, with an examination of the approaches taken to metaphor by two contemporary philosophers of language, each of whom stresses the role played by the interpreter in the activation of whatever meanings a given metaphor potentially brings to its discursive context. After considering the advantages and disadvantages of these visions of the interpretive activity stimulated by metaphorical locutions, I offer my own conception of metaphor, one that insists on regarding the equivalences posited by metaphor *as* equivalences, rather than as implicit comparisons. I contend that metaphors ask less that readers go in search of the similarities between its elements than that they enter a fictional realm which calls for both provisional acceptance and scrupulous interrogation of its imaginative constructions. What I call the "dialogic metaphor" might thus be seen as the kind of figure that stimulates dialogical forms of reading, whereby we seek the means both to identify with and to resist the fictions that metaphors compose.

Literalist Theories of Metaphor

Almost twenty years after the appearance of Richards's *The Philosophy of Rhetoric,* Max Black published a landmark essay entitled "Metaphor" (1955) that many have credited with launching the remarkable growth of subsequent academic interest in the subject.[5] Drawing on Richards's notion that a metaphor consists of "two thoughts . . . active together," Black presents his own version of what he calls the "interaction view" by proposing that a metaphor alters not only our understanding of the subject at hand but also our understanding of the metaphorical term itself. In the statement "Man is a wolf"—to use one of Black's examples—"man" is presented through the unique lens of this metaphor, but so, too, is the "wolf": "If to call a man a wolf is to put him in a special light, we must not forget that the metaphor makes the wolf seem more human than he would otherwise" (291). In other words, the word "wolf," as a result of its part in creating the metaphor, comes to mean something more, and other, than it would in literal discourse. For Black, metaphor produces its effect by changing the literal meanings of its terms into new, metaphorical meanings they do not normally carry.

This notion that words hold metaphorical meanings in addition to their literal meanings has become such a regular feature of the common parlance about metaphor that there may seem little reason to question it. Teachers of literature or composition, for instance, may typically ask their students to identify the difference between the metaphorical and literal meanings of a particular phrase in the text at hand, and most would be surprised to hear that this practice was at all problematic. But in fact a more recent theory of metaphor—at times referred to as "literalist" theory—offers an intriguing alternative to the interactionist (and commonsensical) view that metaphor conveys its own special form of meaning in contrast to that provided by literal statements. For the next several pages, I want to look rather closely at this theory in order to consider both the value it potentially offers teachers of English and the oversight it commits that to a certain extent limits its usefulness. My argument is that literalist theory provides the generative premise with which English studies might *begin* to reformulate its conception of metaphor —even though the direction literalist theory proceeds beyond that premise serves more as a negative than a positive example, one that should remind us to stay aware of the multiple dispositions that readers bring to metaphorical terms, locutions, and texts.

What I am calling a "literalist" position on metaphor was first presented by Donald Davidson at a symposium sponsored by the University of Chicago Extension in 1978.[6] In "What Metaphors Mean," Davidson contends that there is no such thing as a separate, distinct form of meaning called "metaphorical" or "figurative" meaning; rather, "metaphors mean what the words, in their most literal interpretation, mean, and nothing more" (30). In Davidson's view, metaphor "belongs exclusively to the domain of use" (31) rather than to the realm of semantics, so that what is imaginative about metaphor is not its generation of new meanings but its creative employment of standard meanings in order to stimulate further thought about the subject at hand. Consequently, "We must give up the idea that a metaphor carries a message, that it has a content or meaning (except, of course, its literal meaning)" (43). According to Davidson, theories that seek to explain the unique power of metaphor are looking in the wrong direction when they turn toward its supposedly hidden meanings: "Where they think they provide a method for deciphering an encoded content, they actually tell us (or try to tell us) something about the *effects* metaphors have on us" (43). What matters most, in other words, is not the interaction between the elements of a metaphor—as Black presumes—but the interaction between a metaphor and those toward whom it is directed.[7]

The chief merit of Davidson's literalist approach thus lies in the way it shifts attention from the inherent properties of metaphor to the question of what readers do with metaphors upon encountering them. Indeed, the opening lines of Davidson's essay suggest that metaphor is defined as much by its reception as by its production:

> Metaphor is the dreamwork of language and, like all dreamwork, its interpretation reflects as much on the interpreter as on the originator. The interpretation of dreams requires collaboration between a dreamer and

a waker, even if they be the same person; and the act of interpretation is itself a work of the imagination. So too understanding a metaphor is as much a creative endeavor as making a metaphor, and as little guided by rules. (29)

What is involved in this "creative endeavor" on the part of the interpreter of metaphor? Though Davidson observes quite conventionally that "a metaphor makes us attend to some likeness, often a novel or surprising likeness, between two or more things" (31), he stresses that because metaphors do not specify what their likenesses consist of, it is left to readers to pursue on their own whatever resemblances might exist. In this sense, readers continue the work that metaphors only begin—and since such work does not consist of identifying any particular propositional content (as it would were some metaphorical "meaning" to be discovered), there is no reason why the reflection stimulated by a metaphor could not be extended indefinitely. For Davidson, metaphors may *point* to various propositions, but they are not themselves propositional; rather, a metaphor functions much like a work of art, evoking a potentially limitless number of associations: "When we try to say what a metaphor 'means,' we soon realize there is no end to what we want to mention" (44).

While it can certainly be charged, as Black has noted in a rejoinder to Davidson, that this approach returns us in some respects to the "comparison view" of metaphor established by Aristotle ("How" 189)—wherein metaphor becomes nothing more than a condensed simile—its advantage nevertheless lies in the active reader it imagines confronting a metaphorical expression. The trouble, I would argue, arrives less when Davidson draws upon the classical definition of metaphor as a trope of resemblance than when he begins to outline just how readers recognize a metaphor in the first place. Turning to the matter of truth and falsehood in language, Davidson contends that while similes are generally true (since "everything is like everything" in one way or another), metaphors are "usually false" (39)—since to say one thing *is* another is to assert what we know not to be the case. As Davidson goes on to remark, "Generally it is only when a sentence is taken to be false that we accept it as a metaphor and start to hunt out the hidden implication" (40). That is to say, we first take a sentence literally, then recognize that this interpretation produces a false statement, and finally attempt to see what the sentence might imply if taken figuratively. But however "logical" this narrative of reading may initially sound, the problem both here and throughout Davidson's discussion of metaphor lies in the assumption that reading primarily consists of a search for literal truths, which, if not found, signal the presence of figurative language. Metaphor, from such a perspective, must therefore remain, despite Davidson's attempts to demystify its mechanisms, something unusual, a deviation from the norm: like art, it becomes known only through contrast to what precedes and defines it—nonfigurative communication. While Davidson turns us toward the crucial question of what readers do with metaphors, he fails to consider how the reading of metaphor might proceed differently were reading itself not to begin as a search for literal information. The students I referred to in chapter 2, for instance, were looking not for literalism but for metaphor from the moment they began reading Frost's poem. Indeed, given that poetry, fiction, and drama can all be approached as overtly metaphorical discourses—discourses that ask readers to take them *as* metaphors from the moment they begin to read—it would seem imperative to seek a theory of metaphor that can account for such discourses as well as for those commonly considered "literal."

Be that as it may, Davidson's argument that metaphors carry no unusual or extra cognitive content has been highly influential among other scholars who have addressed the subject in recent years, some of whom have examined (in much more detail than Davidson) the issue of what readers do when presented with metaphors in literary texts. One such scholar is Robert Fogelin, who, though he takes issue in his book *Figurative Speaking* with certain aspects of Davidson's essay, agrees that words do not change their literal meanings simply by being in a metaphor. (Fogelin often uses the term *respondent* instead of *reader,* but his examples of metaphor are usually taken from texts, and in his final chapter he applies his theory to poems by Shakespeare and e. e. cummings.) Fogelin's discussion is useful to us here because of the ways in which it further illustrates the importance, on the one hand, of examining how readers do more than merely "receive" the metaphors they encounter, and the problem, on the other hand, of characterizing readers of texts as if they were hearers of speech.

According to Fogelin, both metaphor and simile are instances of what he calls "figurative comparisons"—comparisons that call for a kind of interpretive effort not required in the case of comparisons that are literal. Adopting a position somewhere between those of Davidson and Black, Fogelin argues that readers struggle not only to discern similarities but also to locate the "truth" of a particular metaphor—a task they accomplish by making what Fogelin tellingly labels an "adjustment" or a "correction" that rectifies an otherwise incongruous comparison (87). While figures such as irony and hyperbole demand that readers adjust the statements themselves in order that they make sense (an ironic remark, for instance, must be reversed), figurative *comparisons* such as metaphor and simile demand another kind of response: "With figurative comparisons, the comparison is not rejected. . . . Instead, the context is adjusted to accommodate it" (87–88). In other words, the reader must work to change not the statement itself but the way in which it gets read. Turning to the hypothetical claim "Margaret Thatcher is like a bulldozer," Fogelin contends that understanding the statement figuratively requires that the reader "prune" the features of the object of the comparison (the bulldozer) until only those features which fit those of the subject (Margaret Thatcher) remain—whereupon what first appeared a false statement might now be recognized as true.

The most valuable contribution made by Fogelin's description of readerly response to various figures of speech—a description I have only begun to sketch here—lies in his attempt to account for the rhetorical power of figurative language, which for him results from the ways that figuration forces the reader to participate in the production of meaning. Moreover, Fogelin observes that interactionist theories of metaphor such as Black's may have gone astray by choosing to examine fairly simplistic examples such as "Man is a wolf" rather than the complex effects woven by a series of metaphors in a work of literature—an insight that leads Fogelin to contend: "The chief power of metaphor is not derived from the interaction between two distinct literal realms of discourse, but usually from the interaction of a system of metaphors themselves" (107). That is to say, theorists of metaphor should pay more attention to the ways that the various metaphors found in a single text interact not simply on their own but in relation to one another. In order to illustrate this claim, Fogelin turns to Shakespeare's *Sonnet LXXIII* ("That time of year thou mayst in me behold"), whose metaphors all rely on what he calls "straightforward temporal comparisons, in themselves banal" (109). No reader, after all, is likely to be surprised by a comparison between old age and the onset of winter, or twilight, or the dying of a fire. As Fogelin indicates, the rhetorical effectiveness of this poem lies not in any of these individual metaphors but in "the creation and control of a metaphorical space that gives these metaphors life" (109). It is the way that each metaphor interacts with those which precede and follow it—not the brilliance of any one metaphor on its own—that helps this poem produce such rich evocations.[8]

On the other hand, Fogelin's account of metaphor can also be said to reflect the same problem encountered in Davidson's approach—namely, the presumption that readers recognize a metaphor only after their attempt to make literal sense of a statement fails. For Fogelin, metaphorical discourse, unlike its literal counterpart, becomes language in need of "adjustment" or "correction" on the part of the reader. By contending that "figurative language involves a *departure* from literal language" (77; emphasis added), Fogelin leads himself to construct a reader whose desire, upon confronting the figurative, is apparently to get back to the security of the literal as quickly as possible. This construction is most evident when Fogelin relies on H. P. Grice's theory of the conversational maxims to advance his position on the difference between figurative and nonfigurative comparisons:

> With non-figurative comparisons, the speaker seeks a good fit that will facilitate the easy transfer of accurate information. More fully, the speaker offers his comparisons under the restraints of Gricean conversational maxims. With figurative comparisons the speaker flouts, or at least violates, standard conversational rules and thus engages the respondent in the task of making adjustments that will produce a good fit. (96)

In both scenarios, whether the respondent merely waits on the receiving end of "the easy transfer of information" or actively participates in "making adjustments," the objective is to arrive at a "good fit" between the terms of the comparison.

Now I don't want to deny that this is often the case, especially when

Grice's maxims for conversational cooperation are at least loosely in place —but I do think it important to note that Fogelin turns to a theory of *speech,* not a theory of writing or reading, for his model of communication.[9] Since conversation is more readily conceived (however erroneously) as grounded in the literal, conceptions of metaphor that take "the easy transfer of information" as their norm are quick to imagine "respondents" (be they hearers or readers) who want nothing more than to facilitate the so-called transfer. What this approach overlooks is not only the "linguistic utopia," as Pratt calls it, that informs most theories of speech but also the endless assortment of reasons why people participate in conversation, some of which have little to do with the exchange of information. Might it not be possible, even in speech contexts, that respondents sometimes look for the metaphorical implications of a statement *before* they seek out the literal, and thereby succeed in recognizing its figurative pertinence without having to "correct" a prior act of misinterpretation? How else explain the phenomenon wherein someone replies after initial confusion, "Oh yes, now I see: you must have meant that *literally!*" In such cases it would appear that respondents expect some form of figurative usage, interpret the statement accordingly, and only later realize their error—though it is just the opposite error that theorists of metaphor commonly depict in their versions of verbal behavior.[10]

Ultimately, then, for all there is to admire in the literalist theories proposed by Davidson and Fogelin, they exhibit two significant problems —both of which have implications for teachers of English. The first problem concerns the notion that reading begins as a search for literal truths and only secondarily adjusts itself to the intrusions of metaphor. If we retain this conception of reading, then we never escape from the same old conception of discourse (for surrounding any theory of reading there stands a larger theory of discourse) wherein literalism is granted primacy over metaphor, speech over writing, science over art, reality over fiction.[11] Metaphor, writing, art, fiction—all remain, from this perspective, deviations from the norm, and all therefore continually require a "defense" or "apology" for their existence. But clearly this is not the set of assumptions from which English studies can best define its work, nor do such assumptions recognize the productive interdependence of literalism and metaphor, speech and writing, and any number of other so-called "oppositions" within discursive behavior.

The second problem with literalist theory lies in its conception of what readers do after they identify a metaphor as a metaphor. According to the literalist view, the reader responds to the dissonance between the terms of a metaphor by immediately seeking the means to create consonance—what Fogelin calls a "good fit." In other words, difference is treated as something to be muted or repaired, for the reader supposedly desires (and the metaphor supposedly serves to produce) the pleasures of similarity rather than the tensions of disparity. But what I believe we need to consider is how readers might learn—and teachers of English might teach—an approach to metaphor that *values* the difference between its terms, rather than an approach that merely hopes to get around difference in order to locate the gratifications of resemblance. In the next section, I attempt to delineate a theory of metaphor on which such teaching and learning could be based.

From Resemblance to Equivalence

While my examination of composition textbooks in chapter 1 suggests that such textbooks have trivialized metaphor by presenting it as a condensed simile, there remains a subtle feature of their treatment of the relationship between metaphor and simile that merits a second glance. According to most textbooks, simile serves as an explicit comparison and metaphor as an implicit comparison—this much we find again and again from the late eighteenth century to the present. But in distinguishing between these two figures, textbook authors have long made note of the fact that a metaphor identifies its elements with one another rather than simply asserting their similitude. "In the metaphor," writes David Hill in *The Science of Rhetoric* (1877), "resemblance is not formally expressed, but so emphatically implied as to affirm an identity of the objects compared" (213). That is to say, metaphor pushes beyond mere comparison in order to produce an identification of one term with another. Similarly emphasizing the difference between comparison and identification, John Genung begins his section on metaphor in *The Practical Elements of Rhetoric* (1886) with this observation: "A closer association of objects than by simile is made when, instead of comparing one thing with another, we *identify* the two, by taking the name or assuming the attributes of the one for the other. This figure is named metaphor" (90). Here metaphor seems not a version of simile but a figure of its own kind—as is likewise the case when Adams Sherman Hill remarks in his *Beginnings of Rhetoric and Composition* (1902) that a "simile *likens* a person or a thing to something of a different class; a metaphor *identifies* a person or a thing with something of a different class" (402, emphasis added). From these definitions and many others like them in various composition textbooks of the time, it would appear that metaphor could be approached as a figure whose rhetorical operation is, while related to simile, at the same time quite distinct from it—and that the identifications posited by metaphor might thereby merit attention apart from the resemblances posited by simile.

Unfortunately, this gap between metaphor and simile is almost always closed by textbook authors immediately after they have opened it. A. S. Hill, for instance, follows his statement on the discrepancy between asserting a likeness (simile) and asserting an identity (metaphor) with a claim that arrives with the abruptness of a non sequitur: "The two figures differ in form only, the simile expressing fully a resemblance which the metaphor implies" (402–03). In other words, what initially seems a difference that might *make* a difference suddenly becomes hardly a difference at all: though metaphor fails to "express" a resemblance, it is still declared to "imply" one nonetheless—and therefore to lead us by a parallel path to precisely the same destination sought by simile. As A. R. Ramey puts it in his *Art and Principles of Writing* (1936),

> The metaphor is an implied comparison. Words indicating comparison are not employed as in the simile, but the ideas are identified. The attributes of one object are assumed for the other. . . .
>   Instead of saying one object is like another or resembles another, the writer or speaker says it is the other. The only difference between these two figures of speech is the expression of likeness in the simile and the implication of it in the metaphor. (65)

Intriguingly, while Ramey is quick to discern the difference between metaphor and simile, he is just as quick to cover over this difference by proclaiming that the identification made by metaphor is in fact nothing more than a comparison. Perhaps because he begins, as do most other textbook writers, with the definition of metaphor as an "implied comparison," the distinctions he goes on to observe between metaphor and simile must be forgotten as soon as they are detected.[12]

In *The Holt Handbook* (3rd ed., 1992), we encounter a more recent example of this odd combination of insight and evasion that still characterizes many a contemporary textbook definition of metaphor. After defining simile as "a comparison between two essentially unlike items on the basis of a shared quality," the authors of the *Holt* contend that "a metaphor also compares two essentially dissimilar things, but instead of saying that one thing is *like* another, it *equates* them" (Kirszner and Mandell 314). Yet having observed this potentially critical distinction between likening and equating, the authors immediately thereafter announce: "Metaphors are compressed similes. Because of their economy of expression, they can convey ideas with considerable power" (314). Now there are at least two things to notice in these few brief lines the *Holt* grants to metaphor. The first is that the authors, through their recognition that metaphor goes so far as to equate one thing with another, stand on the brink of shattering what students have been taught about metaphor for well over two thousand years—namely, that its function is to draw resemblances. To equate this with that is not, after all, to declare them alike in certain respects: it is to pronounce them identical. But by subsuming under the category of "comparison" this act of identification, the authors of the *Holt* lose their opportunity to explore the ways in which statements of equivalence and statements of resemblance might lead readers in considerably different directions.

The second thing to notice in the *Holt* approach to metaphor lies in the comment on metaphor's "economy of expression" when compared to simile—for here, too, we find a regular feature of textbook discussions of these figures. Not surprisingly, the observation comes straight from Aristotle, who claims in his *Rhetoric* that "just because [simile] is longer it is less attractive. Besides, it does not say outright that 'this' *is* 'that', and therefore the hearer is less interested in the idea" (186–87). While it might be useful to consider in greater detail why the hearer (or reader) would be more attracted to the "outright" equation of this with that, textbooks tend to pass over this issue as rapidly as does Aristotle, who has little more to say about it other than that people like to "seize a new idea promptly" (187). But does the addition of a comparative term make simile that much more time-consuming than metaphor? Year after year, from one textbook to another, students are told of the advantage that metaphor holds over simile, all because of the absent "like" or "as"—so that the brevity and implicitness of metaphor become de facto signs of its superiority. But what no one ever seems to ask is this: If metaphor is so clearly superior to simile, then why would writers ever use simile in the first place—especially when all they have to do is omit a single word in order to create an implicit, and supposedly more effective, comparison?

The fact that writers *do* use simile, and often to considerable effect ("O my love is like a red, red rose"), suggests that metaphor might more fruitfully be approached not as a shorter, better version of a figure that asks readers to compare one thing with another but as a figure that asks readers to do something else altogether. As we have seen with the literalist theories of Davidson and Fogelin, complex philosophical portrayals of metaphor find it no more enticing than do composition textbooks to investigate this possibility. While the literalists helpfully indicate that metaphors rely on the same form of meaning as that found in literal discourse, their explanation of how readers respond to the literal meanings they encounter in metaphor turns out in large part to be much the same old story: the pursuit of similarities. For Davidson, the form of reading instigated by metaphor may be open-ended and indefinite, but it remains nevertheless a form that is closely aligned with that inaugurated by simile: "The simile says there is a likeness and leaves it to us to pick out some common feature or features; the metaphor does not explicitly assert a likeness, but if we accept it as a metaphor, we are again led to seek common features" (38). As for Fogelin, the bond between metaphor and simile is even closer, since in his analysis both tropes are regarded as instances of "figurative comparisons," with metaphor serving as a simile without the explicit comparative term: "A metaphorical utterance of the form 'A is a Φ just means, and literally means, that A is like a Φ" (75). Indeed, one way to describe the difference between

Davidson and Fogelin would be to say that while Fogelin happily acknowledges that his approach returns him to the "comparison view" denounced by Black, Davidson seem to think that he has staked out a position that rejects, rather than merely repackages, comparativism in favor of something new.[13] This is not to suggest that neither of these theorists make valuable contributions to shifting attention from the internal mechanics of metaphor to the interpretive activity it generates among readers—but it is to submit that they continue to imagine such activity as a search for resemblances.

In contrast to these conceptions of the reading of metaphor, I would like to explore the implications that arise from taking the literalist premise about metaphor at its word. That is to say, if metaphors contain no special meaning beyond their literal meaning, then it would seem incumbent upon us to consider the possibility that readers really do take metaphors *literally*—not as statements of resemblance with the "like" or "as" missing, but as statements of equivalence that mean precisely what they say. As everyone who studies them observes sooner or later, metaphors explicitly claim that one thing is another, not that one thing resembles another. And as Laurence Perrine indicates, a good many metaphors even more boldly present one of their elements in place of the absent other, leaving readers to recognize on their own the equation between the two. In such instances, the effect produced by metaphor seems that much less likely to derive from readers converting an explicit equivalence into an implicit comparison. When Whitman observes in "Song of Myself" that the grass seems to him to be "the beautiful uncut hair of graves," does the metaphor work by encouraging readers to seek out the ways in which grass is *like* the hair of the dead emerging from the ground? An alternative approach would suggest instead that readers are led to consider Whitman's metaphor much the same as they would a work of fiction, wherein imaginary things are transformed (at least temporarily) into the "real": the grass, in Whitman's poem, becomes that with which Whitman equates it:

> Tenderly will I use you curling grass,
> It may be you transpire from the breasts of young men,
> It may be if I had known them I would have loved them,

> It may be you are from old people, or from offspring taken
>   soon out of their mother's laps,
> And here you are the mother's laps. (193)

These lines ask not that readers hunt for similarities between grass and the hair of various dead bodies but that they enter a realm in which grass *is* the hair that "transpires" from these bodies—a realm, that is, where life and death are one and the same. As Denis Donoghue has remarked: "A trope may be the immediate source of a fiction rather than its instrument" (63).

To "enter" a metaphor, as with any fictive text, is to provisionally accept the metaphoric space it sets before us, while to "pull back" often consists of comparing the internal world of the text with the external world beyond. In other words, while similes ask only that we acknowledge (from a distance) how something resembles something else, metaphors ask that we dare to believe (up close, where we ourselves become participants) that something can actually be something else. For Northrop Frye, who made much of this distinction between simile and metaphor, "identity is the opposite of similarity or likeness, and total identity is not uniformity, still less monotony, but a unity of various things" (125). I don't want to underestimate the illumination that can accompany the discovery of similarity in things that initially appear unalike—as with the marvelous simile in Donne's "A Valediction: Forbidding Mourning," wherein the souls of two lovers "are two so / As stiff twin compasses are two"—but I think it important to recognize that much of the persuasive force generated by metaphor derives from its ability to stimulate readers not merely to compare but to cross the thresholds of uncharted fictional territories. In order to do this, readers must make the vision produced by the metaphor their own; they must see as it asks them to see, whereby its two elements become not just comparable but identical.

A similar approach to that which I am proposing can be found in the work of Samuel Levin, who argues in *Metaphoric Worlds* that taking metaphors literally is ultimately a matter not of seeking out resemblances but of altering our epistemological outlook. Levin notes that most theories of metaphor begin with the assumption that "our conception of what the world is like is fixed—a given—and that whenever an expression contradicts or is inconsistent with that conception it is the expression that must be modified, into a form that consists with our conception of the world" (1–2). Thus, "An expression like 'The trees were weeping', say, might be construed to mean that the trees were dripping moisture, shedding their leaves, exuding sap, or something similar" (1). But for Levin, it is equally possible that metaphorical statements can themselves serve as fixed entities, and that our conceptions of the world might therefore be modified by them: "We can try, that is, to conceive, or conceive *of,* that state of affairs that the expression, taken *literally,* purports to describe; we can try to conceive of trees—those very things—as weeping" (2).[14] While Levin's example of weeping trees may sound unconvincing due to its divorce from a particular discursive context—a problem he later remedies with a striking analysis of Wordsworth's *Prelude*—the attraction of his theory lies in its portrayal of the interaction between metaphors and their readers. Rather than presuming that readers adjust the metaphorical expression until it comes into agreement with their already established view of reality, Levin envisions readers who are led to adjust their view of reality until it comes into agreement with the metaphorical expression. As he goes on to comment, his theory differs from others of the literalist persuasion (Davidson's, for instance) in that it contends not only that we should take metaphors literally but that we should accept the "epistemological consequences" that come with doing so (4). That is to say, if a metaphor is taken literally—and not merely converted into a quest for similarities—then the reader must attempt to conceive of a world in which the "state of affairs" described by the metaphor is possible rather than preposterous. To read a metaphor is thus to struggle toward a "metaphoric world" that draws upon but nevertheless challenges the world we ordinarily assume to be factual.

But it is interesting to note that Levin launches his study by portraying metaphors as "expressions that evince a degree of linguistic deviance in their composition" (1). Though in my view he correctly admonishes Davidson for presuming that metaphors display "patent falsity," Levin problematically contends that they nevertheless exhibit what he calls "absurdity" (14): metaphor, for Levin, involves a "lexical misuse" characterized by "improper" attribution (15). In other words, despite his fascinating suggestion that metaphors open metaphoric worlds, Levin returns us in certain respects to the same trouble we encounter in much of the rhetorical tradition that follows Aristotle's *Rhetoric,* a tradition in which the deviant character of metaphor poses a constant threat to the "proper" use of language. While there seems little doubt that Levin's approach to metaphor provides him with fertile ground for reading Wordsworth—and perhaps this explains why Levin so often refers to poetic metaphor rather than to metaphor in general—the question that remains concerns how such an approach might be extended to encompass the reading of any discourse, not just the reading of poetry (for which metaphor has always been regarded as crucial).[15]

Literalist theories of metaphor begin with the assumption that literal language serves as our primary means of communication, and that metaphor, like poetry, therefore occurs as a swerve away from the norm. According to this view, we recognize metaphor because of its falsehood, absurdity, or some other errant feature in its makeup. My proposal, on the other hand, is for a literalist theory that would claim *figurative* language as our primary means of communication—not simply because figures of speech are notoriously difficult to avoid but more importantly because they enable us to "figure" or structure relationships between the subjects and objects of discourse. The relationship figured by simile, for instance, is that of resemblance: this is like that. With metonymy, the relationship is that of association (this keeps company with that), whereas synecdoche involves a relationship of part to whole (this forms a piece of that), and irony a relationship of reversal (this is the opposite of that). While I agree with the literalist principle that none of these figures carries any special figurative meanings apart from their literal meanings, I do not see why they should be considered departures from "ordinary" or "proper" ways of making sense, since, on the contrary, the relationships they establish would seem to constitute some of the most common approaches to connecting one thing with another. Indeed, the construction of relationships is surely one of the primary functions of language itself.[16]

What makes metaphor in particular an especially intriguing form of figurative language is the fact that the relationship it figures between one thing and another is that of equivalence: this is identical to that. Such an equation of subject with object initially appears to challenge the logic of literal discourse, which would seem to rely on the distinctions between separate things being held in place. Yet oddly enough, equating one thing with another borrows (or models) the method of that most literal of all texts: the dictionary. We turn to the dictionary in order to find what something *is,* beyond all figuration—but what we get turns out to be none other than a continuous series of metaphors, wherein this is said to be that which is said to be something else and so on and so forth in a meandering and endless loop.[17] As it happens, metaphor is that figure which most resembles its presumed opposite, literal expression. Metaphor, like literalism, aspires to equate one thing with another and thereby give it unqualified "definition." Or to put this another way: literalism, like metaphor, depends upon readers who are willing to accept the fictive equivalences it presents as if they were facts. To claim what any thing *is* is, however unwittingly, to create a metaphor—as I have just done with this sentence. Metaphor is thus at once the most radical and the most quotidian act of language, for the quotidian is itself radical, in that language can proceed only by equating things whose differences deny the validity of their equivalence.

If literalism works by way of what Nietzsche calls "forgotten" metaphors, and metaphors work by way of constructive fictions, then it follows that in order to learn more about both literalism and metaphor we might look to fictive discourses such as the short story or the novel, wherein whole texts are devoted to negotiating metaphorical space. When they turn to literature, theories of metaphor almost always rush to poetry, where imaginative metaphoric locutions are certainly ample. But prose fiction offers an alternative site for exploring the powers of metaphor, both because metaphors can be approached as miniature works of fiction and because works of fiction can be approached as elaborated metaphors: to read a fictive text is to prolong, and thereby expose, the process of reading metaphor itself. As Cynthia Ozick observes, "Novels, those vessels of irony and connection, are nothing if not metaphors" (282).

Calvino's Fictional Worlds

Surely one of the most intriguing of all Italo Calvino's books is the collection of stories entitled *Cosmicomics* (1965), wherein each story is narrated by "old Qwfwq," a protean being who has apparently endured, in one form or another, the entire history of the universe. From one story to the next, Qwfwq describes his experiences in a variety of fantastical situations—from the time when "all the universe's matter was concentrated in a single point," so that Qwfwq and his companions were "packed like sardines" into that one point in space (43); to another time when the moon would approach so close to earth that, one night each month, people could actually prop a ladder against its underbelly and climb onto it from boats perched in the sea; to still another time when only one dinosaur was left on earth (naturally, it was Qwfwq), who had to hide his identity from a newly dominant species; and so on, through a dozen eccentric moments in the long course of history.

While there are any number of ways we might approach these stories, I would like to consider them here as reflections on the paradoxes and problems of metaphor—which for Calvino can be equated with the paradoxes and problems of language itself. What Calvino confronts again and again, not only in this book but in all his work, is the persistent struggle of language to come to terms with that for which there is no adequate language, despite the most scrupulous endeavors to find the words that could account for it. Take, for instance, the story "At Daybreak," in which Qwfwq and the members of his family, long before the sun grows concentrated enough to radiate light, lie tucked beneath the "fluid, shapeless nebula" that eventually condenses to form the planets of the solar system:

> There was no way of telling time; whenever we started counting the nebula's turns there were disagreements, because we didn't have any reference points in the darkness, and we ended up arguing. So we preferred to let the centuries flow by as if they were minutes; there was nothing to do but wait, keep covered as best we could, doze, speak out now and then to make sure we were all still there; and, naturally, scratch ourselves; because—they can say what they like—all those particles spinning around had only one effect, a troublesome itching. (19)

When the nebula finally begins to condense, the change impresses itself upon the members of Qwfwq's family: his mother feels uncomfortable; his little brother claims for the first time to be "playing" with something solid ("There had never," Qwfwq relates, "been things to play with before" [21]); and his father shouts a warning:

> I heard—I don't know whether awake or asleep—our father's cry: "We're hitting something!," a meaningless expression (since before then nothing had ever hit anything, you can be sure), but one that took on meaning at the very moment it was uttered, that is, it meant the sensation we were beginning to experience, slightly nauseating, like a slab of mud passing under us, something flat, on which we felt we were bouncing. (21)

Part of what Calvino, through Qwfwq, confronts in these passages is the inability of language to depict any "reality" without getting so thoroughly in its own way that we learn more about the language than about that which it hopes to describe. Qwfwq speaks of "counting" the turns of the nebula; but if, as he says, there were no "reference points" to be found, counting would not even be conceivable, let alone possible: indeed, *counting* can only be a metaphor for whatever it was the family was doing at the time. Likewise, as Qwfwq himself observes, his father's cry "We're hitting something!" was a "meaningless expression" without any prior "hitting" to refer to—and yet somehow it made sense in that it was spoken at the same time that they began to experience a new "sensation," which the narrator can in turn only portray through another series of figures: "like a slab of mud passing under us, something flat, on which we felt we were bouncing." Even as we read such a description we know that Qwfwq makes use of terms and concepts that could not have been available to him during the period of the action he represents, so that the gap between his language and the events he details is even more pronounced than it is in typical representations of the past. Thus Calvino not only pokes postmodern fun at the problems inherent in the attempt to "capture" events through language, he also enacts these problems by creating discursive predicaments that force his storyteller to foreground the unavoidable metaphoric distortions that accompany any utterance.

Nowhere is this paradoxical character of language and metaphor more evident than in "A Sign in Space," a story that stunningly anticipates many of the major tenets that Derrida brought to poststructuralist criticism a few years after the publication of Calvino's book. Like all of the stories in *Cosmicomics,* this story is preceded by an epigraph that sets the stage: "Situated in the external zone of the Milky Way, the Sun takes about two hundred million years to make a complete revolution of the Galaxy" (31). Whereupon the narrative begins:

> Right, that's how long it takes, not a day less,—*Qwfwq said,*—once, as I went past, I drew a sign at a point in space, just so I could find it again two hundred million years later, when we went by the next time around. What sort of sign? It's hard to explain because if I say sign to you, you immediately think of a something that can be distinguished from a something else, but nothing could be distinguished from anything there; you immediately think of a sign made with some implement or with your hands, and then when you take the implement or your hands away, the sign remains, but in those days there were no implements or even hands, or teeth, or noses, all things that came long afterwards. As to the form a sign should have, you say it's no problem because, whatever form it may be given, a sign only has to serve as a sign, that is, be different or else the same as other signs: here again it's easy for you young ones to talk, but in that period I didn't have any examples to follow, I couldn't say I'll make it the same or I'll make it different, there were no things to copy, nobody knew what a line was, straight or curved, or even a dot, or a protuberance or a cavity. I conceived the idea of making a sign, that's true enough, or rather, I conceived the idea of considering a sign a something that I felt like making, so when, at that point in space and not in another, I made something, meaning to make a sign, it turned out that I really had made a sign, after all. (31)

Once again, the trickiness (and trickery) of describing that which cannot be described is apparent throughout this passage, as Qwfwq endeavors to delineate how he came to compose the very first sign ever inscribed. Qwfwq knows that his audience will impose their own conception of signs on his use of the term, so he is at pains to distinguish between signs as we now know them and the original sign, which had no precedents or even implements to aid its inscription. And yet Qwfwq has no choice but to use the only language he has at his (and our) disposal, as he informs us that he "drew" a "sign" at a "point" in "space"—all terms that could have had no meaning at the time, and that therefore serve as metaphors for what "actually" occurred.

But beyond this emphasis on the unavoidable impediments to any accurate discursive representation, "A Sign in Space" dramatizes the problematic relations between metaphor, writer, and reader in a number of other ways. After Qwfwq has inscribed his sign, he immediately begins to move away from it, since he is rotating on the edge of the galaxy and will not return to the same point for another two hundred million years. But this absence from the sign only leads him to think about it obsessively, both because there are no other signs with or about which to think, and because "that sign was mine, the sign of me . . . it was the only sign I had ever made and I was the only one who had ever made signs. It was like a name, the name of that point, and also my name that I had signed on that spot; in short, it was the only name available for everything that required a name" (33). In other words, the sign was a *sign*ature, a metaphor for the writer himself: "I carried it with me, it inhabited me, possessed me entirely, came between me and everything with which I might have attempted to establish a relationship" (33). Though Qwfwq begins by imagining himself as the creator of the sign, it subsequently comes to be his own creator, mediating all that he thinks and sees—a predicament made all the more troublesome by the fact that, the further removed in time and space the sign becomes, the less he is capable of retaining it through memory: "I realized that, though I recalled its general outline, its over-all appearance, still something about it eluded me . . . I couldn't remember whether, between one part and the other, it went like this or like that. I needed it there in front of me, to study, to consult, but instead it was still far away" (33). Initially presented as the "writer"—a metaphor if ever there was one, given that his universe had no signaling system to make writing possible—Qwfwq becomes the "reader," anxiously awaiting his return to the text, which will now speak to *him*, even if he once meant to speak through *it*.

But when Qwfwq finally makes it back to the sign, he encounters something other than what he has expected: "At the point which had to be that very point, in place of my sign, there was a shapeless scratch, a

bruised, chipped abrasion of space" (35). Someone has erased his sign
—and, further on in space, Qwfwq finds that this same vandal has inscribed "a similar sign, a sign unquestionably copied from mine, but one
I realized immediately couldn't be mine, it was so squat and careless and
clumsily pretentious, a wretched counterfeit of what I had meant to indicate with that sign whose ineffable purity I could only now—through
contrast—recapture" (35). But of course Qwfwq discovers that he can
never "recapture" the "ineffable purity" of his first sign, for that purity,
to the extent that it ever existed in the first place, has been muddied
forever by the sign itself, which can only *be* a sign if others can copy it
and thereby put it into circulation *as* a sign.[18] A sign, it turns out, must
also serve as a metaphor for a sign—just as Qwfwq's initial sign serves
as a metaphor for all the signs that follow. And now that other beings
have begun to make signs themselves, Qwfwq is soon unable to distinguish his signs from theirs, so that he ultimately arrives at a situation akin
to the contemporary, postmodern predicament described in the story's
final lines:

> In the universe now there was no longer a container and a thing con-
> tained, but only a general thickness of signs superimposed and coagu-
> lated, occupying the whole volume of space; it was constantly being
> dotted, minutely, a network of lines and scratches and reliefs and en-
> gravings; the universe was scrawled over on all sides, along all its dimen-
> sions. There was no longer any way to establish a point of reference: the
> Galaxy went on turning but I could no longer count the revolutions,
> any point could be the point of departure, but discovering it would
> have served no purpose, because it was clear that, independent of signs,
> space didn't exist and perhaps had never existed. (39)

The universe has been "written": it is now composed entirely of metaphors. Attempts to "read" these metaphors, moreover, will be forever
troubled by the fact that "any point can be a point of departure": no
perspective holds an advantage over any other. Even the distinction between "signs" (as intentional productions) and "space" (as natural environment) no longer pertains, for in every attempt to read the space
between one sign and another we find only more signs, more metaphors
for ourselves, who are metaphors as well for things other than ourselves.

Yet if *Cosmicomics* were no more than a set of clever postmodern fables on the inescapable abyss of language (albeit one that preceded the academic movement that later made this abyss so familiar to those in English studies), it would have little to offer the conception of metaphor I am attempting to articulate, beyond confirming what I take to be an important truism—namely, that metaphor forms the material with which we read and write and by which we are written and read. What draws me to Calvino's book lies not simply in his creation of a witty and entertaining series of stories concerning language-as-metaphor, but more significantly in his composition of "fictional worlds"—to borrow a term from Thomas Pavel's book of the same name—that manage to evoke strong currents of emotional empathy as well as intellectual admiration from the reader. Pavel suggests that works of fiction produce imaginative realms that both depart from and depend upon the conditions of the "actual" world; in this sense, he attempts to return our attention to what he calls "the referential purposes of fiction," which have been widely discredited by poststructuralism.[19] According to Pavel, "reference in fiction rests on two fundamental principles that . . . have for a long time constituted the privileged core of the fictional order: the *principle of distance* and the *principle of relevance*" (145). The first of these principles is crucial, for in order to serve its social function, fiction must establish a world set apart from the one we take to be real: "Scandal, the unheard-of, the unbearable tensions of everyday social and personal life, are expelled from the intimacy of the collective experience and set up at a distance, clearly visible, their virulence exorcized by exposure to the public eye. . . . Symbolic distance is meant to heal wounds carved with equal strength by unbearable splendor and monstrosity in the social tissue" (145).

The amount of distance between the fictional and the real is clearly one of the variables that writers can and do manipulate. In most of his books, Calvino leans toward relatively greater rather than lesser distance, to the extent that no reader would consider him, with the exception of his earliest work, a "realist" in any sense of the word. *Fabulist* is the more likely term—and given the scenarios we encounter in *Cosmicomics,* it isn't difficult to see why. Qwfwq, after all, is not even a recognizable form of life in several of the stories; the reader cannot so much as guess what he "looks like," let alone say what he "is." Indeed, this book might easily be classified as science fiction, a category that would thereby inform readers in advance that they could expect to find stories that represent fictional worlds at a considerable remove from the world they call their own. Both for writer and for reader, the advantage of such distance can be located in the opportunities for imaginative play and flexibility that it affords, since the elements in one world are that much less likely to be conflated with the elements in another.[20]

But there is also a risk that comes with increasing symbolic distance —a risk that we might recall from our discussion of the "strained" metaphor in chapter 1. The farther a metaphor stretches to span the distance between two terms, the greater the chance its bond will break, unable to sustain the connection it has attempted to forge. This is not to say, as the textbooks do, that the maker of metaphor should therefore opt for the security of choosing terms that reside in close proximity to one another; but it is to observe that substantial "distance" between what I would call the subject and the object of a metaphor (or tenor and vehicle, in Richards's formulation) can present a special challenge for writer and reader alike. As Pavel remarks,

> Symbolic distance must be complemented by a principle of relevance. Hence the proposition theory of artistic meaning, which, though open to criticism in its more punctilious versions, captures an important, ineliminable intuition, namely that literary artifacts often are not projected into fictional distance just to be neutrally beheld but that they vividly bear on the beholder's world. (145)

Fiction, in other words, must be more than just fiction—or to put this another way, fiction must, in order to reach its readers, bridge the gap between its world and theirs. It must, that is, perform the work of metaphor. Fictive texts that fail to engender some form of recognition of the equivalence between the "fictive" and the "real" will necessarily leave their readers cold.

In the hope that his fiction might help instruct us how metaphor negotiates the difference between its terms—for *distance,* in the end, is simply a metaphor for *difference*—I want to ask how it is that Calvino succeeds in constructing fictional worlds that establish considerable distance from "the beholder's world" while at the same time managing to "vividly bear" on that world. Though Calvino has been accused of reveling in "literary play" at the expense of psychological depth and political relevance,[21] I find his work both deeply moving and socially pertinent, despite the sometimes extreme differences between the realms inhabited by his characters and that of so-called ordinary existence. When the attraction of the earth makes it impossible for Qwfwq to remain with his loved one on the moon; when he experiences the anxiety, while swirling through space, that one of his "signs" will be read in ways that he did not intend; when he fears, as the last dinosaur in existence, that the "New Ones" in power will charge him with guilt by association; when the earth's atmosphere finally grows dense enough to bring radiant colors to his world, yet Qwfwq feels more loss than gain in the disappearance of the "uniform gray" that formerly characterized his environment—in all of these cases and many more, the fictional worlds of *Cosmicomics* seem intimately close to our own. Or rather, they *become* our own, as one world overlaps the other. Pavel contends that the lines dividing the fictional from the actual are permeable, which allows for various forms of interaction between them: "Fictional borders, territories, settlements—all call for metaphoric travelers. These are the fictional heroes who visit our shores in various ways. As models they may influence our behavior as effectively as actual heroes. Did the publication of *Werther* not trigger an epidemic of suicides?" (85). Fictive characters, that is to say, stride from their worlds into ours—just as we readers stride into theirs. Drawing on the work of Kendal Walton, Pavel proposes that

> we participate in fictional happenings by projecting a fictional ego who attends the imaginary events as a kind of nonvoting member. This explanation would account for the plasticity of our relations to fiction: we are moved by the most unlikely situations and characters—Greek kings, Oriental dictators, stubborn maidens, demented musicians, men without qualities. We send our fictional egos as scouts into the territory, with orders to report back; *they* are moved, not us. (85)

As readers, then, we confront the metaphors of fiction by turning ourselves into metaphor—fictive personae who wander near and far. But I would counter Pavel's assertion that "our peregrinations are merely symbolic" (85) by observing that, as metaphor, the "fictional ego" created by the reader must find the means to address the principle of relevance as well as the principle of distance. Fictions call for *identification,* not just peregrination. If our "other" selves who travel in fictional lands have no impact on our "actual" lives, then they are metaphors whose proposed equivalences carry no rhetorical force: we may have played the game, but without any concern as to its value or outcome. The best fictions, like the best metaphors, manage to hold such powerful resonance because the worlds they give rise to matter to their readers, who bring these fictional, metaphoric worlds into contact with a "literal" world that might otherwise seek to abandon all metaphor. Referring to the biblical passage wherein the Hebrews are reminded to love "the stranger" because they, too, were once "strangers in the land of Egypt," Cynthia Ozick comments: "Without the metaphor of memory and history, we cannot imagine the life of the Other. We cannot imagine what it is to be someone else. Metaphor is the reciprocal agent, the universalizing force: it makes possible the power to envision the stranger's heart" (279).

There is, however, a danger in conceiving the reading of metaphor along the lines of the two-part process I have just ascribed to it—a process composed of a journey away from, followed by a return to, one's epistemological "home." Were we to stop here, the reader's identification with the fictional world generated by a particular metaphor might be seen as little more than a taming of that world, an elimination of its vital differences from a world the reader finds more comfortable. From this perspective, metaphor could be regarded as the most ideologically suspect of tropes, for by equating this with that—rather than simply claiming their similarity—metaphor demands an identification that potentially erases all discrepancies both between its subject and object, between its "fiction" and "reality." As Meryl Altman observes, metaphor acquires "tremendous discursive power" by blurring the distinction between analogy and identity, and it "gains both authority and protection from its special generic status" (496). This combination of power, authority, and protection can lead, as Altman indicates, in strikingly opposed political directions—either in service of new forms of understanding (as when a novel metaphor disrupts the hegemony of a certain discourse) or in service of exclusion (as when an equation between one thing and another blithely overlooks the differences between them).[22] The common appearance of this latter phenomenon in student discourses offers a pedagogical opportunity that recent trends in multiculturalist curricular reform seem to have missed. If, as I have argued throughout this chapter, metaphors both stimulate and depend upon the actions of their readers, then it may be that teachers of English can involve students in forms of reading that are informed by, yet also challenge, the ways in which metaphor negotiates difference.

Planned Incongruities

In the fall of 1993, I taught a course entitled "Identity and Difference" as part of a freshman seminar program in which students who wish to be introduced to the practices and methods of a particular discipline can register for smaller classes than they usually encounter in their introductory course work (freshman seminars are limited to twenty-two students). My course was to give students a general idea of the kind of study they could expect to pursue were they to major in English—and I therefore decided to concentrate on issues of identity and difference because of their prominence among recent concerns that have reshaped study in the field. In addition to composing a number of their own texts, students were asked to read and discuss books by Chinua Achebe, Robyn Davidson, and Rita Mae Brown, along with a series of essays and stories by James Baldwin, Nadine Gordimer, Bharati Mukerjee, and David Leavitt, and to watch a film directed by Mira Nair.[23] The guiding theme that informed discussion of all these works was that of dislocation and its effects on one's sense of self and others.

This course remains one of the most rewarding experiences I have had as a teacher, primarily because of the students' enthusiasm for the subject matter and their willingness to listen as well as to speak to one another. But the course also revealed a significant problem that confronts the attempt to engage students in questions of difference. Day after day, whether responding to the African protagonist in Achebe's *Things Fall Apart*, to the lesbian narrator in Brown's *Rubyfruit Jungle*, or to any of the other textual figures with whom most of those in the class seemed to have little in common, students quickly eliminated virtually every difference between themselves and others through the phrase "That's just like . . ." Davidson's months of isolation in the Australian desert became "just like" a weekend spent away from dormitory friends; the secrecy with which South African interracial couples in Gordimer's stories must carry on their relationships became "just like" hanging out with a boyfriend or girlfriend one's parents objected to; the tensions and prejudice endured by immigrants in Mukerjee's fiction became "just like" showing up at a dance wearing the wrong attire; and so on. What I came to find especially frustrating about this reductive gesture was not only that it appeared remarkably short-sighted—in that these comparisons so often trivialized the experiences of those represented in the texts —but also that it seemed unavoidably necessary—in that students *did* need to make connections between themselves and the "Others" of these texts, who would have held little meaning for them had they not made such an effort. When a Caucasian student claims that what Baldwin experiences in the Swiss village is "just like" what he or she has experienced on the first day at a new school in the suburbs, the teacher is faced in certain respects with a no-win situation, for to confirm the similarity is to participate in the neglect of differences, while to reject the similarity may leave the student feeling that his or her own experience has been demeaned. Having experimented with each response, I found both of them (along with various combinations of the two) equally dissatisfactory.

One way to approach the expression "That's just like . . ." would be to see it as an instance of metaphor, wherein the remote resemblances between two seemingly disparate experiences are seized and highlighted. From this perspective—one in which metaphor, like simile, works by way of comparison—we could say that what bothered me about student reactions to the texts they read lay in their penchant for stretching metaphors across realms of experience that were too far apart to be bridged. But as I have indicated throughout this chapter, I believe it both valuable and inevitable that metaphor attempt to cross broad divides, and I resist the notion that the "strained" metaphor constitutes an error. As I see it, the trouble was not that students were making completely untenable comparisons (since in some respect the experience of one form of oppression may be "like" the experience of another), but that they were failing to recognize what tends to get lost when comparison focuses all of its energies on similarity—namely, the *dissimilarities* between the things compared. What occurred in the moment of identification, when students said "That's just like. . . ," was a negligent erasure of the differences between self and Other that I had hoped the course would help them recognize and analyze. If students were to walk out of class with the sense that they "understood" just—or, alternatively, understood "just" (as in *exactly*)—what the experience of an African tribe or an Australian feminist or an Indian immigrant was "like," then my course would have only succeeded in suppressing the very complexity in regard to identity and difference that I had wanted it to promote.

But it is also possible to approach the expression "That's just like . . ." not as an instance of metaphor but as an instance of simile, since the word *like* states a comparison rather than an equivalence. Indeed, it may be that students are prone to rely on simile rather than on metaphor in confrontations with difference precisely because simile offers them safer ground on which to make their identifications. With simile, not only is the recognition of difference muted, but the identification is muted as well, for to say that something is "like" something else merely indicates that they resemble each other in one way or another, whereas to say that something "is" something else is to enter much more precarious territory. While students were all too eager to say that they were "like" Okonkwo (the central character in Achebe's novel), no student would have said, "I *am* Okonkwo"—and thereby replace the simile with a metaphor. Intriguingly, had a more enterprising student made such an utterance, it would have been inescapably apparent both to the speaker and to his or her listeners, in ways that simile obscures, that the statement was a fiction. That is to say, the profound differences between the speaker and Okonkwo would have been brought forward by the same metaphor that presumably sought to hide them. Though the equivalence posited by metaphor appears inclined to erase the distinction between its elements, the ironic effect of certain metaphors is that we are reminded of distinctions even as they are challenged.

Or perhaps we must remind ourselves, when confronted with metaphor, of differences that are otherwise neglected in the act of identification.[24] Given that a metaphor not only identifies one thing with another but also asks that the reader identify with the fiction such an equation inaugurates, the possibility that the reader will overlook what I. A. Richards calls the "disparities" in a metaphorical formulation raises serious ideological and pedagogical questions for the teacher of English—especially in light of the curricular emphasis that has recently been placed on setting before students of various backgrounds the kinds of texts with which they can "identify" (whether immediately or during the course of persistent "exposure" to the Other). While the movement toward inclusion in the literary canon has undoubtedly constituted a significant advance for teacher and student alike, considerable attention must now be given to the forms of identification elicited by different texts and practiced by different readers. If readerly identification, be it with a character, event, theme, or discursive style (all of which serve as metaphors of one sort or another), concentrates entirely on equivalence at the expense of difference, then an education in English studies can offer little more than confirmation of what the reader already knows about self and Other. As the example of my freshman seminar indicates, students who thought they were learning something from the texts they read about people and places different from themselves had actually managed, through the one-sidedness of their identifications, only to convert these people and places into versions of themselves and their most familiar territory.

Kenneth Burke contends in *A Rhetoric of Motives* that "identification is affirmed with earnestness precisely because there is division. Identification is compensatory to division. If men were not apart from one another, there would be no need for the rhetorician to proclaim their unity" (22). Accordingly, it would appear that any act of identification cannot help but carry with it the division from which it has arisen and which it therefore confirms, even as it attempts to overcome that division. The problem, however, is that divisions can be readily ignored by both the writer and the reader of metaphor; indeed, one could say that many writers employ metaphor (wittingly or otherwise) so that readers will ignore the divisions that stand as obstacles to the identifications these writers hope to produce. Advertising, television, popular literature, and Hollywood films are perhaps the best examples of this approach to metaphor, particularly in their drive to reach a "target" audience that can identify without impediments. In reading as they did, the students in my seminar were only reading as they had long been taught to read, both inside and outside the classroom.

Yet just as not all fictions can be said to work toward the same end, not all metaphors can be said to perform the same rhetorical function. In closing this chapter, I wish to make a brief appeal for the value of what I call the *dialogic metaphor*—that is, the metaphor that at least partially inhibits its own movement toward identification. Rather than seeking an equivalence whose appeal is so convincing that the reader completely identifies with its fiction, the dialogic metaphor seeks an equivalence that Burke, in his earlier book *Permanence and Change,* refers to as "planned incongruity" (121). Noting the achievements of the "writers of the grotesque" in the nineteenth century, Burke remarks that these writers succeeded in "giving us new insights by their deliberate misfits" (121). I want to argue that metaphors that retain, rather than eradicate, their incongruities create a dialogic relationship with their readers, whose solace in the comforts of identification is productively disturbed by the intrusion of "deliberate misfits." This is not to say that the best metaphors are those whose elements have the least in common, but that the most resonant forms of identification are those that provoke interrogation of their own metaphoric equivalences. If the act of identification "goes all the way," without any recognition of the differences between this and that, then the dialogue between reader and text has ended before it even begins, with no space for the exploration of further relationships: this simply *is* that—and nothing more need be said. Along these lines, Richards argues that "talk about the identification or fusion that a metaphor effects is nearly always misleading or pernicious" (*Philosophy* 127), for such talk tends to overestimate the role of similarity in the achievement of the metaphor at hand.

But the metaphor generated from the principle of "planned incongruity" stimulates dialogue with the reader by frustrating total identification even as it hopes that some form of identification will take place. Take, for example, Whitman's metaphor from "Song of Myself" that equates grass with "the beautiful uncut hair of graves":

This grass is very dark to be from the white heads of old mothers,
Darker than the colorless beards of old men,
Dark to come from under the faint red roofs of mouths.

O I perceive after all so many uttering tongues,
And I believe they do not come from the roofs of mouths for
    nothing. (193)

Part of what makes this figure so evocative and memorable is the oddity of its equivalence, which might certainly be considered a "deliberate
misfit." Yet if its oddity formed the whole of its attraction, the metaphor
that equates grass with the hair of the dead would have as little to "say"
as those that rely on a supposedly perfect match. Dialogue, in other
words, depends upon that which enables identification as well as upon
that which impedes it. Unlike metaphors that we might dismiss as
merely bizarre, Whitman's metaphor generates a dialogic relationship
with its readers because it encourages them both to identify with its fictional world—by joining the poet in imagining that the grass "transpires," as he puts it, from the bodies of the dead—and to recall the
peculiarity of that world, which remains incongruous with the "literal"
world readers take for granted. Similarly, Calvino's anomalous metaphoric domains, wherein nebulae, atoms, and other unpopulated realms
are filled with humanized beings of unknown size and shape, manage
to retain a tension between the strange and the familiar that allows readers to "enter" these fictional spaces even as they consider them from
afar. As so many commentators on metaphor have observed, figurative
language turns readers from recipients into participants in the production of meaning. But the dialogic metaphor, as I conceive it, requires
something more—that *readers also be made spectators of their own forms
of participation.* It is in this nexus of participation and spectatorship that
dialogue is born.[25]

One could argue that my conception of the dialogic metaphor nevertheless returns metaphor to the same marginal position it never seems
to escape, for surely it would appear that a figure of the kind I have attempted to describe constitutes a departure from more prevalent forms
of discourse. When a person takes interest, as Burke suggests, in challenging "the vestigial congruities still upheld by language," that person

"has necessarily vowed himself to conflicts with the classifications of everyday speech, which is primarily designed for calling things *good or bad, intelligent or stupid, this or that,* and being done with it" (*Permanence* 144). But here I find it crucial to remember that even "the classifications of everyday speech" are *potentially* open to dialogue; it is only our complacency as readers and writers (shaped, to be sure, by the complacency of the culture at large) that prevents us from questioning what we are expected to accept. For Bakhtin, as Ken Hirschkop and others have indicated, dialogism is both a characteristic of certain discourses and the very nature of language itself, which can always be submitted to interrogation and subversion.[26] Hirschkop's observations on this double meaning of dialogism are especially pertinent in our examination of metaphor:

> If we are going to continue using "dialogism" as a theoretical term denoting a general quality of linguistic practice, then some revision of the term is needed, so that specifically monological cultural forms are understood as *forms* of the dialogical—dialogical in some profound sense —rather than as some inexplicable perversion of the dialogical. But this also means that monologism must itself be recognized as a strategy of response toward another discourse, albeit a strategy which aims to "ignore" or "marginalize" the opposite discourse. We are thus led to a very different vision of what Bakhtin meant by "dialogue," one which includes not only the liberal exchange of views but also questions of cultural oppression and power. (674)

Similarly, a revision in our understanding of metaphor must include a revision in our understanding of literal discourse, which serves not simply as a "perversion" of metaphor but as a *form* of metaphor. As metaphor, literalism composes fictive worlds whose equivalences are susceptible to resistance and critique; the fact that such fictions seek identification alone—that they hope to work by way of monologue rather than dialogue—only goes to show the importance of addressing "questions of cultural oppression and power" in any attempt to read either the literal or the metaphorical dialogically.

Bakhtin writes that "every word is directed toward an *answer* and cannot escape the profound influence of the answering word that it anticipates" ("Discourse" 280). From this perspective, all metaphors are in some sense dialogic, not only those that strive to create the productive tension between equivalence and difference that I have cited here. As Louise Smith has observed, "all metaphors . . . invite the reader to participate in exploring their enigmas and constructing their intelligibilities" (163). Ultimately, metaphor might be approached less as a specific feature of discourse than as a dialogic attitude toward discourse—an attitude that holds serious implications for the English studies curriculum.

4

"OTHER FORMULATIONS"

Reading and Writing the Fragmentary Text

> "The dream: to know a foreign (alien) language and
> yet not to understand it: to perceive the difference
> in it without that difference ever being recuperated
> by the superficial sociality of discourse, communica-
> tion or vulgarity; to know, positively refracted in a
> new language, the impossibility of our own; to learn
> the systematics of the inconceivable; to undo our
> own 'reality' under the effect of other formulations,
> other syntaxes; to discover certain unsuspected posi-
> tions of the subject in utterance, to displace the
> subject's topology; in a word, to descend into the
> untranslatable."
>
> Roland Barthes, *Empire of Signs*

IN ONE OF HIS most celebrated novels, *If on a Winter's Night a Traveler*
(1979), Calvino creates a narrative structure that places the act of reading itself at the center of attention. As a writer who revels in complicated
fictional patterns, Calvino accomplishes this metatextual feat through
two unusual techniques—first, by designating the second-person protagonist of his book as, quite simply, "the Reader," whose adventures
we follow from one chapter to the next; and second, by interrupting
these chapters with ten different texts that the Reader reads, all of which
are themselves interrupted just as they reach their moments of greatest
tension. Since both the Reader and the woman he pursues (whom
Calvino comically and problematically names "the Other Reader") can
be read as metaphors for actual readers reading Calvino's book—indeed,
the opening statement of the text discloses: "You are about to begin reading Italo Calvino's new novel, *If on a Winter's Night a Traveler*"—every

line from beginning to end implicitly calls for readers to self-consciously examine their own habits and proclivities in response to the text. In this sense, the Reader (Calvino's character) is thoroughly entangled with, and potentially displaced by, readers themselves, whose own stories of reading help compose the plot of this supremely reflexive text.

Yet while Calvino's novel contributes imaginatively to the study of reading,[1] his book might also be productively approached as an experiment in fragmentation—one that has much to teach us about the possibilities for a curriculum in English studies. The ten separate narratives that the Reader encounters in *If on a Winter's Night* are each written in different narrative styles and by supposedly different "authors"; but what is most intriguing—and, for the Reader, most frustrating—about all of them is that each is terminated before reaching its conclusion. The first story has been defectively bound at the printer's and must be returned to the bookstore; another was never finished by its writer, who committed suicide; another is partly read aloud in a discussion group and then set aside; and so on. After reading or hearing the opening pages of each story, the Reader goes in search of the pages that follow, only to be lead to another story altogether. What he accumulates, in other words, is a series of fragments—bits and pieces rather than whole stories. Similarly, the interruptions that so often intrude upon the tale of the Reader himself (for Calvino alternates this tale with those of the texts that the Reader reads) remind us of the fragmentary status of the novel itself, for by inserting fragments of other texts into the supposedly unified narrative of the Reader, we see that this larger narrative is likewise composed of fragments whose seams would ordinarily be covered over by the author.

I hasten to indicate, however, that though poststructuralist literary theory might claim that Calvino's novel takes its readers straight into the abyss of language—where, as Paul de Man has remarked of readers in general, they are forever left in "suspended ignorance" (*Allegories* 19)— my interest in his book concerns the ways in which its fragmentary structure manages to sustain rather than deconstruct the fictions it generates. While the fragment is often approached as a sign that the writer has lost control over his or her discourse—or at least that the writer has admitted that the subject at hand is too difficult to grasp except in smaller pieces—the striking architecture of *If on a Winter's Night* suggests that Calvino uses fragmentation not to confess defeat at the hands of language but to construct a discursive pattern considerably more inventive and intricate than those we generally find in texts that rely on the semblance of unity for their effect. Fragmentation here signals an ambition on the part of the writer, not a plea to be excused in the face of overwhelming complexity. If anything, fragmentation becomes Calvino's triumphant means for creating complexity rather than his resignation when confronted by it.[2]

Yet despite the impressive achievements of fragmentary texts such as *If on a Winter's Night,* the fragment, like the metaphor, continues to occupy a contradictory role within the English studies curriculum. On the one hand, students are often asked to marvel at the fragmentary prose of Sterne, Joyce, Woolf, and Faulkner (among many others), and to appreciate the fragmentary poetry of Eliot, Stevens, Plath, and Ashbury (also among many others). On the other hand, these same students are told to avoid the fragment at all levels—sentence, paragraph, and discourse—in their own writing.[3] The justification generally offered in support of this double message is that student writers should first and foremost learn to bring separate bits of text into a coherent whole, and that only *after* they have mastered the art of unification does it make sense to provide them with opportunities to do something more "creative" by way of form: "Writers need to know the rules before they can go about breaking them." While fragments of various kinds are at times permitted in student journals or in preliminary "prewriting" (as it is often called in textbooks), such texts are precisely those that teachers tend to read without rendering commentary or with mere content-related encouragement. In other words, the very fact that the fragment is tolerated in student writing only in an initial stage of drafting reflects its low status even when accepted, for the assumption appears to be that, since such texts constitute "informal" compositions, form is not an issue. Form is supposedly what comes later—and when it comes, the fragmentary character of earlier work is expected to be replaced by a rhetoric in which all parts fit neatly into a single totality. From this perspective, the fragment may serve temporarily as a heuristic tool, but it must also know when to step aside.[4]

To be sure, the attempt to gather the scattered fragments of an early draft into an identifiable whole can pose a considerable challenge for any writer, and students have much to gain from the practice. But at the same time, it may well be that teachers of English have made this practice all the more difficult on their students by divorcing it from the crafting of fragments—an endeavor whose relationship to the struggle for textual unity could be described as interdependent rather than oppositional. In this chapter, I suggest that the fragment should be actively embraced, not renounced, by those seeking to help students with their writing. As this is an extremely tricky proposition, I should say from the start that I have no intention of celebrating either "radical indeterminacy" or "the free play of signs," nor do I wish to argue that teachers regard their students' failures to integrate the disparate pieces of their writing as successful examples of fragmentary prose. ("Congratulations," we can humorously imagine a teacher commenting on a student paper, "on your brilliant display of the abyss over which all readers hang! No part of your text has any connection to any other part—a marvelously ingenious enactment of the fragmentation which defines the textual exchange!") Rather than ask that we praise the scattered remains of a student essay as the sign of postmodern heroics, I propose that we broaden the range of texts we elicit from students to include the "fragmentary" as well as the "unified." I recognize the oddity of this idea: why would a teacher ever *request* a class filled with relatively inexperienced writers to produce texts composed of fragments? To begin to respond to this question, I turn to a writer whose life's work is in large part a tribute to the fragment, and from whose example teachers of English might reconsider the parameters of student writing.

Why Teachers of English Should Always Remember Roland Barthes

In *Roland Barthes: The Figures of Writing*, Andrew Brown observes that "the decline of interest in Barthes's work that has followed his death . . . is not just a posthumous slump: it does not seem to have affected Lacan or Foucault, for instance, to anything like the same degree" (3). Rather, the "general unease" about the value and achievement of Barthes's contribution has become one of its defining elements—an element that therefore calls for closer investigation. In Brown's view, Barthes is in certain respects himself responsible for the decline of his popularity, particularly through his acts of tragicomic self-criticism, wherein he appears to ask that he not be taken too seriously. This insistent interrogation of his own identity leaves critics unsure of his theoretical project, which thus "makes it difficult," as Brown puts it, "to see what to do with Barthes" (3).

The result is that unlike Lacan and Foucault (or Derrida, for that matter), Barthes has not spawned a "school" of followers, nor has he remained fashionable, as he was in the seventies and early eighties. But it may be that Barthes's very inability to produce an identifiable theory (or at least a theory to which he remained loyal) provides good motive for teachers of English to take another look at his work, especially in light of what Brown calls Barthes's "fascination for writing itself—writing, as it were, rather than what the writing says" (8). More than any critical theorist who emerged in the heyday of the French wave of influence, Barthes can be best approached as a *writer* (or what he would prefer to call an *author*[5]) rather than the progenitor of a coherent set of ideas—and perhaps the most prominent feature of his writing lies in its commitment to fragmentary form. Indeed, Barthes's fragments, especially in the last decade of his career, could be said to represent his attempt to enact, and not just argue for, a form of meaning-making that poses an alternative to what he repeatedly disparages as the "arrogance" of discourse.[6] Unlike the text that seeks to contain all of its potential meaning by explicitly revealing the various relationships between its parts, the fragment invites readerly participation in the construction of meaning by severing itself from all that it precedes or follows. What the unified text attempts to eliminate or conceal—namely, its gaps and fissures—the fragmentary text willingly acknowledges as an inevitable characteristic of both its composition and its reading. Moreover, if texts and their readings are all to some degree constituted by disjunctions as well as connections, then the difference between intentionally fragmentary texts on the one hand and ostensibly unified texts on the other lies primarily in the ways that the latter struggle to provide the appearance of smooth, untroubled access. According to Barthes, such texts are duplicitous because they present no awareness of the conventional, cultural basis of their writing and reading. In short, clarity in writing may often be little more than discourse shaped by "a community of stereotypes" (*Criticism* 48)—and the accessible text at times akin to a plagiarism not of content but of form.

By contrast, the openly fragmentary text foregrounds its construction by writer and reader. Through its discontinuities and dislocations, the fragment inaugurates what Barthes calls the "drift" of meaning, thereby resisting the static structure imposed by any attempt to establish and grab hold of a signified. In other words, the fragment signals a refusal of a particular kind of rhetoric—which Barthes labels "classical" —but not of rhetoric itself. In a fragment in his "autobiography" (if that is how the intriguing *Roland Barthes* should be classified), he writes of himself: "Speaking of the text, he credits its author with not manipulating the reader. But he found this compliment by discovering that he himself does all he can to manipulate the reader, and that in fact he will never renounce an art of *effects*" (102). Effects, Barthes implies, are inevitable; at issue are the kinds of effects writing makes available. The fragmentary text does not divorce itself from effect but instead sets out to invoke another realm of effect, one wherein the disparity of textual elements paradoxically manipulates readers toward their own acts of imagination. Barthes recognizes his desire to lead his readers in a certain direction—but the direction he leads is toward a space in which readers are left to their own devices among disparate pieces of text. While all readers must discern structure in order for a text to make sense—and in our compulsion for sense, it may be that we can eventually find *some* structure in (or invent a structure for) any text—fragmentary texts make this recuperation of sense more circuitous and thus more self-conscious: the fragment will never let us forget that there is nothing "natural" about reading and writing.[7]

Barthes's fascination with fragmentary form thus represents an attempt to reinvent the relationship between the text and its meaning. For Barthes, meaning is never that which stands "behind" writing, waiting for the curtain to be drawn or the skin to be peeled; nor is it that which the writer "expresses" from some interior realm, thereby granting readers access to the writer's self. In other words, meaning belongs neither to the text nor to the writer. And yet the third possibility—that meaning belongs to the reader—is also rendered problematic by Barthes. While he is often considered a champion of reading and the reader, a return to his work reveals an ambivalence toward certain forms of readerly interpretation, an uneasiness not immediately apparent in his otherwise confident analyses of everything from the discourses of advertising and fashion to those of wrestling and love. The reader that concerns Barthes is, after all, the critic—and therefore a writer—as in this memorable passage from *S/Z:*

> The text, in its mass, is comparable to a sky, at once flat and smooth, deep, without edges and without landmarks; like the soothsayer drawing on it with the tip of his staff an imaginary rectangle wherein to consult, according to certain principles, the flight of birds, the commentator traces through the text certain zones of reading, in order to observe therein the migration of meanings, the outcropping of codes, the passage of citations. (14)

Here we find the reader, in the guise of a soothsayer, drawing on the sky —the text—with the tip of his staff, which thus serves as both a writing implement and the key to his powers of discernment.[8] That is to say, it is precisely because of his own patterns, his own inscriptions, that the reader-critic's observation of "the migration of meanings" becomes prophetic or culturally significant. Moreover, while the emptiness of a text "without edges and without landmarks" would appear to privilege the reader in any struggle for power, meanings are nevertheless said to "migrate" on their own: the reader merely "traces" their movements and mutations (the Latin *migratus* is related to the Greek *ameibein*—to change). As soothsayer, the reader is given ambiguous status: on the one hand, he brings a certain wisdom to the text through his ability to observe and predict; on the other hand, he lacks the authority of science and may in fact be something of a charlatan—one who performs rather than holds authoritative knowledge.

My point is that meaning as Barthes envisions it exhibits an unusual independence, for it belongs neither to writer nor reader nor text. Rather, it is variously passed among these agents and at the same time exceeds the grasp of any one of them. Even during what Annette Lavers has called his "structuralist phase," Barthes at times defines reading more by its amorous relation to the text than by its ability to identify textual meaning:

> For nobody knows anything about the sense which reading attributes to the work, nor anything about the signified, perhaps because this sense, being desire, is established beyond the code of language. Only reading loves the work, entertains with it a relationship of desire. To read is to desire the work, to want to be the work, to refuse to echo the work using any discourse other than that of the work: the only commentary which a pure reader could produce, if he were to remain purely a reader, would be a pastiche. (*Criticism* 93–94)

And in the later Barthes, reading continues to be alternately active and passive, both a transformation of the text and a transformation of the reader himself:

> Paradox of the reader: it is commonly admitted that to read is to decode: letters, words, meanings, structures, and this is uncontestable; but by accumulating decodings (since reading is by rights infinite), by removing the safety catch of meaning, by putting reading into freewheeling (which is its structural vocation), the reader is caught up in a dialectical reversal: finally, he does not decode, he overcodes; he does not decipher, he produces, he accumulates languages, he lets himself be infinitely and tirelessly traversed by them: he is that traversal. ("On Reading" 42)

What these passages illustrate is that Barthes, despite the power he clearly ascribes to reading as a productive process, never gives readers the kind of autonomy or authority we find envisaged by reader-response criticism of the time.[9] Rather, readers appear as part of a scene of language in which the very writing they enact places them into a complicated and far from controllable relationship to meaning.

For Barthes, the ideal state of language is that in which meaning "floats" away from all attempts to pin it down—hence his preference for what he calls the "writerly" over the "readerly" text. While readerly texts, which Barthes claims "make up the enormous mass of our literature" (*S/Z* 5), are products to be consumed by readers, writerly texts, such as the novels of Robbe-Grillet or Philippe Sollers, are productions that at this stage can only be written, since we do not yet know how to read them. (Or to put this another way: our standard protocols for reading prove inadequate when confronted by writerly texts like the *nouveau roman*.) Writerly texts set meaning into motion: their very illegibility is in Barthes's view their value. Readerly texts, to the contrary, hold meaning still: in their effort to transmit a dominant message to the reader, they work in the service of bourgeois culture, which seeks a stabilization of the forces of language. From Barthes's perspective, the most dismal state of affairs for writing—what he calls in one of his interviews "an apocalyptic vision of the end of the book"—would not be the disappearance of the book but the "triumph [of] its most abject forms: the book of mass communication, of consumption, the capitalistic book. . . . And that would be complete barbarism: the death of the book would correspond to the exclusive reign of the readerly, legible book and the total defeat of the 'illegible' book" (*Grain* 147).[10]

Of course the danger with an opposition like this one lies in the temptation to endlessly celebrate the signifier that never meets its signified— and there are certainly numerous passages in Barthes's work where he appears to do little more than revel in meaning set adrift.[11] But elsewhere, particularly in *Roland Barthes,* he complicates his position by observing that what he calls "the thrill of meaning" can be found in two somewhat antithetical places. On the one hand, there is the thrill that comes when meaning begins not to drift but to solidify, to take shape and identify itself, as "the machine of languages starts up" and "the 'natural' begins to stir" (97). On the other hand, there is the thrill to be found in meaning that "before collapsing into in-significance, shudders still: there is meaning, but this meaning does not permit itself to be 'caught'; it remains fluid, shuddering with a faint ebullition" (97). In both instances of this "thrill," then, we find meaning in a liminal, unstabilized existence—either at the incipience or near the end of its embodiment, but never when it can be "seized." As he goes on to comment,

> The ideal state of sociality is thereby declared: an enormous and perpetual rustling animates with countless meanings which explode, crepitate, burst out without ever assuming the definitive form of a sign grimly weighted by its signified: a happy and impossible theme, for this ideally thrilling meaning is pitilessly recuperated by a solid meaning (that of the *Doxa*) or by a null meaning (that of the mystiques of liberation). (98)

Here Barthes puts forward, even as he recognizes the forces that stand against it, his utopic vision of language, one in which meaning avoids being either captured or completely released. The forms of meaning that Barthes seeks—and that he believes writing, rather than speech, is best suited to provide—are those that stand outside the traditional opposition between the clear and the opaque. Barthes's metaphors for meaning (as that which "rustles," "explodes," "crepitates") draw as often on auditory as on visual phenomena, and the very multiplicity of these figures seems intended to dissolve the ubiquitous fixation on degrees of transparency.

The fragment, then, becomes Barthes's means of exploring an alternative rhetoric, one in which writing offers mobile rather than settled meanings:

> The implication from the point of view of an ideology or a counter-ideology of form is that the fragment breaks up what I would call the smooth finish, the composition, discourse constructed to give a final meaning to what one says, which is the general rule of all past rhetoric. In relation to the smooth finish of constructed discourse, the fragment is a spoilsport, discontinuous, establishing a kind of pulverization of sentences, images, thoughts, none of which 'takes' definitively. (*Grain* 209–10)

Yet at the same time, Barthes remains conscious of the fact that the rhetoric of the fragment is not the writer's alone to control:

> I have the illusion to suppose that by breaking up my discourse I cease to discourse in terms of the imaginary about myself, attenuating the risk of transcendence; but since the fragment (haiku, maxim, *pensée*, journal entry) is *finally* a rhetorical genre and since rhetoric is that layer of language which best presents itself to interpretation, by supposing I disperse myself I merely return, quite docilely, to the bed of the imaginary. (*Roland Barthes* 95)

Barthes admits that however disruptive the fragment, it remains entrapped by the ambition of any rhetorical enterprise, which ultimately consists of communicating to another through "the imaginary"—an "illusory unitary subjectivity," as Michael Moriarty describes it, that is "supposedly external to the structures of language" (170). For Barthes, this unitary subjectivity provides the readerly security and comfort that the writer of fragments has hoped to upset by frustrating any "transcendence" of the medium of writing itself. But in this passage, the frustration becomes his own as he realizes the extent to which even the fragment "presents itself to interpretation"—that is to say, gives itself over to readers, who seek to make it intelligible—and thus "returns" Barthes's own discourse to the very "bed of the imaginary" he wishes to escape.

The lesson, I believe, is an important one: whatever its anarchic potential, the fragmentary text remains subject to the recuperative energies of the reader, who may strive all the harder to put back together what the text aims to pull apart. The fragment, in other words, is no panacea for the discursive habits of a culture. Nor does it offer any easy solutions for the teaching of writing in composition, literature, or creative writing courses. As I believe to be the case with metaphor, attention to fragmentary discourse creates a more, not less, complicated predicament for teachers and students of English. But this also seems just the kind of complication we might welcome.

Student Writers and Fragmentary Texts

It would be a mistake, of course, to give the impression that the fragment has received nothing but condemnation from those concerned with postsecondary writing instruction. In an essay published over twenty years ago, Charles R. Kline Jr. and W. Dean Memering attempt to come to terms with the fact that sentence fragments appear in formal and professional writing of virtually all kinds and therefore must serve an important rhetorical function. Working from the linguist Elizabeth Bowman's classification of utterances, Kline and Memering divide written units into "major," "minor," and "broken" sentences. While the major sentence consists of what most teachers consider a sentence proper —with subject and predicate forming an independent statement—the minor sentence comprises what teachers often identify (and mark on student papers) as a fragment: a unit either without a subject, or a predicate, or grammatical independence, yet punctuated as if it held the status of a complete statement (106). (To cite an example the authors find in Eldridge Cleaver's *Soul on Ice:* "That is why I started to write. To save myself." The second unit lacks a subject and therefore constitutes a minor sentence.) According to Kline and Memering, minor sentences, despite their rejection by the majority of English teachers when they appear in student texts, serve as a legitimate form of written expression that in no way impedes communication. In the authors' view, only the broken sentence—that which represents "fragmented, discontinuous, and/or noncontinuous thought"—should be considered a "fragment" and therefore treated as an "error" by teachers (108). As long as minor sentences establish their own form of independence or are implicitly connected with other independent sentences, they should create no cause for alarm. Even more provocatively, Kline and Memering conclude that "'fragments' will largely disappear if teachers will read student papers rapidly, attending to the substance of sentences" rather than seeking to condemn what are otherwise "perfectly acceptable minor sentences" (109).

Yet for all the insight offered by their essay—which by turning to issues of reading in its closing gesture faces us in precisely the right direction—I find it intriguing that the place Kline and Memering reserve for their redefined "fragment" remains that of the misguided creation. Acceptable fragments become examples of the "minor sentence," while unacceptable fragments continue to be called "fragments": the territory is not as vast as before, but it is still to be avoided. In a sense, what Kline and Memering contribute is a revised approach to punctuation more than a revised approach to fragmentation, for the discontinuous, the broken, the detached—all of which signify the fragment in its most radical form—are still rejected as inadequate. The minor sentence is found admissible because it brings no interruption to the flow of discourse and no challenge to the unity of the text. But the "broken" sentence remains a troublemaker, disrupting the cohesion and coherence of language and hence the reader's access to authorial meaning and intent.[12]

A more generous approach to the fragment, and one with significant implications for the college curriculum, can be found in Philip Keith's "How to Write Like Gertrude Stein." Keith observes that the emphasis on communicative efficiency in writing—an emphasis that continues to dominate freshman composition programs across the country—leads teachers to believe that the primary goal of writing instruction is to help students acquire "stylistic devices . . . that make it easier for a reader to read what has been written" (229). While Keith admits that students need to learn how to use techniques such as parallelism, repetition, paragraphing, punctuation, and whatever else will help their readers to "clarify rather than obscure relationships" (229), he does not believe the teaching of these skills should come "at the expense of seeing writing as an invitation for the reader to make meaning" (229–30). To the contrary, Keith asserts that the teaching of writing should provide students with "language experiences that are . . . calisthenic for the reader and aim at reflexivity or even opacity of style, rather than transparency" (230) —a commitment that leads him to bring excerpts of Gertrude Stein's writing to his classroom, despite their fragmentary and elliptical form. Initially, Keith admits, his students read Stein's writing as a "farce," with her sentence fragments "implying that the writer did not know her grammar" and her lack of question marks serving as "signs of either illiteracy or infantile rebelliousness" (231). But by looking closer at the inadequacy of making "corrections" to Stein's prose—that is, by seeing what meanings are lost when her writing is made to comply with certain standards or conventions—Keith's students begin to recognize "how it might be useful to think of grammar and mechanics more as resources in the system than rules or maxims to be followed, and even how one might command some special power as a user of language-acts when one can work with rules in this way" (231–32). Rather than reflecting her failure to write as she should, Stein's "errors" display just how carefully she has considered the relationship between writer and reader: "Stein subverts conventions of meaning to throw readers back on an intensified experience of their own reading processes and ultimately to challenge the expectation that meaning is merely referential" (233).[13]

Keith concludes his essay by noting that he looks forward "to seeing chapters in future freshman composition texts on how to write like Gertrude Stein" (236)—an unorthodox vision of the textbook if ever there was one. But since the bulk of Keith's discussion addresses only the question of *reading* Stein in the first-year course and not that of *writing* like her, it remains to be seen just what it would mean to use avant-garde authors such as Stein as models for composition students. Would we ask student writers to be intentionally obscure? to violate grammatical conventions? to ignore their usual responsibilities as writers within the academy? What can they gain from rejecting the very qualities of writing that might later help them find employment or succeed at further study? And how, precisely, would teachers ensure that "writing like Stein" did not further disorient students who may be said to already harbor any number of confusions?

In order to address these questions, I would like to turn to a contemporary textbook—entitled, simply (or grandly) enough, *Text Book*—that gives an idea of how teachers of English might responsibly ask their students to compose fragmentary texts.[14] As the authors Robert Scholes, Nancy Comley, and Gregory Ulmer explain in their preface,

> The title of this textbook is not a joke. It is meant to signify our intention to offer an alternative approach to the traditional course called "Writing about Literature" or "Introduction to Literature." By substituting the concept of *text* for the traditional concept of *literature,* we accomplish a number of things. We allow for the presentation of a wider range of material and a broader spectrum of approaches to literary study. And we close or reduce the gaps that have separated reading from writing, creative from critical work, and literature from ordinary language. (v)

While we might at first greet such assertions with the skepticism born of experience with textbook prefaces, perusal of the chapters that follow tends to confirm rather than undermine their validity—for unlike any number of textbooks that claim to provide a substantial "alternative" to traditional study, *Text Book* actually manages to do so. Furthermore, I would argue that its utility lies not so much in the selection of readings (which, through the inclusion of writers such as Benjamin, Goffman, Freud, Sontag, Derrida, and others, clearly denotes a concern with "theory") as in the selection of writing assignments, which reveal an unusual willingness to lead students into adventures with form and not just with content.[15] In many of these assignments, the "creative" and the "critical" do indeed meet in ways that numerous literary and composition scholars have hoped they might.

Take, for instance, the penultimate chapter, "Experiments with Texts: Fragments and Signatures." At the beginning of this chapter, Scholes, Comley, and Ulmer observe that the experimental use of a text in a sense reverses the relationship between writing and knowing, in that you start out with a form and a procedure and use them to invent an idea, to produce or generate a text whose features you may not be able to predict in advance. Instead of trying to make the language conform to what you already know, now you may let the form lead you, let the form tell you something or show you something about your cultural existence. (209)

One of the forms that the authors have in mind is the fragment, which they go on to exemplify for students with a series of excerpts from Barthes's *A Lover's Discourse,* a book that resists the narrative "flow" of its love story by taking up various themes (or what Barthes calls "figures") of love in separate fragments—themselves fragmented into numbered paragraphs—that are arranged alphabetically according to subject.[16] The mere fact that the authors of an introductory textbook would include passages from such an eccentric and elliptical volume is reason enough to give serious consideration to their approach, but even more compelling are the assignments that follow the reading, for here students are asked to make Barthes's fragmentary discourse a part of their own methods as writers. Scholes, Comley, and Ulmer begin by suggesting to students that they "select one of Barthes' figures and replace it with your own numbered paragraphs" on the subject at hand (219). Then, noting that they have reproduced only four of the eighty fragments in Barthes's book, the authors ask that students "try to add some of the missing pieces" by composing "a list of some of the other objects, events, and expressions that constitute the lover's 'scenes of language'" (219). Finally, they propose that students "test the validity and value" of Barthes's experiment by replicating it: "Write a set of figures, entitled *Fragments of a Student's Discourse,* . . . applying Barthes' form and procedure to the discourse of a student. You are to write about the conventions and stereotypes of the student experience, identifying the conventions and clichés, figures and poses, myths and expectations of the student life. Do for the student's life*style* what Barthes did for the lover's style of conduct" (219).[17]

As the authors of *Text Book* recognize, part of the value of such assignments lies in their ability to give students a sense of "text as *productivity* rather than as representation or communication" (210). Ask any

English major the function of writing and he or she will more than likely offer some version of what Catherine Belsey in her book *Critical Practice* calls "expressive realism," whereby language serves either to reflect some preexistent reality or to express some preexistent thought (7). But the fragmentary text, by virtue of its discontinuities and separations, can help students to experience the ways in which language produces, not merely "communicates," thought—for in the absence of the kinds of constraints that leave them preoccupied with clarifying a position they already hold, the fragment allows students the opportunity to use writing as a means for exploring positions they have yet to assume or even to imagine. If the unified compositions generally assigned to students require that they "compose themselves" (in the sense of demonstrating self-possession), then the fragmentary text can be seen as a *de*composition—a form of writing that works against the attempt to make oneself whole and self-sufficient.

Yet experiments with the fragment such as those found in *Text Book* have more to offer than their subversive charm. Beyond the challenge they pose to currently dominant pedagogies of writing, assignments that ask students to write in fragments can contribute as well to their understanding of and proficiency with the dynamics of *unity*. As Bakhtin has observed so eloquently in "Discourse in the Novel," "unitary language" operates not in isolation but "in the midst of heteroglossia" (271) —that is to say, in the midst of diverse social forces that work against its drive toward monologic authority: "Alongside the centripetal forces, the centrifugal forces of language carry on their uninterrupted work; alongside verbal-ideological centralization and unification, the uninterrupted process of decentralization and disunification go forward" (272). Though Bakhtin does not here refer specifically to fragmentary texts, I would argue not only that the fragment participates in "the uninterrupted process of decentralization and disunification" but also that the social life of any piece of writing—its life, in other words, among the various readers who interpret it—ultimately leads to the break-up or fragmentation of its rhetorical power. In other words, the unified and the fragmentary indicate not so much opposing discourses as opposing forces within *all* discourse in social circulation. If language, as Bakhtin claims, truly is "dialogic," then there can never be any such thing as a completely unified text, a text that entirely eliminates the cracks and fissures that help create different interpretations of its meaning and different responses to its form.[18]

From this perspective, the pedagogical obsession with driving students toward the production of seamless texts appears to curtail more than it enables. Indeed, students who imagine that they should or even could avoid writing in fragments can be said to be laboring within the confines of a formidable delusion, whereby the ideal text supposedly silences its (teacher) reader with perfection rather than partaking in an always imperfect dialogue. My suggestion is not that we lead students to believe that there is no sense in worrying about unity, but that we enable them to recognize the inevitable struggle between unity and fragmentation in all forms of writing, so that they come to see fragmentation as a characteristic and not simply an abuse of language. As Susan Miller observes, writing is "a living fiction of, not an achievement of, stability" (*Rescuing* 19). Along similar lines, I wish to contend that fragmentary writing is a fiction of *instability*—for when written with care, the collection of fragments is always more than a chaotic dispersion of words. Just as unified texts conceal their fragmentation, fragmentary texts conceal their unities. Accordingly, we might wonder why students should not be asked to design, alongside texts that attempt to erase all ambiguity, texts that attempt to remain relentlessly ambiguous. Or why they should not construct, alongside essays that attempt to cover over their gaps, essays that expose their gaps for all to see. Why not use fragmentary writing as a way to sharpen the writing of unified texts (and vice-versa)? Faced with the considerable challenge of composing in fragments, students might gain a new sense of the power and necessity of unifying devices even in writing that appears to ignore them. After all, if the fragmentary text is too diffuse, the reader will have no "access" whatsoever. The fragment, in other words, is not simply a disruptive deviation from the norm but an alternative approach to communication, one that requires an extremely sensitive awareness of readerly desires and needs.

Given that there are any number of ways in which teachers might invite students to explore the fragmentary in their own writing, I don't want to be too prescriptive about specific classroom practices. But I will suggest a couple of possibilities, the first of which consists of a deceptively simple syntactical exercise. To complete the exercise, students compose a brief argument of one or two pages on any matter of concern (perhaps in response to a text they have read)—with the only stipulation being that *every* sentence of their argument must be written as a sentence fragment. Initially, it may be useful to say nothing more before students write their papers, since the papers themselves can then become the focus of class discussion over the question of just what constitutes a sentence or a fragment to begin with. As I've attempted to indicate throughout this chapter, this kind of exercise might have considerable value not simply for the production of eccentric or unusual writing but also for the pursuit of more conventional goals such as composing in "complete" sentences. Despite all of the workbook drills students may have endured in middle school and high school—or perhaps because they were members of "advanced" classes that "didn't do grammar" (as I'm often told by the students I teach)—the fact is that most college students have never had the opportunity to investigate the architecture of sentences through a close examination of the sentences in their own texts. They have all heard, for example, of the "subordinate clause," but even those few who can still identify one have little idea how to recognize the crucial contribution subordination makes to the shaping of meaning. My proposal is that we help them to recognize and discuss such things by strategically overturning our usual request for sentences that are "whole." Indeed, one of the results of the exercise I've described is that students tend to find it surprisingly difficult to write a full page of sentence fragments and still help the reader to "follow" their argument—a predicament that helps them begin to understand the relationship between syntax and meaning. When they see a subordinate clause standing, fragmentary, all on its own, they are given the means to reflect on how subordination sets up readerly expectations and why they may then satisfy or upset those expectations with what comes next.

The second possibility begins from the other side of the fence, as it were. With this assignment, students first compose an essay that attempts to meet the standard requirements for unity and coherence (whatever those might be in the context at hand); then, after these essays have been submitted and returned, students are asked to take the same essays and "chop" them into fragmentary blocks that make no explicit connections between one another. This may mean that students have to rewrite the essays entirely or that they retain certain portions that are cut around the edges—but the object in either case is to create an essay that excludes all transitional, coordinating, and subordinating devices between the separate fragments into which the text has been divided. Students can also be encouraged to experiment with the sequential arrangement of these fragments, so as to determine the effects created by different patterns of organization. Once again, though it may initially seem counterproductive to have students eliminate the very procedures by which they might make their texts hold together, the point is to lead students into a deeper engagement with the tensions between "holding together" and "falling apart" that all writing must negotiate. By placing their unified and fragmentary essays side by side, students can begin to recognize the rhetorical functions of each, rather than extolling one (mostly because the institution insists on it) at the expense of the other.

But beyond these particular pedagogical practices, attending to the subtle rhetoric of fragmentary texts might make a valuable contribution to current discussions regarding the very purpose of the English department curriculum. As many have observed during the past twenty years, critical theories of various sorts have not only reinvented English studies as a discipline, they have also left the discipline deeply divided over its relationship to its own object of inquiry. Why study "literature" —or, if one prefers, "texts"—in the first place? The fragment offers new ways to respond to this question.

Politics and Pleasure: A Reconsideration

One of the more intriguing articles to appear on the teaching of English in recent years is Frank Lentricchia's "Last Will and Testament of an Ex-Literary Critic." In this essay, Lentricchia repudiates his past life as someone who claimed literature to be "a political instrument" (59) and who believed that a literary critic "could be an agent of social transformation, an activist who would show his students that, in its form and style, literature had a strategic role to play in the world's various arrangements of power" (60). Now reformed, Lentricchia asserts that he no longer teaches such ideas, in part because of the moral superiority that often accompanies them and in part because of their eradication of the pleasure that literature is designed to provoke. What currently interests Lentricchia, he tells us, is literature in its own right, apart from its political subtexts—an interest he claims to hold in common with undergraduate students, who likewise "believe that literature is pleasurable and important, as literature, and not as an illustration of something else" (60). Confessing that he has "nothing new to offer the field of literary theory," Lentricchia goes on to describe the process of appreciating literature: "If you should happen to enjoy the literary experience of liberation, it's not likely that you do so because you're able to take apart the formal resources of literature. All you know is that you live where you live and that you are who you are. Then you submit to the text, you relinquish yourself, because you need to be transported. . . . Even if you can't say what it is, you know when you're in the thrall of real literature" (63).

While it might be tempting to discount Lentricchia's essay as the sad tale of a formerly brilliant leftist theorist who has lapsed into the conservative discourse of those whom he once refuted, I think it crucial that teachers and scholars disillusioned by the explicit political cast of recent criticism be heard with empathy rather than condescension. If Lentricchia has here oversimplified what critical theory instructs us about the relationship between literature and politics, it is also true that critical theory has often oversimplified what traditional literary criticism instructs us about the relationship between literature and pleasure.[19] Neither side, so to speak, has appeared sufficiently motivated to come to terms with the other, and I think it safe to say that virtually every English department in the United States has experienced the tensions that have resulted from this mutual antagonism between "old" and "new" approaches to literature. Yet somehow the gap between politics and pleasure must be addressed—if only so that students will not continue to be subjected to a curriculum that asks them to choose between critique and delight. It is not that all divisions within English studies should (or could) be overcome, but that this particular division ignores the potentially productive interaction between issues of politics and issues of pleasure in the study of literary texts.

Ironically, it may be Barthes—a writer whom Lentricchia once accused of "poststructuralist hedonism" (*After* 145)—who provides the best place to begin a reconsideration of the politics and pleasures of discourse. Barthes is, after all, both the author of a book entitled *The Pleasure of the Text* and a theorist who insists that ideology shapes not only reading and writing but all forms of cultural production. While this dual interest in politics and pleasure potentially offers a fresh vision of the relationship between the two, it is commonly assumed—as appears to be the case in Lentricchia's essay—that a concern for one cannot exist alongside a concern for the other. Consequently, Barthes's career is often regarded as split between the early Barthes for whom politics matters and the later Barthes for whom pleasurable indulgence has supposedly replaced serious reflection on ideological realities. As Jonathan Culler describes it, Barthes's "celebrations of the pleasure of the text seemed to point literary criticism towards values the traditionalists had never abandoned, and his references to bodily pleasures created for many a new Barthes, less forbiddingly scientific or intellectual. . . . Strategic and radical in certain ways, Barthes's hedonism repeatedly exposes him to charges of complacency" (*Roland Barthes* 100). For many, the Barthes who contends that "the pleasure of the text does not prefer one ideology to another" (*Pleasure* 31) betrays the very ideas that he formerly did so much to cultivate.

What remains at issue, however, is whether Barthes's exploration of the pleasures of reading and writing (and the pleasures of the fragment in particular) represents a denial or an extension of his prior convictions. Though it may appear that his late writings display a lack of attention to matters of history and politics, it is not altogether certain that Barthes relinquishes his political commitments during the final decade of his work. In order to consider a different explanation, we might begin by observing that Barthes divides pleasure into two sorts: *plaisir* ("pleasure") on the one hand and *jouissance* (often translated as "bliss") on the other. These terms can cause confusion since *plaisir* in Barthes's work refers at times to the general domain of pleasure that includes *jouissance* (as in the passages noted above) and at other times to a narrower realm that stands opposed to *jouissance*. In the latter usage, Barthes links *plaisir* with the "readerly" text or what he calls "a comfortable practice of reading," while *jouissance* derives from "the text that imposes a state of loss, the text that discomforts (perhaps to the point of a certain boredom), unsettles the reader's historical, cultural, psychological assumptions, the consistency of his tastes, values, memories, brings to a crisis his relation with language" (14). *Plaisir,* then, is that form of pleasure that stems from an approach to reading whereby the reader seeks the confirmations that come with cultural identification, while *jouissance,* to the contrary, appears in certain respects divorced from culture altogether—a matter of the individual body and its unpredictable rhythms. For Barthes, *jouissance* is "atopical, asocial . . . one cannot account for one's own bliss, no one can classify it" (*Grain* 176). Or, as he asserts in *The Pleasure of the Text,* "pleasure can be expressed in words, bliss cannot" (21).

Jouissance thus stands for the radically unknown and unknowable in our relationship with texts: it is what comes of its own accord, what lies beyond cultural recuperation. If *plaisir* works to constitute our sense of self, then *jouissance* marks a loss of identity—"the dissolve," as Barthes puts it, "which seizes the subject in the midst of bliss" (7). In other words, through the concept of *jouissance,* Barthes seeks to explore the ways in which engagement with certain texts can transform who we are: texts of bliss, he claims, are "texts that may displease you, provoke you, but which, at least temporarily, in the flash of an instant, change and transmute you, effecting the expenditure of the self in loss" (*Grain* 207).

Given that such a metamorphosis in perception and self-constitution could well contribute to a political project that resists the status quo, it becomes apparent that Barthes's supposed rejection of politics in the last years of his work might be examined in another light. Indeed, when an interviewer once observed that in Barthes's writing his relation to politics seems "extremely discreet," Barthes replied,

> Discreet, but obsessed. I would like to make a distinction which may seem somewhat specious to you, but it is quite valid to me: between "the political" and "politics." To me, the political is a fundamental order of history, of thought, of everything that is done, and said. It's the very dimension of the real. Politics, however, is something else, it's the moment when the political changes into the same old story, the discourse of repetition. My profound interest in the attachment of the political is equaled only by my intolerance of political discourse. Which doesn't make my situation very easy. (*Grain* 218)

Barthes's situation is difficult, he goes on to explain, because the discourses of both the Left and the Right have become what he calls "arrogant," rather than exploratory, in their relationship to knowledge. Political discourse tends to assume that it has already found the answer: we should do this, we should do that. Consequently, the presumptuous reiterations that characterize politics confront Barthes, situated on the Left, with a thorny contradiction: "The heart of my personal problem is that there is an arrogant leftist discourse: I'm divided between my situation within a political site and the aggressions of discourse coming from this site" (219).

Rather than relinquishing his awareness of politics, Barthes devotes his final decade to the thoroughly political endeavor of articulating and practicing an alternative to "the aggressions of discourse." What Barthes repeatedly repudiates, beyond the obvious assaults inherent in overtly political discourse, is the more subtle violence of interpretive reading and writing in general—that is to say, reading and writing intent on "uncovering" or "penetrating" meaning. As I indicated earlier in this chapter, Barthes contends on numerous occasions that he desires not to "capture" meaning but to set it adrift—while at the same time preventing it from completely eluding all contact with readerly understanding. His ambition, in other words, is to locate a politics of language that would escape the reckless excavations wrought by hermeneutic projects on the one hand and the useless suspensions devised by deconstructive projects on the other. This search for an alternative realm of meaning is evoked in his admiring description of the haiku as a form that "engenders no sense, but at the same time it is not non-sense. It's always the same problem: to keep meaning from taking hold, but without abandoning meaning, under the threat of falling into the worst meaning, nonmeaning" (211). Barthes would have us "read" and "write"—but neither for the purpose of arriving at a stable signified, nor for the aim of swirling in the poststructuralist abyss.

The composition of fragmentary texts may thus be seen as Barthes's attempt to defamiliarize reading and writing, to loosen the tyranny of dominant discursive practices both within and beyond the academy. For Barthes, this tyranny was characterized not only by aggression but also by asceticism—by a determination, especially on the part of the Left, to banish pleasure as a matter of concern:

> An entire minor mythology would have us believe that pleasure (and singularly the pleasure of the text) is a rightist notion. On the right, with the same movement, everything abstract, boring, political, is shoved over to the left and pleasure is kept for oneself: welcome to our side, you who are finally coming to the pleasure of literature! And on the left, because of morality (forgetting Marx's and Brecht's cigars), one suspects and disdains any "residue of hedonism." (*Pleasure* 22)

It is as if, from a leftist perspective, to speak of the pleasure of reading or writing were merely to indulge in trivialities at the expense of "higher" intellectual obligations. Against this view, Barthes prefers the position of Brecht, whom he claims "never thought that pleasure was in any way contradictory to revolutionary responsibilities" (*Grain* 163). Furthermore, Barthes goes on to contend that the intellectual "is not a proxy, he doesn't speak in the name of the proletariat: he must speak in his own name, in a revolutionary perspective, to account for what he needs, what hinders his intellectual activities, the alienations imposed upon him as an intellectual by our present society. He will be all the more a revolutionary if he measures the extent of his own alienation, and not just that of others" (163).

Barthes's revaluation of pleasure thus reflects not a rejection of his early political ideals but a consequence of them. For Barthes, pleasure becomes not merely an aftereffect of discourse, but part and parcel of its production and reception: "The important thing is to equalize the field of pleasure, to abolish the false opposition of practical life and contemplative life. The pleasure of the text is just that: claim lodged against the separation of the text" (*Pleasure* 59). Aestheticism traditionally divides the text from the "real"—but Barthes sees the text as material, as "an object of pleasure like the others" (58). And the most intense pleasures come from the unexpected, from that which we cannot anticipate. As he remarks in *Roland Barthes,* "Bliss is not what corresponds to desire (what satisfies it) but what surprises, exceeds, disturbs, deflects it. One must turn to the mystics for a good formulation of what can cause the subject to deviate in this way: Ruysbroek: 'I call intoxication of the mind that state in which pleasure exceeds the possibilities which desire had entertained'" (112). This, it seems, is what Barthes would have us find in his own fragmentary writings: the deflection, the disturbance, of our desire for fixed understanding, for a firm hold on meaning. With the fragment, as with metaphor, meaning is always just out of reach, never firmly in our grasp—which is precisely what enables a dialogic relationship between reader and text.

The teaching of English in large part commits itself to the project of enabling students to get meaning firmly in hand. The premise of most pedagogical work in the field is that if teachers are not careful, meaning will be dangerously on the loose, well beyond students' desperate attempts to pin it down as readers or writers. But Barthes helps us to imagine another possibility—namely, that students' limitations with texts stem not from a negligent or lax approach to meaning but from an approach that zealously constricts its movement, to the extent that many of the practices they encounter in literary texts are denied them in their own writing: "I'm always sorry that the dimension of pleasure is not more perceptible in the language of students, who have in other regards such a true impression of life and society. It has been remarked, with a glance in my direction, I believe, that *these residues of hedonism should be liquidated.* Not at all, they should not be eliminated; pleasure should not be reduced to this residual status in the first place" (*Grain* 163). Illustrating both the pleasures of the fragmentary text and the politics of pleasure itself, Barthes opens a new avenue for student writing, one that has been largely ignored in the quest for textual unity and flow. By engaging in the centrifugal as well as the centripetal forces of language, students may gain a better understanding of each, and thereby learn to produce not merely "proficient" but also surprising, suggestive, and supple forms of written discourse.[20]

In addition to the pedagogical options made available through Barthes's appreciation of the fragment, his approach to the pleasures of reading and writing suggests that teachers of English might reconsider the cost of divorcing pleasure from politics and politics from pleasure in their conceptions of what it means to work as a member of this profession. If the political analysis of texts becomes a joyless affair, one in which all "residues of hedonism" are "liquidated," then such analysis will ultimately alienate more than it will instruct. Conversely, if the aesthetic response to texts overlooks the political dimension of that which gives various readers pleasure, then it will ultimately prove no more than an escape from direly significant social responsibilities. English studies, in other words, could provide a forum for discussing both the politics of certain textual pleasures and the place of textual pleasure itself in certain political sensibilities—subjects on which all need not agree but to which all can surely contribute. Rather than giving up politics for pleasure or pleasure for politics, teachers of English might construct a relationship to literature that recognizes the connections that bind each to the other.

5

PERFORMING SELVES

The Writer as Metaphor

> "The author of every book is a fictitious character
> whom the existent author invents to make him the
> author of his fictions."
>
> Italo Calvino, *If on a Winter's Night a Traveler*

IN HIS TOUR DE FORCE, *Exercises in Style,* Raymond Queneau presents a deceptively simple narrative in ninety-nine different ways, each of which represents an alternative stylistic approach to the "same" set of characters and events. Since the plot, which describes a minor conflict on a bus, seems relatively innocuous, the various styles themselves take on all the more importance, as Queneau illustrates the many registers through which a story may be told and hence the profound impact matters of style—often considered of secondary importance—can have on even the most trivial of tales. What makes these "exercises" all the more fascinating is the realization that none of them represents *the* story, not even those that attempt decisively spare or literal approaches to their subject: all versions of the story serve as metaphors for a story that cannot be told without coming to form through some sort of style.

Consider as well the endeavors of Florentino Ariza, the central character of Gabriel Garcia Marquez's *Love in the Time of Cholera,* who, after losing Fermina Daza—the love of his life—to another man, takes up writing love letters for the illiterate citizens of his town. Ariza subsequently becomes so successful as a ghostwriter of these letters that "he had to establish a system of appointments made in advance so that he would not be swamped by yearning lovers" (171). Eventually, his talent for imagining what a lover longs to express to his or her beloved leads him into an unusual predicament:

His most pleasant memory of that time was of a very timid young girl, almost a child, who trembled as she asked him to write an answer to an irresistible letter that she had just received, and that Florentino Ariza recognized as one he had written on the previous afternoon. He answered it in a different style, one that was in tune with the emotions and the age of the girl, and in a hand that also seemed to be hers, for he knew how to create a handwriting for every occasion, according to the character of each person. . . . Two days later, of course, he had to write the boy's reply with the same hand, style, and kind of love that he had attributed to him in the first letter, and so it was that he became involved in a feverish correspondence with himself. Before a month had passed, each came to him separately to thank him for what he himself had proposed in the boy's letter and accepted with devotion in the girl's response: they were going to marry. (171–72)

Such, it seems, is the power of the stylist, who can make his own writing appear to have been written by another—or even by several others.

What interests me in these displays of stylistic flexibility are the questions they raise about the act of writing in general and the performance of student writers in particular. Though style, like metaphor, has long been approached as mere overlay or embellishment—a belated attempt to dress up the "substance" at the core of thought—the achievement of a writer like Queneau (or, however fictive his existence, Florentino Ariza) suggests that this separation of style from substance overlooks the ways in which substance is discovered *through* style, not apart from or prior to it. As Susan Sontag observes, "Practically all metaphors for style amount to placing matter on the inside, style on the outside. It would be more to the point to reverse the metaphor. The matter, the subject, is on the outside; the style is on the inside" (17). Once again, such a comment comes as no surprise when applied to the teaching of literature, for literature is so often heralded as precisely that discourse wherein form means as much as, if not more than, content. But when we look to the teaching of writing, be it in composition or in literature courses, style remains a minor concern, usually ignored until students are imagined to reach a more "advanced" proficiency as writers.[1] Erwin Steinberg, for instance, has recently responded to Richard Lanham's contention that introductory students should learn a variety of prose styles by arguing that "most of today's students . . . need to be taught first about such things as invention, organization, argument, and the concept of audience before they should be asked to deal with the niceties of style that Lanham proposes teaching" (272). In other words, attention to style should come later, once the so-called fundamentals (invention, organization, and so on) are firmly in place. Moreover, Steinberg's telling phrase "the niceties of style" suggests that stylistic choice in writing is a kind of social privilege, one not to be granted "most of today's students," who are apparently fit only for lower-order instruction.

My aim in this chapter is to explore the possibilities generated by a pedagogy that refuses to distinguish between "style" and that which supposedly precedes it. More specifically, I want to investigate just what it is that the kind of writing exhibited by Queneau and Florentino Ariza —writing capable of transforming itself into an entirely different mood, syntax, and sensibility at the drop of a hat—requires its writer to do, or what such writing requires its writer to become. How, that is, do writers manage to move effectively from style to style, mask to mask, to the extent that they write as adroitly and convincingly under one guise as under another? The metaphor of *persona,* commonly applied in discussions of stylistic expertise, suggests that the issues at hand concern not only the arts of manipulation but also the tensions of subjectivity: Queneau does not simply take on a new style each time he writes another version of his narrative; he takes on a new *character,* through whose eyes he "sees" and whose voice he "speaks." What attracts me to this view of the writer is the hope it offers for helping students to establish some useful distance between themselves and their texts. While it might be claimed that the problem is just the opposite—that students feel so distant from their writing that they cannot make it matter to them—I want to contend, against this common observation, that students who are the most alienated by writing are in many cases those nearest to it. Indeed, many students are pressed up so close against their language that it smothers their sense of linguistic power, their capacity to step back and do something with a piece of writing to make it different. At the other end of the spectrum, where writers feel relatively "empowered" to make language work for them, it is much less difficult—in fact, it is essential—to set writing at a distance, to observe its movements and undercurrents, so that revision becomes both desirable and stimulating.

Examining the processes that inform his own acts of writing, Barthes asks: "Can one—or at least could one ever—begin to write without taking oneself for another? For the history of sources we should substitute the history of figures: the origin of work is not the first influence, it is the first posture: one copies a role, then, by metonymy, an art: I begin producing by reproducing the person I want to be" (*Roland Barthes* 99). In the pages that follow, I examine both the opportunities and the challenges that confront a pedagogy in which student writers are encouraged to adopt a posture or role: to "produce by reproducing" the language of someone different from themselves. What I have in mind is not the attempt to "imitate" the writing of admirable composers but an endeavor that normally finds itself reserved for courses in creative writing —namely, the intentional construction of fictional narrators, whereby writers "metaphorize" themselves into other beings and other discourses. If, as Barthes implies, it is impossible to write anything at all "without taking oneself for another," then it may be time to reconsider the wisdom of a curriculum in which the writing of fiction is approached as an elective rather than a requirement for students of English.

Role-play: Possibilities and Limits

The idea that writers enter some form of role when they write is surely one of the most familiar metaphors in discussions of writing instruction. (Allow me to reiterate: I mean not only the discussions of writing instruction found within composition studies but also those that appear throughout the discipline of "English" in its broadest sense.) Almost thirty years ago, Walker Gibson contended in *Persona* that "our decisions about the language we use are, in part, calculated to present our reader or listener with a recognizable character who is to do the communicating" (xi)—a comment echoed by several prominent scholars in the years thereafter.[2] Wayne Booth, for one, claims in his essay "LITCOMP" that "the most important thing is to get [students] quickly into seeing that every speaker 'makes' a self with every word uttered;

that even the most 'sincere' statement implies a self that is at best a radical selection from many possible roles; and that we are thus in some degree free to choose which of our 'selves' to present" (66). Arguing forcefully for the integration of composition and literary studies, Booth proposes that the college curriculum begin with a course in "the making and remaking of people" (65), wherein students would both study the roles adopted by writers of literature and "[try] out voices they have never before dared to be" (69). For Booth, these experiments with role-play form "the best way I know to get students to enjoy their writing and care about succeeding with it" (69).

Perhaps the most ambitious attempt to articulate a pedagogy based on role-play can be found in Judith Summerfield and Geoffrey Summerfield's *Texts and Contexts,* which offers both a nuanced theoretical justification for conceiving writing through the metaphor of role and a wealth of role-oriented assignments for the classroom.[3] From the Summerfields's perspective, to write in role is not so much an "option" as an inescapable reality: just as in the course of an ordinary day we act and interact by way of various roles—parent, teacher, administrator, customer, colleague, friend, and so on—so, too, we write through the roles constructed by the various social contexts within which our texts operate. Though "the same person" may serve as, say, both an academic and a lawyer, to write as an academic addressing fellow specialists in the field is not to write as a trial lawyer addressing members of the jury: different contexts call for different identities. The Summerfields observe that "we are, none of us, never nobody, always somebody; and that somebody involves role, whatever it may be. In our daily lives we move easily from one role to another without even having to think about the shift. . . . We notice the fact of congruence between role, context, and discourse only when the congruence breaks down" (27). Accordingly, it would appear that if we are to write any discourse effectively, we must learn to enter the role whereby the conventions of that discourse become familiar, even unconscious—for only then will we be able to adopt or challenge these conventions as we see fit.

Like Gibson and Booth before them, the Summerfields argue that this conception of writing can help students engage in a broader range of discursive activity than they normally encounter in their English courses: "It is our case that if we wish to involve students in the production of a greater variety of texts, to nudge them toward *repertoire expansion,* the best way to do it is to involve them in a variety of roles that will themselves, inescapably, generate a variety of modes of discourse" (28). Letters, poems, newspaper articles, paratactic ramblings, memoranda, academic essays, dramatic dialogues, riddles, definitions—all, in the Summerfields's pedagogy, are placed before students as "generative frames" for experimentation and discovery. The result would appear to be a form of writing instruction that thrives on the *differences* between the many discourses students are asked to employ—differences that help them to recognize, produce, and assess the salient features of any one discourse in particular. Moreover, the Summerfields claim that what they call the "enabling constraints" (6) of taking on a specific role manage paradoxically both to discipline and to loosen the range of student writers' verbal expression, for while students begin these assignments with "nothing to lose" by way of emotional investment—after all, the role-play is but a fiction—they often find themselves projecting their own experiences and values into the role they come to inhabit. In this sense, role-enactment reverses conventional assumptions about subjectivity and writing: rather than proceeding from an inner core of sincerity already present within the self, writing-in-role could be said to *create* the writer's honesty about and commitment to her words. As Richard Lanham has remarked, "Sincerity begins not in feelings but in sentences" (*Style* 117).

The key contribution of the Summerfields's work, then, lies in its alternative conception of the writer's relationship to the act of writing—a conception that counters common teacherly injunctions for students to write in "their own voice" about what they "really" feel or think or believe. As the Summerfields indicate, when the search for one's true voice is made the focus of the writer's struggle, that voice becomes all the more elusive: "If indeed there can be said to be such a thing as one's own voice . . . then its pursuit, like that of happiness, is a waste of time and effort. For like happiness, it will come not out of willed effort but as a mostly retroactive discovery and as a donnée. And if it comes at all, others will be more likely than oneself to recognize its arrival: 'Ah,' they will exclaim, 'you have finally found your own voice!'" (197). For the Summerfields, the self is not so much "found" as *actualized* or brought into being by the attempt to use language to social effect. It follows that the writing assignments given to students in their English classes might allow them to explore what Geoffrey Summerfield elsewhere calls "hitherto unsuspected, inarticulated, selves" ("Luminous Realms" 11)—that is, selves that they would not otherwise imagine they could become.

Yet despite the pedagogical possibilities that the metaphor of role would appear to offer, I think it fair to say that its influence in the teaching of either literature or composition has been surprisingly limited.[4] While the textbooks designed for courses in both fields occasionally suggest some form of role-play among their recommended writing assignments, they usually do so only to indicate how teachers can offer students an "exercise" in preparation for more serious kinds of discourse. Writing-in-role, in this view, serves as a form of "prewriting" alongside other heuristics (brainstorming, outlining, and so on) intended to help students warm up before the real work begins.[5] The presumption here is that writers take on roles entirely by choice—not that they invariably inhabit a role whether or not they are aware of doing so. As a result, the great majority of writing assignments continue to assume that students should write as "themselves," sharing their private, hidden thoughts on the subject or text at hand. Writing thus remains a process of revelation —an exposure of what lies inside the writer. Or even more irresistibly: writing gets figured as a process of self-discovery whereby students writers come to know who they "really" are through locating what they "want" to say.

At issue, however, are not simply the ways in which certain textbooks have obscured the opportunities that role-play might bring to student writers, but, more importantly, the ways in which the pedagogy of role-play itself presents a problematic conception of both the writer and the act of writing. In other words, it may be that the failure of this pedagogy to obtain a more prominent place in the teaching of English stems as much from its own shortcomings as from those of a curriculum that has trivialized them. I want to concentrate on two of these shortcomings, which together suggest not that role-play assignments should be abandoned but that they must be substantially reconceived if they are to make a significant contribution to postsecondary writing instruction within English studies.

The first problem ironically stems from what advocates of role-play generally consider one of its most important attributes—the beneficial effect that writing-in-role can have on the writer's awareness of audience. When the Summerfields, for instance, list the virtues that role-play brings to the act of writing, "a clear sense of audience" is among them (*Texts* 188); and they go on to contend that role-play is especially useful for student writers, who are often inhibited or derailed by the fact that their primary reader is the teacher: "Our case is that one of the most valuable *products* of writing in role is, precisely, that the writer-reader relationship is more clearly defined, delimited, contextualized, constrained than it is when a student *in propria persona* writes for an instructor who is more or less a stranger, indeterminate and threatening —threatening because indeterminate" (204). In other words, by defining the audience as someone other than the teacher, role-play grants students both the freedom to imagine themselves writing in contexts beyond the classroom and the enabling certainty that comes with knowing one's reader well: "The desires of the *persona* who writes the text are understood, and so are the needs of the *persona* to whom the text is addressed" (204). By making the intended audience more explicit than assignments that merely ask students to "discuss" an issue or "write in response" to a text—without specifying to whom these writings should speak—role-play assignments supposedly help students to write with a keener sense of context and purpose than they do otherwise.

But what of situations that place the burden of inventing an audience much more squarely on the writer's shoulders? Even if, as Walter Ong has famously claimed in the title of one of his essays, "the writer's audience is always a fiction," some audiences are clearly more fictive than others. When we write a letter to our congressional representative, we no doubt have to imagine, to fictionalize, his or her attitude toward our text—but this is a significantly different, and less taxing, proposition than attempting to imagine, when writing an essay for a widely read periodical, the multiple attitudes of a largely unparticularized audience, one that may include any number of people with any number of perspectives and concerns. As Douglas Park has observed, it might be useful to distinguish between "transactional" discourse—that is to say, discourse intended for a very specific audience—and discourse that presumes a "general" audience of unspecified individuals (485). Both the writer of the letter and its reader (in this case, the congressional representative) can rely, as Park indicates through his own examples, on the respective roles provided by a well-known social institution, wherein the conventions of discourse are relatively clear. But the writer of the periodical essay confronts a much different situation, one in which the audience, of its own volition, "comes . . . to the discourse to participate in the social relationship—a sort of one-sided conversation—that is offered there" (485). Along similar lines, Robert Roth observes that "a writer's audience may be more protean and malleable than we normally assume. . . . If one's audience may emerge during composing, we are no longer looking at a static entity: we can consider how it changes as composing proceeds—and what writers do to make it change" (47–48). The interest here lies not so much in how to specify an audience that will make writing more immediately purposive, but in how to help student writers attend to the ways in which they construct their audience—and hence their purposes—during the act of composing. Rather than simply determining the dominant characteristics of their readers in advance, students need to examine self-consciously the process of constructing unknown readers even as they write, and to consider more carefully just whom they imagine these readers to be.

What this line of thought suggests is that, by sharply defining the intended audience, role-play assignments tend to evade one of the most difficult challenges a writer confronts—namely, how to address a diverse and unpredictable group of readers and to anticipate the conflicting forms of their response. While it is surely possible to design role-play assignments that incorporate this challenge (one could, for example, invite students to play the role of the "essayist" or the "critic" addressing the general public), to do so would not make the writer's struggle to invent her audience any less difficult. Indeed, it may be that we should search not so much for the means whereby role-play assignments can improve student writing as for the ways in which the metaphor of role can assist in revising our image of "improvement" itself.

Take, for instance, what is probably the most widely assigned genre in college English classes across the country: the argumentative essay, a category in which I include the research paper, wherein students must not only report on but also argue for an interpretation of the material they investigate. As so many scholars have recently observed, the anachronistic discourse that tends to structure classroom discussions of argumentation is in dire need of overhaul—and I would point in particular to the problems with that endless refrain, invoked by students and teachers alike, about "supporting" one's position.[6] Again and again, students come away from their English courses with the idea that to write a "convincing" argument means nothing more than bolstering their opinion with enough "evidence" that the argument becomes, of its own accord, not necessarily correct but, more importantly, "well-argued." What matters here is the solidity and immobility of one's stance; consideration of counterarguments serves merely as a formal maneuver performed for the sake of further "strengthening" one's powers of persuasion. In other words, argument is a matter of building one's case in a social vacuum, completely devoid of political or social consequences: "weaknesses" arise not from the relationship of one's position to alternative positions but from the failure to provide sufficient "examples" where they are called for. Accordingly, both the drafting and the revision of student writing often comprises a single procedure: *shoring up one's claim.*

But if an appealing argument must be appealing to *others*—to those who, despite their differences, can in some sense become the readers that the argument desires—then to argue adeptly has much to do with creating a generous social space, one in which people holding any number of views find it possible to become engaged with a view unlike their own. From this perspective, *inclusiveness,* not "support," becomes the test of a well-written argument: writers who have intelligently thought about their positions are those who have imagined—and demonstrate that they have imagined—how people from other positions might respond. To argue is not to construct an impenetrable fortress but to envision a relationship with those who might well argue otherwise. It is, indeed, a valid critique of many an argument to reply: "But this completely overlooks the experience and values of Group Z, who would certainly think and feel otherwise. How does the writer propose to address them?" As Andrea Lunsford and Lisa Ede have recently observed, arguments primarily bent on "success" are often those most likely to narrowly define their rhetorical context—and thus to be characterized not only by the audiences they "address" or "invoke" but also by "audiences ignored, rejected, excluded, or denied" (174).

This is not to say that texts should, or even could, address all groups at once; indeed, it may be that certain groups *must* be ignored in order for others to be addressed at all. But such a recognition only goes to show how imperative it is that the discourse of role-play, like the discourse of argumentation, find ways to account for rhetorical predicaments characterized by the heterogeneity of their audience. We simply cannot talk anymore about roles or arguments that are "effective," but only about those that are effective *for certain readers*—an achievement which necessarily entails, to a greater or lesser degree, the alienation of other readers. If the differences between readers are recognized as more than superficial—as more, that is, than matters of individual preference or personal "opinion"—then there is no escaping the profound complexities that currently surround the act of composing for a "general" (which means multicultural, divided, incompatible) audience. No textual role, however skillfully enacted, can attain unqualified success, since its attraction for one group is likely to ensure its repulsion for another.

Which brings me to the second reason why I believe the pedagogy of role-play has failed to gain a more significant place in the teaching of English. By emphasizing, in its assessment of texts, the technical proficiency with which various writers "inhabit" their roles, this pedagogy potentially depoliticizes the act of writing and ignores the ethical implications of role-play itself.[7] If we limit the goal of writing instruction to that of enabling student writers to enter effectively, even brilliantly, a variety of social roles, then they may acquire the ability to move from one role to the next, but they will be left with little sense of why certain roles should be assumed in the first place or of whether mastering these roles is not just another way to capitulate in the games their society would have them play. It follows that the pedagogy of role-play can be accused of seeking nothing more than to help students "convincingly" employ the discourse demanded by those with the power to establish

precedent and convention. Student writers who can adopt the custom-
ary syntax and locutions of the available roles are pronounced merito-
rious: they know what manner of composition each situation calls for.
But they have yet to explore the values that inhere in composing this
way or that.

None of which is meant to underestimate the difficulty of helping
students to recognize the discursive conventions of various roles and
put them into practice. But it is also useful to consider the ideal writer
that a given pedagogy hopes to produce, and I am suggesting that the
ideal writer produced by the pedagogy of role-play does not necessarily
learn how to critique the roles she learns to inhabit with such grace and
charm. In *Texts and Contexts,* the Summerfields note the importance of
having their students write "metatexts" that evaluate their own texts
written in role; but for the most part these metatexts appear to serve an
explanatory rather than a critical function—that is to say, students use
the metatext to explain the discourse they have appropriated or the experience they have had while writing the primary text, but they do not
evaluate the role itself, its potentially problematic cultural function, or
its conflict with other roles they have also played. What is missing, in
other words, is an interrogation of the ethical and cultural issues at
stake both in certain roles and in certain forms of role-play. For what
are we asking student writers to do when we suggest—to cite two possibilities the Summerfields endorse—that they "take on" the persona of
someone who has survived the Holocaust or of someone condemned to
years of solitary confinement because of their political beliefs?[8] How
might role-play, as with metaphor, lead students to forget about the
differences between those who *have* experienced or *are* experiencing such
suffering and those who pretend to experience it as writers? I ask these
questions not to suggest that role-play assignments of this sort should
be avoided but to note the importance of helping students to engage in
them critically, so that they will become alert to more than simply creating a viable impersonation. As I observed in chapter 3, students (as
with all of us) can be quick to tame the difference of another's experience by claiming it to be "just like" something already a part of themselves: by retrieving their own loneliness, for instance, they may learn
to write as if they were political prisoners—and then conveniently ne-

glect just how crucial that *as if* remains. In the absence of extensive reflection on the complicated ethics of role, students may get the idea that writing means nothing more then glibly sliding from one discourse to the next, without ever questioning the power that some discourses wield over others and how this power constructs relationships that are often not to the good of all involved.

Role-play, as the Summerfields indicate, offers the teaching of English an inviting pedagogy that provides students both the distance to examine the social conventions of various discourses and the proximity to experiment with these conventions as writers. But in addition to committing themselves to writing-in-role, students might commit themselves to critical projects that interrogate the ideology of various roles and of role-play itself. What are the consequences, both good and bad, for a culture that rewards mobile as opposed to anchored selves? Should those who are more "attached" to the roles to which they've grown accustomed in their home environments be judged inadequate? Do we as teachers want to introduce students to as *many* roles as possible or to a few, carefully selected roles that they might practice more extensively? How will we determine what those roles should be? Any pedagogy that encourages role-play in the writing class will need to confront these questions, among others, if it is to form not simply a method *for* writing but a reflexive inquiry into various methods *of* writing and the cultural politics that attend them.

On the Uses of (Meta)Fiction

When it came time to plan my freshman composition course for the past academic year, I decided to attempt an experiment. Rather than selecting from an ever-wider assortment of textbooks filled with fairly predictable samples of nonfiction prose, I chose instead a single novel —Tim O'Brien's *The Things They Carried*—to serve as the reading material for my course. The reasons for this choice were many, but certainly one of the most important was the fact that O'Brien's book alternates, from chapter to chapter, between the various stories told by the narrator and the narrator's commentary upon his stories. In other words, O'Brien's narrator intrudes upon and fragments his own narrative, jumping back and forth between events that occurred twenty years in the past and his present existence as a writer retrieving these events. Because of this self-consciously reflexive approach to its own composition, I hoped that O'Brien's book would serve as a catalyst for helping students to read and discuss their own writing and the ways that they might revise it.

I was also interested in the ways that *The Things They Carried* might help students to reconsider conventional distinctions between fact and fiction. Given that the narrator's name is "Tim O'Brien," and that the stories he relates take place either in Minnesota, Vietnam, or Massachusetts (where, respectively, O'Brien *the author* grew up, went to war, and now resides), it is extremely tempting to read this book as an autobiographical text. Yet time and again, O'Brien draws readers toward such an interpretation, only to deny it by suddenly asserting that the story he has just told is entirely imaginary. For example, the chapter entitled "How to Tell a True War Story" begins: "This is true"—whereupon the narrator proceeds to tell a gruesome tale of how a fellow soldier, not long after his best friend has been blown to pieces by a booby trap, kills a baby water buffalo, shooting off its body parts one at a time. This, readers are repeatedly told throughout the telling, is a "true" war story —except that, as the narrator later admits to a woman who has admired the story at a public reading, "Beginning to end . . . it's all made up. Every goddamn detail—the mountains and the river and especially that poor dumb baby buffalo. None of it happened. *None* of it" (91). By no means for the last time, readers have been set up to believe and trust, only to have the rug pulled out from under them. Thinking about potential subject matter for my course, I imagined that this tension between belief and disbelief, and between the "real" and the "true," might make for some productive discussions with students.

But the reading for the course constituted only a part of my experiment. The more important part concerned what I decided to ask students to write. It is not that unusual, after all, to have students read fiction in freshman composition; any number of textbooks add short stories, and even poetry, to their anthologies of nonfiction prose. What *would* be unusual, it seemed to me, would be to have students write fiction as well as read it—moreover, to write fiction not just as a supplement to the writing of essays but as a (or even *the*) major component of their work for the course.[9] Erika Lindemann has remarked that "examining literary language has limited usefulness in a writing course because our students do not *write* literature; they write about it or respond to it" ("Freshman" 314). But what if teachers of freshman composition —and, as I will go on to argue, teachers of literature as well—were to insist not only that students respond to fictive discourse but that they attempt to compose it themselves? What might this activity teach students about writing that they often fail to learn from instruction that primarily attends to the ways and means of (so-called) nonfiction? While it is generally assumed that those who wish to write fiction can do so by enrolling in courses in creative writing, I wanted to see how the English department curriculum might change for the better were we to *require* the writing of fiction rather than to marginalize it as an elective. If the reading of fiction has much to offer by way of lessons in language and literacy, then surely the writing of fiction could give students even more intimate lessons of this kind.[10]

But that wasn't all: it would not be sufficient merely to have students compose their own fictions. As I knew from previous composition courses in which I had given students the occasional opportunity to write a "made-up" story, such forays into fiction writing can produce texts that are considerably more naive, banal, and awkward than almost any essay written by the same set of students. There are at least two readily available explanations for this phenomenon: the first is that most first-year students are more familiar with composing essays, which may have been presented as five-paragraph formulas during the course of their secondary education; and the second is that, not having read much fiction, students know little about its structural conventions and even less about how to employ them with any dexterity. Consequently, the fictional narratives composed by college freshmen often appear exceedingly immature, with their obvious plots, two-dimensional characters, and superficial moralisms. And the fact that students seem to *enjoy* composing these narratives (and regard them as personal "expressions" of their inner selves) makes the teacher's obligations that much more difficult to fulfill. Ironically, some students can be much more sensitive to criticism of their fictions than they are to criticism of their essays, even though the latter supposedly illustrates what they "really" think—an observation which suggests, as noted in my discussion of the fragment, that students are in dire need of productive distance from their words. The challenge of teaching a composition course that stresses the writing of fiction would be to find the means to establish such distance, so that students might begin to look at their fictive discourse with a critical eye and ultimately demand much more of themselves than a mere "story."

Here again it appeared that O'Brien's book could come to my aid, for this text is not simply a work of fiction, it is a work of *metafiction*—however problematic the distinction. As Mark Currie asserts, metafiction serves as "a borderline discourse, as a kind of writing that places itself on the border between fiction and criticism, and which takes that border as its subject" (2).[11] By inserting chapters that comment on the chapters that precede them, O'Brien critiques his own fictions, thereby exposing the "border" between one discourse and another. What makes *The Things They Carried* all the more intriguing, however, are the *ways* in which O'Brien engages in self-criticism: rather than simply "stepping forward" as the narrator—that is to say, as one who has left behind the production of fiction in order to "tell it like it is"—the figure named "Tim O'Brien" offers his critique in the form of *another story*. In this manner, fiction and criticism are portrayed not as two separate discourses but as discourses that are inextricably intertwined.

Take, for instance, the second chapter, "Love." Following an opening chapter that has described, in "realistic" detail and with no hint of postmodern antics, the guilt experienced by first lieutenant Jimmy Cross after a member of his platoon was killed in Vietnam, the second chapter begins: "Many years after the war Jimmy Cross came to visit me at my home in Massachusetts, and for a full day we drank coffee and smoked cigarettes and talked about everything we had seen and done so long ago, all the things we still carried through our lives" (29). Since the first chapter was told from a third-person omniscient point of view, the sudden appearance here of the narrator comes as a surprise. The narrator goes on to relate how he told Jimmy that he wanted to write a story about him, and that Jimmy didn't object. At the end of the chapter, Jimmy prepares to leave: "He got into his car and rolled down the window.

'Make me out to be a good guy, okay? Brave and handsome, all that stuff. Best platoon leader ever.' He hesitated for a second. 'And do me a favor. Don't mention anything about—' 'No,' I said, 'I won't'" (31). Now we already know from the story told in the first chapter that the narrator has *not* portrayed Jimmy Cross as the "best platoon leader ever"; to the contrary, he has represented Jimmy as a young man who was so absorbed by his longing for a woman back in the United States that his attention often wandered far from the war—until the death of one of his soldiers made him feel that his irresponsibility was the cause of this loss. The question therefore becomes whether the narrator has lied when he tells Jimmy that he won't mention anything about . . . what? The soldier's death? If Jimmy is referring to this death, then the narrator is confessing that he eventually did exactly what he promised not to do, and thus appears to be making a statement both about fiction writers and the writing of fiction—namely, that writers mine the lives of others for material; that their attachment to writing is greater than their attachment to those who provide this material; and perhaps that the writing of fiction *requires* that writers ignore the ethics of this behavior.

Thus it is that O'Brien manages to engage in criticism even as he composes fiction, for of course we have no way of knowing whether the story of Jimmy's visit to the narrator in Massachusetts "really" happened any more than we know the amount of fact in the story with which the book begins. Indeed, it may even be that the narrator has *not* told us anything about whatever it was that Jimmy did not want him to mention, and that his promise as a writer to his friend was kept. Since we're not explicitly told what Jimmy wished to hide, we cannot say whether or not the narrator has exposed it. And this means that we must consider the possibility of another message within O'Brien's implicit commentary on writers and writing—that writers need to mine the lives of others in order to write, but that they must also know where to draw the line. Though we may find this contention far less provocative than its counterpart, it is the ambiguity that counts: O'Brien refuses, in producing commentary on his own methods, to write with any more transparency than we find in his fictions themselves. The criticism *is* a fiction, and the fiction *is* criticism.

What good could metafiction of this sort do for student writers? Not much, it seemed to me, if it were restricted to a "topic" for discussion or for the writing of essays; the point would *not* be to have students accrue knowledge of various metafictional precepts and practices. Rather, in keeping with my sense that students should study the textual endeavors of professional writers *for the sake of engaging in such endeavors themselves,* I decided to design a sequence of assignments that would invite students to compose their own metafictions. Thus it was that after two weeks of reading and discussing O'Brien's book, they were given the first of ten writing assignments:

BACKGROUND

Imagine that you have been asked to produce a fairly extensive piece of writing by the end of this semester—a mini-book of sorts (let's say 30–40 pages), complete with chapters, characters, events, and so on. Imagine as well that your teacher has said that in this "book" you may mix fact and fiction in whatever ways you wish.

But you have also been given two imperatives:

(1) that you tell a "war story" of one sort or another; and

(2) that your story be as "true" as you can make it.

Regarding the first requirement, the teacher has said that you may interpret the term "war" literally or figuratively. One approach would be, like O'Brien, to write about war in the literal sense—complete with guns and bombs and death. But alternatively, you might write about war in the figurative sense, as in a "war" fought at home, in school, on the streets of your neighborhood, or elsewhere. There are "battles" of all kinds that we fight everyday—in our minds or with others—and people constantly wage "struggles" for rights, liberties, and justice. "War," then, is a term that can be applied not only to Vietnam or the Persian Gulf or Bosnia but also to daily life, families, groups, communities, schools.

As for the second requirement—that your war story be "true"—the teacher has offered no further guidance.

You have, however, been given one final piece of information: your teacher has said that your "war story" need not necessarily draw upon segments of your own life and/or the lives of people you know. It may be, that is, that you choose to write not about yourself or those close to you but about people (past or present, actual or invented) who interest you enough to explore and imagine the dimensions of their "war." Then again, it may be that you do decide to write about "yourself"—either throughout the book or in bits and pieces. The point is that the extent to which autobiography enters your story is entirely up to you. Furthermore, you are free to use the first-person pronoun ("I") whether or not that "I" refers to *you*.

ASSIGNMENT

Write the first chapter of this book.[12]

Though the assignment begins by asking students to *imagine* that they have been asked to produce a "mini-book" by the end of the semester, the composition of such a text was exactly the goal I intended to set before them in the weeks to come. As for this first assignment, it should be apparent that I was attempting to create what the Summerfields call an "enabling constraint"—that is, a constraint that guides, without unduly restricting, the movement or growth of the venture at hand. I wanted the students' texts to productively interact with O'Brien's, which, after reading in full during the first two weeks, they would now reread slowly, a chapter or two each week. While writing their opening chapter, for instance, students would read again and discuss in detail O'Brien's opening chapter, exploring how it is that he brings readers into his war story and leads them to invest themselves emotionally in its outcome. It was here, in other words, that students would try their hands at the production of a "metaphoric world"—a fictional space in which illusions are provisionally accepted as equivalent to the "real." In so doing, students would have the opportunity to draw upon their own lives to whatever degree they wished, yet without the burden of "sticking to the facts" that more strictly autobiographical writing might impose upon them. Like O'Brien, they could experiment with *pretending* to divulge their personal histories even when relating imaginary events—and thereby investigate ways in which language creates its own realities.

The assignments that followed were designed to lead students into further experimentation with the structure and methods of O'Brien's novel while at the same time allowing them enough room to create "their own" fictions. Here are all ten assignments in abbreviated form:

1. Compose chapter 1: the "war story" *in medias res*
2. Compose chapter 2: the narrator interrupts his/her story to discuss its composition.
3. Compose chapter 3: the narrator returns to a time *prior* to the "war."
4. Revise chapter 1.
5. Revise chapters 2 and 3.
6. Compose chapter 4: the narrator continues the "war story" begun in chapter 1.
7. Compose an essay comparing and contrasting the textual strategies found in the student's own text with those found in O'Brien's novel.
8. Compose chapter 5: like O'Brien's chapter entitled "How to Tell a True War Story," this chapter must alternate between fragments of the story itself and fragments in which the narrator comments upon the story.
9. Revise chapters 4 and 5.
10. Write a foreword to the completed "book," under the guise of a critic who explains both its attractions and its problems.

At the end of the semester, then, students were to submit a five-chapter metafictional novella, a foreword that introduces this novella, and an essay that discusses the novella in light of O'Brien's book.

Perhaps at this point I should remark, before describing what I find valuable in these assignments, that the course in which I used them was by no means a "success": this is not a story of pedagogical triumph. Only a handful of students managed to produce stories of any complexity or subtlety, and all encountered serious trouble with composing chapters 2 and 5—those requiring that they comment on their own writing while at the same time making this commentary an integral part of their novella. But I don't think that the difficulties that emerged as a result of the unusual project with which these students were confronted necessarily means that such a project should be deemed unworthy or frivolous. Rather, it may be that these difficulties demonstrate precisely why it is that the writing of metafiction has much to offer students of both composition and literature. While the common presumption in most discussions of teaching seems to be that we should look to those courses in which students have performed exceeding well, I would counter that we might also look to courses in which the failure of most students to produce accomplished texts reveals a parallel failure in the curriculum—in this case, an English studies curriculum that has in large part missed the opportunity to allow the ambitious enterprises of "literary" writers to shape the forms of writing it requires of students. Though I do not wish to suggest that the troubles students experienced in my course had nothing to do with my own oversights as a teacher (about which I will have more to say later), I think it important to recognize that, given an education in which students are generally assigned to write narratives only as a prelude to the supposedly more demanding requirements of exposition and argument—and, furthermore, given that the narratives solicited from students are usually expected to be nonfictional or even confessional—we can hardly expect that college freshmen (or college seniors, for that matter) will be prepared to compose an extended piece of metafiction in the course of a single semester.[13] Yet I am convinced that the curriculum *should* prepare them to engage in just such an endeavor, however extraneous it may initially appear when we consider the writing that students are most likely to perform both in other academic disciplines and in their working lives beyond the academy.

In order to explore the value of asking students to write fiction, I want to turn briefly to one of the texts produced in my course. As a first draft, this is not an "accomplished" text in virtually any sense of the word—nor can I say that the writer went on to improve it much when he revised his work later in the term. But it provides an idea of the struggles with discourse that students confront when they attempt to compose a fictional world. In this particular text, the writer has responded to the assignment that required him to continue in chapter 4 the "war story" he had begun in chapter 1:

CHAPTER FOUR

As soon as I got home, I called Keenan. I knew he wasn't in the house yet but this is something that was done after school, either he would call me or I would call him. I wanted to tell him not to do anything stupid. I also wanted to remind him that he was not a Stone and that he should not get caught up in the madness. After my short stay, I ran out the house and down the street to the bus stop. I asked a couple of people that I saw along the way if they had seen Keenan or a large group of people walking around. When I got to the bus stop there was not anybody in sight. As I was making my way down to the park, I started to hear people shouting and yelling ahead of me. At that point I knew it was Keenan.

There were a lot of people at the park that day. The folks that were out there acted as though there was supposed to be a prize boxing match going on or something. The atmosphere was like an electrifying mass hysteria. There was a variety of people out that day, ranging from little kids running around to gang members who were doing the actual fighting. I was not at the park a long time before some boy kid from another town got stabbed. It didn't really phase me that he got hurt because I didn't know him and he really should not have come to the Ville that day.

I was not ready for the events that unfolded before me when I arrived at the park. I saw "gangstas" running around with bats and knifes. It did not take me long to pick out Keenan from the rest of the thugs and hoodlums. He was sitting on the ground and was leaning his back against the fence and his face was bleeding. It looked as though he had been cut really bad.

I could not even say anything to him at first because the shock had set in that my friend was cut so bad. Finally I got up enough strength to say something to him even though it was not very appropriate for the time.

After a brief moment of silence between him and I, he told me, "I'm going to kill one of those dudes for messing up my face."

I asked him, "What are you fighting for anyway? I don't see why you are out here."

He simply replied, "This ain't none of your business," and then he walked off to where some of his friends had caught a couple of GDs and were beating them up. That is when the police rolled on the scene. They came from every direction. It was like they had an army. A majority of them were on foot but a lot of them came in cars with their lights flashing and the sirens blasting. After noticing that the police were all over the place one of the Stones started to shout, "Lets be up!! Five-O, Five-O!!" Then everybody started to run. While I was running through the confusion, I saw this GD fall on his hands and knees ahead of me. He was stabbed right in front of me. The boy screamed and cried like the pain was excruciating. When I was close enough to see the boy's face, I heard a couple of boys laughing while they were running in the opposite direction. One of them said fairly loud, "Yo dude, you stuck that kid somthin nice." It shocked me that one of those boys was Keenan.

I remember leaving the boy that got stabbed in the spot where he fell. I also remember running home with the police on my back for most of the dash. When I saw Keenan later on that day I asked him if he stabbed the boy. He did not want to tell me for some reason, so I left the subject alone until the other day when he brought the incident back up.

"In a way I am sorry that I hurt that boy, I even almost regret it, but on the other hand I am very glad I did it. On everything dude, I tried to ram that knife into him as deep as I could. Just so that he could feel me!! He was the one."

"He was the one that did what?" I asked him.

While pointing to the long scar on his face, Keenan replied, "He was the one that messed my face up."

This conversation brought up a couple points about that crazy afternoon and evening like who was shooting and who was the person that got shot.

I can remember when times were much simpler. Back in the day when everybody watched cartoons and let their parents worry about everything. Life just is not the same anymore due to the responsibilities that we all received when we grew up.

While it would certainly be possible to produce an extended critique of this text, I want instead to describe the conversation about writing that it enabled during a thirty-minute class discussion devoted to this writer's work.[14] In order to launch this discussion, I began class by commenting that one of the fiction writer's most challenging tasks is to produce a "convincing" account of physical activity. How is it, I wondered aloud, that mere words can come to create and sustain the illusion of tangible action, be it something as seemingly simple as the protagonist walking down the street or something as obviously complicated as a gang conflict in a park? Students were then asked to explore how this particular text confronted this challenge from one line to the next, and whether its various strategies offered any lessons about the art of representation.

What followed was a detailed examination of two passages in the text at hand: the opening paragraph and the paragraph that concludes the third section. Attending to the precise wording of the former, several students maintained that after a promising beginning in which the upcoming violence is foreshadowed, the text begins to lose credibility when it speaks of the narrator asking those on the street "if they had seen Keenan or a large group of people walking around." Since this phrase seems to presume both a certain intimacy with the people being asked (who would have to know who Keenan is in order to reply) and distance from them ("a large group of people" suggesting no common knowledge of the group's members), the reader is left unsure of the narrator's relationship to those he encounters in his neighborhood. Even more confusing are the two sentences that follow: "When I got to the bus stop there was not anybody in sight. As I was making my way down to the park, I started to hear people shouting and yelling ahead of me." So at first there is "not anybody in sight"; and then there are "people"—still not visible?—"shouting and yelling" up ahead. Just what is the narrator seeing as he hears the stirrings of violence? How large does he imagine the group that is making all the noise? The reader is not told.

Responding to the paragraph that concludes the third section of the text, students concentrated on the lines in which the narrator describes the stabbing. Here the problem was identified as a contradiction: the boy was stabbed "right in front of" the narrator, and yet he fails to notice that the one who did the stabbing was Keenan. Though most students found the line spoken by one of the gang members—"Yo dude, you stuck that kid somthin nice"—an effective way to portray casual attitudes toward violence, they noted that the writer had missed an opportunity to have his narrator prolong the dramatic tension of the events in the park. Were the narrator, for instance, to begin by saying not that he saw the boy stabbed but that he saw the boy *fall*, the reader would share the narrator's incomplete knowledge of what had occurred —whereupon both might subsequently find (through word of mouth or perhaps by the narrator's turning the victim over himself) that the boy was bleeding from a stab wound. In other words, students were starting to recognize that writers can find ways to *play* with the key moments in their texts by keeping alert to the minutia of deftly providing readers with information one piece at a time. If, as Barthes contends, "the dynamics of the text . . . must set up *delays* (obstacles, stoppages, deviations) in the flow of discourse" (*S/Z* 75), then students were here investigating just how such delays might be mobilized without losing coherence or leaving the reader completely in the dark.

Though I cannot do justice to all that was said during the course of this class (there was a fairly elaborate conversation, for instance, about the text's representation of dialogue and its inconsistency with the use of contractions), I do wish to take note of the attention students gave to the last two paragraphs of the text. Though several students admitted to having lightly passed over the first of these paragraphs on their initial reading, they now observed that it had suddenly, and without explanation, replaced the stabbing incident with a reference to "who was shooting and who was the person that got shot." Either the author had committed an egregious error or he was attempting to make an allusion to something the reader would learn more about in the next chapter—no one could say for sure. Given the latter possibility, students went on to converse about how certain writers (Stephen King, for one) manage to drop hints at the end of chapters that make it difficult for readers not to read on: what were the exact methods by which this rhetorical technique could be performed skillfully? and how might it have been done in this particular text? I suggested that we keep an eye on this matter as we reread O'Brien's novel.

As for the final paragraph, wherein the narrator nostalgically longs for "the days when everybody watched cartoons and let their parents worry about everything," there was considerable debate about whether the text would gain from the omission of its final sentence: "Life just is not the same anymore due to the responsibilities that we all received when we grew up." While most agreed that the essayistic "due to" should be replaced with language more in keeping with the story's prior discourse, a surprising number of students argued that this instance of "telling" does not detract from the "showing" that precedes it. Drawing upon contemporary film for their examples, these students held that pointing to the message of the narrative demonstrates the author's (or director's) commitment to communication and the shared emotional resonance that accompanies it. Indeed, had they been familiar with

Wayne Booth's *The Rhetoric of Fiction,* they could have ushered forth scholarly authority to support their contentions, for Booth says much the same in his numerous illustrations of how even the most "impersonal" of texts must discover the means to tell as well as to show. Which doesn't mean that I agreed (or that Booth would agree) with their assessment of the final line in the student text before us; rather, it means that their investigation of the relationship between rhetoric and fiction enabled me to help them complicate their ruminations on the role of "communication" in narrative. Turning to the question of whether "showing" itself cannot also "tell," I asked whether the contrast between this writer's fourth chapter and his third (in which Keenan and the narrator are presented as young kids harmlessly playing in the neighborhood) had not *already* told us that "life is just not the same anymore" in addition to a number of other potential "messages" made more rich by remaining implicit. What mattered here was not how many students were led to change their minds—as far as I could tell, the grand total was zero!— but how far they found themselves taking this exploration of language, method, and value. To the extent that such concerns should inform *any* course in the English studies curriculum, assignments in which students are invited to write fiction (and/or poetry, for that matter) may offer possibilities we ignore when we imagine that these endeavors should be relegated to courses in creative writing alone.

Some might argue that, though they have nothing against the kinds of assignments I am proposing, my subsequent emphasis on issues of form comes at the expense of more significant issues of content that often appear in student papers. In class discussion of a paper about gang conflict, for instance, many teachers believe it imperative to lead students toward further consideration of ghetto violence, racial segregation, and police hypocrisy, so that the student text serves as a springboard for exploring positions on matters of social and political consequence. (These discussions often begin with students being asked how they feel about the events in the text they've read and whether they've ever experienced or witnessed anything similar in their own lives.) While I do not wish to completely oppose such an approach, I do wish to indicate that close attention to form can serve as a way *toward* content rather than an abdication of it. By investigating the precise means whereby content is made believable and compelling through marks on a page, class discussion of supposedly "formalist" concerns such as diction, syntax, and rhetorical technique offers students the opportunity to see themselves as writers—not just students writing—whose work can substantially affect their readers.

Nor should it be assumed that representation is the only game in town. In the class I've described, the writer may have invented characters and happenings that many of his classmates were initially prepared to take as historical realities (perhaps all the more so because, as European Americans, they expected authentic revelations about African-American life from this student, who was one of only two African Americans in the class). Indeed, whether or not the episodes he depicted were "made up," the writer was *making* them as he wrote. An emphasis on form can thus help students to see this act of making for what it is—not merely a "report from the field" but a creative construction, an artistic design. And it is here, I believe, that some sort of empowerment, however humble, might be derived from writing instruction, for by recognizing the ways in which they shape and interpret experience through words, students may begin to understand the power of words to transform worlds.

Nevertheless, it must also be said that, in designing this course, I committed any number of oversights. I failed to anticipate that most students would eventually grow bored with sticking to a single book (however much they were initially attracted to O'Brien's novel) for the entire semester, just as they would eventually grow bored with sticking to a single writing project (their novella) for the same period. I also failed to anticipate that the chapters in which they commented on their own work would not prove an adequate substitute for the writing of essays —as became clear when the one essay they *did* write proved much weaker, in most cases, than I had expected. While I had hoped that the fictive element in their self-referential chapters would lead students to take a more inventive approach to the essay assignment, almost all of them reverted to a bland, perfunctory compare-and-contrast model when considering their own work alongside O'Brien's novel. As with the "advanced" students I discuss in chapter 2, these "introductory" students held tightly to their conception of the essay as an exemplar of literal discourse—a discourse that for them stood starkly opposed to the domain of the metaphorical. In other words, perhaps my most significant oversight lay in my failure to anticipate how deeply invested students can be in the separation of "fact" from "fiction": those who chose to write about events from their own lives kept trying to relate "exactly what happened," while those who chose to write about fictive characters and occurrences kept wandering into a fantasy world that revealed no connection to the "real." In short, I underestimated just how profoundly difficult students would find it to create a compelling metaphoric space through their writing.[15]

Yet surely these troubles are not such that the writing of fiction should be denied to students of composition or literature. Though some of the students in my course grew restless during the second half of the term with composing their novellas (either because their stories lacked sufficient intricacy or because they wanted to be free of the structural constraints I placed on these stories), all demonstrated remarkable interest in the question of how to construct a powerful narrative—much more interest than I have ever witnessed in the question of how to construct a powerful essay. Whatever their "actual" level of commitment, these students certainly appeared deeply engaged in finding the means to make their stories work for the readers in our classroom, and this meant that the rhetorical dimension of their prose was highly visible to them from the beginning. Furthermore, the metafictional chapters in the assignment sequence *forced* them to be self-conscious about the reception of their work, if only because this self-consciousness had to be explicitly built into the structure of their text. Given this combination of student desire and rhetorical awareness, the writing of fiction may deserve considerably more attention in the teaching of English than it generally receives.

Writing as Performance

Anticipating the charge that to engage students in role-play is to have them become nothing more than actors on a stage—actors whose words are thus divorced from what they might "really" want to say—the Summerfields claim that it is essential "to discriminate clearly between the environmental determinants and acts of mind that characterize role, and those that are required in acting" (*Texts* 201). Acting, according to the Summerfields, is "a process of replication," since actors speak lines written by another—while role is "an act of retrieval," one in which "we speak lines that come out of ourselves, lines that we have already made our own or are in the process of making our own" (202). In other words, while acting works to create a theatrical illusion, the roles we adopt in the course of everyday social interaction work to create a "reality" that can and should be distinguished from the pretense of the stage. To cite an example the Summerfields provide: a doctor may be said to play the "role" of the surgeon in the operating room, but we do not say that she then "pretends" to perform an operation, complete with fake blood and all the contrivances used in the latest television hospital drama. Borrowing from Marianne Moore, the Summerfields contend that "if acting is the presentation of imaginary toads in imaginary gardens, then role begins as the presentation of real toads in imaginary gardens and moves toward the presentation of real toads in real gardens" (202).

Yet the crucial question that arises from this separation of the roles played by actors and the roles played in the social dynamics of "real life" is whether *writing* is best understood as excluding the kind of role-play that occurs on the stage or screen. Though the Summerfields sensibly wish to defend writing-in-role against those who see it as nothing more than hollow pretense—a mere "front" put on with little or no personal investment—to place writing in opposition to acting may overlook a number of possibilities. After all, the writing of fiction is quite clearly in the business of producing illusions, and it could also be argued that the writing of any text requires a verbal sleight of hand—for, unlike a real operating room, a text has only words with which to perform its operations. While this does not mean that there is no difference between a person who writes a letter and an actor who pretends to do so on film, it does mean that the former seeks to construct a set of images that are no less "manufactured," in their own ways, than the latter. The letter-writer, for example, who "sets the stage" by beginning "I am writing in my attic on a cold December night" is not necessarily expected to reveal later on that the last two paragraphs of his letter were composed on a much warmer afternoon the next day—nor will his failure to mention other details that might compromise the atmosphere his letter creates be held against him. In this sense, as Erving Goffman remarks, "the representation of an activity will vary in some degree from the activity itself and therefore inevitably misrepresent it" (65). Since part of what any text does is (mis)represent, however implicitly, its own composition, it may be that parallels with the arts of illusion—even in the case of "nonfiction" writing—are not so misguided as they initially appear.

An alternative to segregating social roles from stage roles—and then aligning the act of writing with one or the other—might be to adopt a metaphor that encompasses both forms of role-play and recognizes their inevitable intersections. I am thinking here of the metaphor of *performance,* especially as articulated by Richard Poirier in his remarkable book, published over twenty-five years ago, *The Performing Self.* Unabashed by its connections with the stage, Poirier turns to performance as the most significant, yet pedagogically the most ignored, dimension of writing and literature. What the English studies curriculum needs, he contends, is "admiration for, exploration into, the effort which is literature, the act which is writing" (69)—in other words, a recovery of the performative "energy" (a favorite word of Poirier's) that instigates and sustains written composition. Indeed, though Poirier primarily addresses himself to the teaching of literature, his vision of the classroom is such that literature and composition, reading and writing, observation and participation, all merge in the study of what he calls "the mysteries of performance" (84)—which include not only "those acts of presentation when the author, spruce, smiling, now a public man, gives the finished work to the world" but also those "acts of local performance, carried out in private delight and secret plotting" that constitute the unseen feat of *composing* the text. To study writing as performance is thus to study texts for their "manifestations of energy" (72), their "exertions of vitality" (77), rather than for their unity or clarity or honesty or any of the other shibboleths that characterize conventional evaluation both of literature and of student writing.

Part of Poirier's potential significance for the teaching of English can be located in the way he investigates the act of writing without becoming caught up in the kinds of issues that tend to preoccupy what is known in composition studies as "process" pedagogy, wherein teachers attend to how students handle tasks like planning, prewriting, drafting, proofreading, and so on. In other words, Poirier would have us concern ourselves less with the idiosyncrasies of each writer's personal habits than with how a text reveals its author's attention to the performative quality of writing—that is, to the "pacing, economies, juxtapositions, aggregations of tone, the whole conduct of the shaping presence" (86–87). This concentration on how the text performs, and on its productive anxiety over the effects of its performance, might lead to an altogether different approach to student writing, one that offers not a series of heuristics intended to address the student's supposed inadequacies as a composer but a form of reading intended to enliven the student's sense of textual activity. By positing writing as "a dimension of action" (69), Poirier helps to challenge the words/deeds dichotomy that keeps so many students uninterested in the study of language—especially when they imagine power to lie not in speech or writing but only in money, property, beauty, and muscle. The fusion of writing with action can help students to see that texts not only communicate but also work, play, build, destroy, worship, denigrate, elude, and embrace (to mention just a handful of textual behaviors).

None of which may sound all that surprising these days, particularly in light of speech-act theory and various sociolinguistic conceptions of language. But Poirier does much more than merely assert the priority of the performative over the constative. The most provocative element in his conception of writing lies in his thoroughly unsentimental awareness of the aggression, even the violence, of written performance—quite in contrast to the cooperative realms of speech envisioned by J. L. Austin and John Searle.[16] If writing is a struggle to *make* something out of performance with the written word, then it has little to do with the purity of motive imagined in metaphors of expression or communication: "If this [emphasis on performance] sounds rather more brutal than we imagine writers or artists to be, then that is because performance partakes of brutality" (87). Nor will writing, as Poirier indicates more than once, conform to the political ideology generally endorsed by the academic establishment:

Writing is a form of energy not accountable to the orderings anyone makes of it and specifically not accountable to the liberal humanitarian values most readers want to find there. Such an idea of literature excites a blind and instinctive resistance in most quarters, and for good reason. It makes literature not a source of comfort and order but rather, of often dislocating, disturbing impulses. (xxiii)

While this comment might at first sound like the recent (and not-so-recent) outcry for an "apolitical" approach to literary studies, Poirier strongly censures those who make such an appeal. Rather than seeking to drive politics from the study of literature, he wants us to recognize that the political significance of a text lies not only in its "message" but even more so in its performance, in the ways it composes—or, alternatively, de-composes—itself. Thus he can return to T. S. Eliot and find the hesitant, as well as the proclamatory, character of this poet's prose; and he reads Norman Mailer—controversially, to be sure—as someone who by taking on the identities of, rather than denouncing, various demons makes it all the more possible to move beyond them. In a similar vein, I imagine Poirier would be able to read the performance of someone like Richard Rodriguez in more interesting ways than those who simply wish to condemn his opposition to bilingual education.[17] For Poirier, the politics of any text is less its stated "position" than its body of verbal actions—actions that tell us far more about the text's political sensibilities than mere statement ever could.

Central to Poirier's approach to writing is his vision of performers as those who shape their own selves during the course of a performance. And this is where his decision to embrace rather than exclude associations with the stage—along with painting, dancing, athletics, and so on—becomes crucial to the value of his contribution. While the notion that writers inhabit what are often unconscious social "roles" can be criticized as an oversimplification of subjectivity,[18] the idea of writing as a self-conscious, dramatized performance acknowledges the discontinuities of subjectivity without altogether relinquishing the powers of agency. If writing is a staged performance, then the self can never be entirely equivalent to what it writes, for there always exists a gap between the performer and the performed. Indeed, the performing self is anything but a coherent identity; rather, it undergoes numerous transformations not only as it moves from performance to performance but even within the duration of any single performance, wherein shifts in "character" are often part of the performance itself. Moreover, in performance the self communicates indirectly, not through an unbroken conduit but through a staged activity that the audience must creatively interpret in order for it to take on meaning: performances are always something other (or at least something more) than what they claim to be. In this sense, the performing self is as much possessed by its materials, history, and culture as it possesses them—an awareness of which has led much of twentieth-century literature, as Poirier indicates, to concern itself primarily with the problems and possibilities of its own existence.

In his more recent work, Poirier further complicates these ruminations on performance and selfhood by noting the ways in which any number of writers (he is especially interested in Emerson and his inheritors) at times propose "to do away with the self" and the cultural burdens that attend it (*Renewal* 182). Poirier reminds us, for instance, of Emerson's "transparent eyeball" passage, wherein the writer declares, "I am nothing; I see all . . . I am part or particle of God"; and of Wallace Stevens's "The Snow Man," who, "nothing himself, beholds / Nothing that is not there and the nothing that is." As Poirier indicates, the paradox of any such text lies in the projection of self that obtains in the very attempt to erase it: Emerson and Stevens come through most strongly just as they claim to disappear. Yet the paradoxical tension that marks these textual moments is precisely what makes them so intriguing for Poirier, who believes we should seek to locate in literature "points of rhetorical stress or discontinuity, moments where the language, and the cultural presuppositions that empower it, seem to thwart rather than facilitate an idea" (183). Indeed, it is by turning to literature that Poirier brings unexpected insights to the study of literacy, for by exploring the linguistic struggles which literary texts tend both to enter and to display, he suggests that discursive authority often stems as much from efforts to cast off one's performative self as it does from efforts to embrace it. As he elsewhere says of Emerson, "self-reliance . . . insofar as it is insufficiently understood to refer to the assertion of one's unique personality, gives way recurrently to its opposite, to self-dissolution, to the abandonment of any already defined Self" (*Poetry* 20).

What, then, are some of the curricular possibilities that emerge from Poirier's conception of written performance? As a former undergraduate in the English department at Amherst College, where he encountered the highly unconventional first- and second-year curriculum designed by Theodore Baird, Ruben Brower, and Armour Craig, and later as a section teacher in Brower's Humanities 6 course at Harvard, Poirier comes from a pedagogical tradition devoted to encouraging what he calls in *Poetry and Pragmatism* "a habit of enjoying the way that words undo and redo themselves to the benefit of social as well as literary practice" (173). Though for the most part he refrains from presenting classroom techniques or assignments—perhaps out of the recognition that teachers should generally discover these for themselves since teaching practices must answer to particular situations and constraints—Poirier makes clear his commitment to asking students to *do* things with texts, to investigate the acts of reading they stimulate, rather than to unveil their supposedly hidden meanings. Quirky, difficult, elusive texts (and for Poirier this often, and unapologetically, means canonical texts) therefore become material to be sought rather than shunned by the curriculum—the introductory curriculum as much as the advanced. Such texts are valuable, according to Poirier, not because they put us in touch with some venerable cultural heritage but because they invite a special kind of work with language, "work that requires a skeptical excitement about the past as it still vibrates round us in words" (33).

I would add that Poirier's attention to the performative dimension of writing might lead teachers of English to reconsider the questions they invite student writers to confront in regard to their own texts. In place of queries about their composing habits and the "points" they wish to communicate, students might learn to ask themselves instead: How can I work with a language that is simultaneously working on me? What are the possibilities for written performance at this moment in its history? How do these possibilities respond to or take their cue from or reject those that have come before? In what ways can I not simply perform as a writer but make reflection on my performance a part of how I write? Other questions could take on a more specific cast: What forms of "energy" does this piece of writing manifest? Where do they come alive and where do they die? How can I tell? What does my text attempt to excite or enable in its readers? How might I craft my performance in other ways and toward other ends? My point is not that such questions are never asked but that the more common emphasis in the teaching of writing, be it in the composition or the literature class, lies with issues of meaning rather than with issues of action. Students are endlessly instructed to clarify, revise, expand, develop, and/or detail what they "mean," but only rarely are they urged to describe what a paragraph, sentence, or phrase *accomplishes* as part of a theatrical performance before a noncaptive audience—that is, before readers who want (as both teachers and students should) to be not just informed but also engaged. Indeed, were English teachers to decide they have a right to be engaged by their students' writing, the whole curriculum might well be revolutionized.

I will have more to say about comprehensive curriculum reform in the epilogue. Here I want to conclude with a few thoughts on the hazards of performance, in spite of all that it offers our reflections on the act of writing.

"Where You Yourself Were Never Quite Yourself"

In one of the first college courses I ever taught, a student approached me at the end of the opening session, a class in which I had said that I would encourage students to write in a number of styles and voices. With a look of grave concern in her eyes, the student almost whispered, "I just want you to know that I may not be able to write what you're looking for in this class. You see, I can only write in one voice—the voice of the heart."

I've thought about this remark quite a lot in the years that have followed, and though I initially considered it the product of naiveté, it has come to represent to me a strikingly adroit rhetorical gesture on the part of this student. For what can be said to one who claims to speak or write nothing but what she truly feels? that she should give this up in favor of writing what she does not believe? that as a woman she should relinquish her identity at the behest of her teacher (who in this case was a man)? Similarly, when Jane Tompkins reported in *College English* several years ago that she had turned away from the "performance model" of teaching in her classes—which implied that she had found a way to be who she *really* is in front of her students—how could anyone successfully counter the appeal of this move toward the genuine? By setting performance in opposition to authenticity (like the student who placed voices that would merely pose as her own in opposition to her "voice of the heart"), Tompkins made performance seem almost shameful—an act of self-protective deception that those who are sufficiently brave and honest eventually learn to relinquish.[19]

As I have indicated, I don't think of performance as something one can escape, especially not in writing. Like metaphor, performance is ubiquitous—a constitutive element of any discourse. On the other hand, I don't wish to claim that either my former student or Jane Tompkins is entirely mistaken in her rejection of performance; rather, I see their embrace of the "true" as an equally inescapable component of our relationship to language. If the metaphorical can only be defined through its relationship to the literal, then the same must be said of performance: authenticity is to performance what literalism is to metaphor—its necessary accomplice. Consequently, resistance to the notion that everything is performed—or, more specifically, that all writing is a performance—will always be offered from one quarter or another, if only because to imagine what it means to perform requires that we also imagine what it would mean *not* to perform: performance and authenticity share an interdependent bond. As with the metaphorical/literal bond, we must respect the integrity of both terms. It is not enough just to say that every text represents a performance, for readers also seek to know the personal "engagement" of the one who performs in the words performed—which means that they remain endlessly curious (as the popularity of television shows, magazines, and biographies devoted to Hollywood actors appear to verify) about the potentially "authentic" features of performance.

At the beginning of this book, I noted that Wallace Stevens's poem "The Motive for Metaphor" can be approached as either a celebration or a critique of metaphor. In listing the clear, definitive images from which metaphor "shrinks," the speaker of the poem asserts either his appreciation of or his dissatisfaction with this movement toward the obscure: metaphor works against the desire to say what things really are. Likewise, performance works against the desire to *be* who we really are— or at least who we are before the performance begins. When the speaker of Stevens's poem refers to a realm "Where you yourself were never quite yourself / And did not want nor have to be," he may be reveling, as I suggested earlier, in the liberties that come with taking on the guise of another—in the marvelous play, that is, of performance. But he may instead be directing an accusation against those who perform, those who avoid the responsibility of being who they are and saying what they mean. Performance, as we know from daily enactments, serves as perhaps the most enticing form of evasion, excepting outright disappearance, at our disposal; concealed within our roles, we escape all manner of confrontations. Which is not to suggest that I accept the wholesale condemnation of performance offered by Tompkins. My point is not that performance could be traded in for baring our souls, but that to perform is to construct a relationship—indeed, a bewildering array of relationships—between the performing self and whatever it performs. If performance is inevitable, then the gap can never be fully closed: self and word are never one and the same. But gaps can be narrow or wide, and at times we *experience* such a proximity between self and word that the gap between them seems to vanish altogether, as I think was clearly the case with the student who approached me after class, convinced that her writing emerged from the heart of her existence. Nor is it uncommon for people to declare, as Tompkins has, that they are tired of all the pretense—performance can be exhausting as well as invigorating —and will henceforth follow "their own" inclinations. Of course, the irony of such declarations lies in their performative quality: some of the best performances are found in denials that performance is taking place.

What does all of this mean for the teaching of English? On the one hand, it means that teachers might encourage students to recognize and value, rather than attempt to erase, the "distance" between themselves and their texts. While this might initially seem a recipe for alienation, it is only through an understanding of the disparity between self and text that writers begin to work on their own texts with the "brutality"

Poirier attributes to artistic performance. If students assume that what they write on the page represents their "true self," then it is little wonder we find them defensive and uneasy about putting those pages under strenuous critique or revising them to the extent that the "originals" are no longer recognizable. But if students approach their texts as dramatic performances, as staged productions of possible selves, then they may come to appreciate the ways in which writing resembles the performances—musical, filmic, televisual, and otherwise—that they observe and evaluate with such enthusiasm throughout their daily lives. Many a teacher has tried in one way or another to get students to write *about* such performances; why not ask them to engage *in* performance themselves, discarding the pose of sincerity in favor of other, more enabling, masks? Through these dramatizations, students may come to find not that the literal self hides—secure, stable, unified—behind the cloak of its "disguise," but rather that metaphoric selves—vulnerable, inconstant, fragmentary—discover their ever-changing contours in the very course of performing. As Poirier observes, performance "must go through passages that both impede the action and give it form, much as a sculptor not only is impelled to shape his material but is in turn shaped by it, his impulse to mastery always chastened, sometimes made tender and possibly witty by the recalcitrance of what he is working on" (xxii).

On the other hand, I don't think that the pedagogical potential of performance renders the concerns of Tompkins or of my former student beside the point. Whatever the flaws of the *Phaedrus,* Plato was right, I believe, to worry about sophistry in writing, about the weaker argument made the stronger, not because (as Socrates apparently thought) the rhetoric of deception threatens to contaminate the rhetoric of pure truth, but because all rhetoric, as performance, enables the writer to use the distance between self and word for whatever ends are sought—cruel, humane, or otherwise.[20] In teaching students the performative dimension of writing, we teach them how indifferent writing can be to moral responsibility. As Wayne Booth has remarked, "Some students soon feel they have been liberated to lie to the world at will: 'If I can mimic *anybody,* maybe there are no limits'" ("LITCOMP" 69). Indeed, there *are* no limits—which offers us another reason why teachers of English have yet to embrace the concept of student writing as performance: if students are allowed to "become" whomever they wish through their writing, whom might we find them becoming? This is a question that our assignments, with their focus on truthful and diligent response, generally do not give students the opportunity to explore.

To conceive of writing as performance is not to discover a panacea for the difficulties students encounter with reading and writing texts; it is instead to open the door to a whole new set of problems. But these are the problems that readers and writers who care about their work have the privilege to struggle with—a privilege that students who come to the English studies curriculum should share.

EPILOGUE

Toward a Metaphoric Curriculum

THE PRECEDING CHAPTERS have proposed that a reconception of the English studies curriculum might begin with a reconception of metaphor, both because of its overlapping position among the disciplinary domains within that curriculum (literature, composition, creative writing, and so on) and because of its unique way of negotiating "difference" —a matter of considerable significance in recent attempts to reimagine the teaching of English. While literalism responds to difference by putting things in their "proper" places, metaphor responds to difference by putting things together, not by merely juxtaposing them but by *equating* them despite, or even because of, their disparities. Literalism separates, arranges, and classifies, so that things that are less different are situated in relative proximity and things that are more different are situated at a relative distance. Through the lens of the literal, we are presumed to see things as they "are" and where they "belong." Metaphor, by contrast, dispenses with the proprieties of literalism and takes the risk of merging elements and discourses that are supposedly incompatible: the metaphorical impulse might thus be described as dialogic, novelistic, carnivalesque.[1] Furthermore, metaphor not only flouts the "rules" by which literalism operates; it sneaks its way into literalism itself, which is unable to sustain the production of discourse without recourse to that which it ostensibly shuns.

But as I have indicated throughout this book, the audacity (and, simultaneously, the commonality) of metaphor call not simply for celebration but also for reflective hesitation. After all, by fusing one thing with another, metaphor overlooks their differences and passes on to writers and readers the responsibility for bearing those differences in

194

mind—a responsibility that entails not, as is frequently thought, an insistence that the metaphor is "only" a metaphor, but rather an *entry* into the fictive space generated by the metaphor, where dialogue about equivalence and difference can begin. Metaphor, in other words, does more than identify one thing with another; it asks that we ourselves identify with the "world" of its fiction, that we provisionally take that fiction as literally true. Thus it is that literalism works its way back into metaphor and demonstrates that the literal is as inescapable as the metaphorical. The challenge that confronts writers and readers of metaphor is therefore the same paradoxical challenge of literacy itself, which requires that we continually relearn how both to accept and resist, to enter and withdraw from, the persuasive force of texts.

My claim has been that this conception of metaphor, literalism, and their crucial role in literate activity holds certain implications for the English studies curriculum. I have suggested, for instance, that students might be asked to *write* and not just read fragmentary texts, so that they can experiment with the rhetorical tensions that characterize both the centrifugal and the centripetal movements of language, each of which approaches equivalence and difference in its own ways. And I have also suggested that students might be asked to write, in composition and literature courses as well as in creative writing courses, overtly fictive or metaphorical discourses rather than or in addition to those considered nonfictive or literal. Yet even were a number of individual teachers to bring such practices to their classrooms (as many may already have), the resulting changes would still leave untouched the general structure of the departmental curriculum as a whole, which arguably communicates the contents and contours of English studies more forcibly (or at least more intractably) than any particular course by itself. As Gerald Graff indicates, English has evolved as a discipline over the past hundred years through a system of "growth and accumulation" ("Other" 826), so that new approaches to texts tend to enter the curriculum alongside the old, and students are left to intuit the larger picture as best they can as they move from course to course. While teachers often imagine the possibilities for altering the curriculum through changes in their own pedagogy or the contents of their own courses, Graff argues that the "reduction of education to teaching, which goes hand in hand with the glorification of the autonomous, self-contained course as the natural locus of education, fails to see that educational problems are systemic ones that involve not just individual teaching but the way that teaching is organized" (831). Graff contends that "individual teaching is arguably the least promising place to start in transforming education" (831), and he goes on to call not for the "dialogical classroom" sought by critical pedagogy but a dialogical *curriculum* that would remove courses from their isolated positions and put them into conversation with one another. Graff believes that only by turning to this larger context can departments of English (and the academy at large) bring significant change to what students experience in the course of a college education.

Recent curricular modifications in response to the rising disciplinary status of composition illustrate at the programmatic level the same kind of problem that Graff identifies at the level of individual courses. In a recent survey of over sixty colleges and universities that provide an undergraduate major in composition, rhetoric, professional writing, technical writing, expository writing, or (the most common term) writing, I found that the overwhelming majority of these majors are housed not by independent composition or rhetoric programs but by English departments that offer special "tracks" (also called "concentrations," "options," "specializations," or "emphases") in writing—tracks that run parallel to, but apart from, tracks in literature and in teaching certification.[2] Though these tracks in writing would certainly appear to indicate an achievement on the part of composition faculty across the country, who now play a more prominent role in the curriculum than in years past, the movement to multiply student tracks within the English major, like the tendency to multiply courses within a particular track, demonstrates the persistence of the separatist impulse that Graff derides. It is also worth noting that while several of the writing majors in my survey require that students take a handful of courses in literature, very few of the literature majors require that students take courses in writing beyond the freshman year, and there is nothing to suggest from catalogue descriptions that courses in the two fields have anything in common. Indeed, the impression received from such a survey is that many of those departments now granting degrees in writing have in some respects *further* entrenched the division between the study of composition and the study of literature by institutionalizing their dissociation not simply during the freshman year but throughout the entire four-year curriculum. "Advanced" study in writing may have become an acceptable, even marketable, path through English studies—but it remains a separate path nevertheless.[3]

Much the same can be said for the increasingly visible presence of composition and rhetoric in the graduate curriculum. According to a 1994 report by Stuart Brown, Paul Meyers, and Theresa Enos, at least seventy-two graduate programs now offer doctorates in composition and/or rhetoric, and well over a thousand students are currently pursuing these degrees (240). Again, such figures clearly point to the striking viability this long-subordinate field has acquired within English studies over the past quarter-century. Yet looking through the curricular descriptions provided by the report, we find that the core courses for virtually every program—which often include those such as "Approaches to Teaching Composition," "The History of Rhetoric," "Research Methods in Composition," "Seminar in the English Language," "Topics in Rhetorical [or Composition] Theory," and so on—suggest little, if any, connection to the graduate literature courses that are offered by these same departments. This is to say not that relationships to other parts of the English curriculum cannot be or are not being forged by courses in composition and rhetoric, but that the graduate curriculum, like the undergraduate curriculum, has been constructed in ways that leave it up to the enterprising teacher (or student) to discover the links between one program or track and another: there is nothing in the *structure* of the curriculum as a whole that insists that such links be made. Like the undergraduate students who must piece together on their own whether (and if so, how) one course is conversant with another, graduate students are often left to figure out for themselves the relationships between a semester of courses in, say, postmodern theory, eighteenth-century British literature, and the teaching of composition (among countless other combinations)—except that here the stakes are extremely high, with careers on the line and complicated departmental politics to negotiate. Even when, as in the department in which I teach, the core curriculum for graduate students requires them to take courses in literary history, composition, film, and textual practices, there may be nothing that ensures these courses will be taught in ways that generate dialogue between them. Consequently, students may be more likely to receive a tour of each discrete field than an exploration of how the different fields that comprise English studies can productively interrogate and respond to one another's interests.[4]

Graff's widely discussed solution to this predicament at the undergraduate level is for professors to "teach the conflicts" that divide them by arranging for clusters of courses that share a theme and engage in periodic meetings modeled on the academic conference, wherein teachers and students can openly present their views and debate their differences. While I agree with Graff that some such forum could lead to several of the advantages he cites—perhaps the most important being the possibility that students might see connections between arguments within the academy and arguments beyond its walls—I question whether *conflict* should serve as the metaphor on which cross-course interaction is designed.[5] Graff imagines a predominantly agonistic curriculum, one that thrives on argument and contestation; a primary function of the symposia he envisions is for the oppositions that currently characterize English studies to become discernable through confrontation on a public stage. In this sense, though he calls his proposed curriculum "dialogic," I regard it instead as a *literalist* curriculum, one that works largely in the service of identifying "the way things are" in the discipline rather than the way things might be transformed. Or perhaps it would be more accurate to say that Graff's curriculum is such that the latter must always wait for—and consequently receive much less attention than—the former. As he remarks in *Beyond the Culture Wars,* the reform Graff advocates seeks to "clarify the real controversies in the academy and dispel the myths surrounding them" (36). In other words, the goal is to clear away the clouds of confusion, to eliminate the "myths" (the metaphors) so that the "real" (the literal) academic battles might be seen for what they are—as if doing away with one set of myths could be accomplished without the aid of another.[6] Students are to be enlightened through a process in which opposing positions become visible and the intellectual landscape solidifies under their feet, whereupon they can locate themselves and determine where they want to stand.

Not that I want to minimize the productive changes that the implementation of Graff's scheme might bring about: literalism, as I have argued throughout this book, is both necessary and potentially productive —not something to be scorned as invariably simpleminded or totalizing. The current curriculum in English studies does indeed needlessly mystify the conflicts, both internal and external, that have shaped and continue to shape the discipline. Moreover, virtually any kind of forum in which otherwise separate courses made regular contact would help address the individualism and isolationism that structures the present curriculum. As Graff observes,

> the greater the degree of collective interaction, the greater the likelihood of generating and sustaining self-criticism of whatever in that interaction is problematic or debatable, including its relevance or the lack of it to students' needs. Given a faculty that is reasonably representative of the current diversity of academic culture, an integrated curriculum figures to be more theoretically, historically, and politically self-aware than a faculty that teaches in isolation. Instead of repressing the history and politics embedded in it, such a curriculum would tend to bring that history and politics into the foreground and open it to debate. (194–95)

But while public debate can certainly have transformative effects on its participants, it can also lead to defensive attitudes and the rigidification of intellectual positions. Graff has responded to this charge by suggesting that an argumentative conversation is nevertheless better than no conversation at all—but such a response overlooks the possibility of holding *another* kind of conversation between courses, one that would envision the differences between teachers, courses, and programs not simply as the antagonisms of a discipline in conflict but also as the mutually illuminating forms of inquiry by which English studies investigates the reading and writing of texts.[7] To put this in a personal light: what I regret about the current curriculum is not that I so rarely get to confront my rivals in a public forum but that I so rarely get the opportunity to learn from those who are doing very intriguing, and substantially different, work in classrooms just down the hall from mine. One can always take the extra time to see the teaching of one's colleagues, but the curriculum itself does nothing to motivate such a commitment. Nor does it urge teachers and students to connect, rather than oppose, one approach to English studies with another. Graff's proposal for a dialogical curriculum might thus benefit from a crucial revision of its methods—namely, an emphasis on the potential *alliances* between courses and not merely on their enmities. From this perspective, the discrepancies between various courses could be treated not just as signs of disciplinary disagreement or discontent but as instructive displays of diverse literate practices, each of which converses with and draws upon the others.

What I am suggesting, in other words, is that we consider the possibilities offered by a *metaphoric,* rather than a literalist, curriculum. On the one hand, such a curriculum would ask, as noted in the last two chapters, that students in individual courses explore the resources of metaphorical discourse instead of simply attempting to ascertain their literal views of the subject matter or texts before them. On the other hand, such a curriculum would also ask that courses vacate the safe havens of their detached classrooms in order to come into contact as do the elements of metaphor—that is to say, in ways that forge unusual equivalences between them. While a literalist curriculum keeps courses in their established places, a metaphoric curriculum brings them together in striking and unexpected combinations. Graff, I am contending, takes an initial step away from literalism by claiming that separate courses should periodically meet in the same room, but his curriculum remains literalist to the extent that it brings together a predictable set of foes (multiculturalists versus traditionalists, feminists versus humanists, and so on) whose job is to "clarify" their ideas on particular themes or texts. In contrast, the metaphoric curriculum I am proposing is one in which courses would meet not merely to discuss their differences but to *share practices* ordinarily reserved for just one of them. Thus, a cluster of courses in, say, composition, Renaissance literature, and creative writing might ask that students compose a narrative essay, read a comedy by Ben Jonson, and write a poem at different moments during the semester, whereupon these otherwise separate courses would intersect, encouraging students to explore the similarities and differences in their various approaches to the assignments. Rather than waiting for their professors to describe the contours of a conversation that will go on whether or not students choose to join it, the students in these courses would participate in a conversation created by the *work*—the literate endeavors —in which they are involved as readers and writers.

Such a curriculum is predicated on at least two significant assumptions about the teaching of English, the first of which concerns the relationship between teachers and students. As so many of those who have sought to reconceive this relationship in recent years have observed, the crucial determinant in any pedagogy consists of the extent to which it engages students in the production of knowledge.[8] Accordingly, it is imperative that a curriculum that seeks to bring courses into more frequent contact consider carefully the *form* of contact it hopes to provide —specifically, the role that students will play in the knowledge-making produced by such contact. Though Graff's model invites students to partake in (or even to organize) panel discussions and to make up their own minds in response to professorial debates, their contributions remain no more than supplemental when compared to that of their teachers, who clearly continue to hold most of the cards when it comes to defining and presenting the conflicts within their discipline. Again, I am not contending that Graff's curriculum would not make a difference; I am contending that it would not make *enough* of a difference in redefining the standard relations among teachers, students, and knowledge. But an integrated curriculum whose primary interest is in particular *acts* of reading and writing—rather than merely in their *outcomes,* when opinions have been formed and issues established—offers the possibility of opening multicourse discussions in which student work is central, not peripheral, to the knowledge these discussions attempt to produce. While Graff suggests that students in a given cluster of courses write papers after a conference-style forum has been held, I would suggest that they write *before* as well as after their courses come together so that their ventures and struggles with language can be studied alongside those of the writers on their reading lists.[9]

This attention to student writing constitutes more than a minor revision of Graff's proposal; rather, it reveals a vital difference between what I am calling literalist and metaphoric curricula. In a literalist approach, student writing is brought forward primarily for the "points" it has to make, the "views" it has to argue—which may be taken as seriously as the views argued by teachers, but which remain no more than views. In other words, samples of student writing enter the classroom to be read for what they literally *say* (and, for purposes of assessment, how well they say it). By contrast, a metaphoric approach to student writing insists on reading for what that writing *does,* for the *action* it takes—intertextually, historically, sociopolitically, culturally—and not just for the message it delivers. Here student texts are treated *as* texts, not as "papers" that can be taken at their word. (It is no accident that Graff would have student writing adopt the form of the conference paper.) As I have indicated through this book, to read a text as a text is to read it as a metaphor—a metaphor in which word and deed, saying and doing, stating and performing, are made equivalent even as their differences remain in view. While such an approach to texts is taken for granted in the study of literature, student texts are generally considered suitable for "response" rather than study, even in composition courses that strive to give the work of students more prominence.[10]

But if student writing is to be read *as* writing, with the same concerns that animate the reading of those texts on course syllabi, then teachers of English will have to be willing to mix their metaphors. That is to say, they will have to be willing to merge student texts with the official material of their courses, so that the disjunctive discourses of student writers and experienced writers can be investigated together, often in the same class meeting and with the same set of terms. And this will require, moreover, that teachers relinquish their sense of superiority when in the presence of student writing in order to acknowledge and respect the institutional and cultural pressures under which it labors. Indeed, until student writing can be read without condescension, it may be that the effects of other forms of curricular change will be significantly curtailed.

Which brings me to the second assumption on which a metaphoric curriculum relies—namely, an assumption that the so-called "strained" metaphor (that is, the metaphor that reaches precariously across the divide separating supposedly irreconcilable elements) serves not as an error but as the prerequisite for fresh insight. Thus, in addition to grouping together courses that sound immediately compatible or well-suited to one another (courses on the same theme, or from the same period of history, or within the same sub-disciplinary program, and so on), the metaphoric curriculum I have in mind would also create clusters of courses that initially appear, or even in some ways remain, *in*compatible or *ill*-suited for partnership. Imagine, for instance, the possibilities that could emerge from a cluster that included one introductory, one intermediate, and one advanced-level course, each of which were housed by a separate track in the English department. Though such an arrangement might seem a recipe for disaster, it would provide, if well-designed, opportunities for learning that students rarely obtain within more conventional course groupings, which usually match up freshmen with freshmen and seniors with seniors. But consider what might be gained by asking seniors in a course required for teaching certification to read, discuss, and comment in writing upon the essays composed by members of a freshman composition course, who in turn might be asked to critically assess the value of such commentary for their work as writers. Similarly, those enrolled in an upper-division course in literary theory might be invited to explain the tenets of a particular poetics to those enrolled in a lower-division poetry workshop, who would in turn converse and write about the implications of this poetics for poems they themselves had written or would now attempt to write. Nor is this to say that advanced students would always be located in the position of authority, since their own work might benefit from being placed under the scrutiny of their peers in introductory courses, who would thereby face the difficulty of creating a critical discourse with which to talk about discourse. The point, in other words, would be not to dissolve all prospects for specialization into one melting pot of generalism—for specialization can be productive, not merely limiting—but to ensure that each branch of specialization is enriched and informed by the various literate practices that comprise English studies.[11] Different tracks of study now present in many departments might remain intact, but not in isolation, as if they had nothing to offer one another.

Perhaps I should add that I do not mean to suggest that the more farfetched the metaphorical link between one course and another, the better. Rather, I am attempting to imagine a curriculum that would not simply show students which ideas in English studies belong where and how they disagree, but that would help students begin both to draw upon and to interrogate the various practices through which readers and writers address what Robert Pattison calls "the problems posed by language." As I discussed briefly in chapter 2, Pattison offers an intriguing two-pronged definition of literacy, one that disputes the notion that literacy primarily consists of proficiency in reading and writing. While Pattison admits that literacy includes skill with whatever technologies of expression are made available by a given culture, such skill is secondary to that which he considers the foremost component of literacy: consciousness of the *problems* that language presents to all who use it. In his book *On Literacy*, Pattison explores a number of these problems (the gap between language and event, the conflict between speech and writing, the antagonism between formal and informal discourses, and so on) as part of his historical survey of the ways in which different societies have attempted to resolve them. But what matters for my purposes here are the implications Pattison's definition of literacy holds for the English studies curriculum, which by and large separates one component of literacy from the other, to the extent that teaching students skill in reading and writing rarely coincides with an investigation of "the problems posed by language"—a subject reserved for courses in "theory" or other "advanced" courses in literature.[12]

If departments of English are to meet the many challenges that confront them as the twentieth century comes to a close, then they will have to find the means to connect engagement *in* literate practices with the study *of* literate practices. Currently, I think it fair to say that even when the undergraduate curriculum manages to produce students who can meet the demands of various contexts for reading and writing, most of these same students have almost nothing to say about language itself. By this I mean that even those students who appear to have "mastered" the conventions of different academic discourses, and who may speak knowingly about their own composing processes, can barely begin to address questions about, say, the relationship of writing to speech, or the rhetoric of the sentence, or the issues of language and dialect that presently confront the United States, be it in the home, the workplace, the media, or the schools. Of course, such questions befuddle many otherwise impressive students because, though they have been taught how to deploy language for personal gain and academic achievement, they have not been taught (or have been taught too sporadically) how to reflect on language as a nexus of social, political, and cultural problems. Yet without this further inquiry into the complications of language, they will be unable to build a more intricate and perceptive understanding of themselves and the world they inhabit.

The "metaphoric" curriculum I have proposed represents an attempt to bring those dissatisfied with the factionalism that has characterized English studies into dialogue about the diverse literate practices that constitute their fields of interest. Such a curriculum need not require the sanction nor the participation of all members of a given department; indeed, it may be that beginning on a smaller scale (with just one or two clusters of courses) would present fewer administrative difficulties and enable greater cooperation among those involved. If the initiative were successful—by which I mean if the teachers and students who chose to participate found it illuminating and energizing—then others would no doubt be attracted to it, and the various forms of curricular collaboration could expand to include a larger number of courses. A broader consensus, in other words, might be generated by such innovations, even if they did not begin with it.

The time is ripe—the time for teachers of literature, composition, creative writing, critical theory, cultural studies, and all other instructional realms within "English" at large to reach beyond their disconnected classrooms in order to create a curriculum based not only on how these realms differ but also on what each has to educate the other. In the years to come, the capacity for forging some such alliance may determine whether the study of reading and writing continues to be regarded as necessary merely for the sake of "functioning" in society, or whether it becomes something else altogether: a sphere for the investigation, re-creation, and critique of metaphor, of literalism, of language itself.

NOTES

WORKS CITED

INDEX

NOTES

Prologue

1. As it turns out, Bloom hears Shelley rather than Keats in Stevens's poem, which he claims is "remarkably like Shelley's late lyric *To Night*. . . . Stevens's love for that moment in the day when light has come but the sun has not yet risen is a thoroughly Shelleyan passion, related to all of Shelley's visions of the morning star fading in the dawn light" (*Wallace Stevens* 221). In suggesting that Bloom "might observe" in "The Motive for Metaphor" a revision of Keats's "Ode to a Nightingale," I am simply noting that Bloom, among others, has taught us to look for such revisions of the British Romantics in the American poetic tradition.

2. The colleague I refer to here is Stephen Carr.

3. Consider that in 1971 Warren Shibles found it possible to compile an annotated bibliography of metaphor in less than three hundred pages that began with the Greek Sophists and moved all the way through the 1960s; while recent bibliographies by J. P. Van Noppen et al. and Van Noppen and Edith Hols, which cover just twenty years, contain well over seven thousand entries.

4. See Bartholomae, "Freshman English, Composition, and CCCC," 47.

5. See Ohmann, "Literacy, Technology, and Monopoly Capital" and Stuckey, *The Violence of Literacy*. For a less Marxist but to my mind more insightful discussion of this subject, see Coles, "The Literacy Crisis."

6. A good example is Deborah Brandt, who argues in *Literacy as Involvement* that literate practices should be conceived as demanding not (as is often presumed) a detachment from the social world but rather a more alert connection to it:

> literacy learning requires intensifying—not subordinating—reliance on social involvement as a basis of interpretation in reading and writing. It requires heightening understanding of how human beings create reality together. In oral exchanges, this joint reality-making is at once both more obvious (because speakers are physically together) and more hidden (because we tend to think of the oral context as already "there" and so are less conscious of the degree, even in talk, that language contributes to the forging of a shared world). In written language, these illusions are less tenable; the social foundations of reality (how we work together to bring reality into being)

become more fully crystallized. . . . The radical social foundations of the literate orientation compel a reanalysis of literacy failures in school. (6–7)

7. See, for example, Atkins and Johnson, *Reading and Writing Differently;* Bizzell, "On the Possibility"; Booth, "LITCOMP"; Culler, "Imagining Changes"; Horner, *Composition and Literature;* Nan Johnson, "Rhetoric and Literature"; Lanham, "One, Two, Three"; Scholes, *Textual Power;* Slevin, "Connecting English Studies"; Waller, "Polylogue"; and Young, "Rebuilding Community in the English Department."

8. A ready example would be the department in which I teach, where five tenure lines were recently lost as part of an administrative decision to reduce such lines across the arts and sciences.

Chapter 1. Aberrant Figures

1. For an illuminating discussion of the consequences of identifying composition with the teaching of *freshman* writing, see Susan Miller, *Textual Carnivals,* esp. 45–76.

2. For the purposes of this chapter, I have performed an extensive—but by no means exhaustive—search of nineteenth- and twentieth-century composition textbooks. My central resource was the Nietz Old Textbook Collection of Hillman Library at the University of Pittsburgh. This collection houses over fifteen thousand volumes, most of which are primary and secondary school texts, but some of which are postsecondary composition and rhetoric textbooks. With the help of Juli Parrish, who served as my research assistant during summer 1997, I consulted eighty-four textbooks in the Nietz collection and in the library stacks, covering every decade from the 1820s to the 1990s. I also consulted at least fifty additional textbooks from my personal collection and that of Joseph Harris, director of the composition program at the University of Pittsburgh. While there are surely textbooks that take a different approach to figurative language than those I go on to document in this chapter, my survey suggests such textbooks provide the exceptions rather than the rule for the treatment of figures in college writing instruction over the last two centuries.

3. Not that John F. Genung's approach to style should be seen as typical for its time. According to Connors, *Practical Elements* was "the last really popular textbook to valorize style. . . . Despite Genung's early popularity, however, his sort of rhetoric was backward-looking, theoretical, discursive. He could not save the canon of style for very long" (*Composition-Rhetoric* 267).

4. The taxonomic approach to style identified the desirable qualities of style

by way of vast, valorized abstractions, such as Perspicuity, Energy, and Elegance —to cite those offered by Richard Whately in *Elements of Rhetoric*. See Connors, *Composition-Rhetoric* 257–69.

5. Ironically, the only handbooks I have encountered that make no mention of metaphor are those I consider the best: Pat Belanoff et al., *The Right Handbook;* and Jay Silverman et al., *Rules of Thumb: A Guide for Writers.* Both of these handbooks take a calm, reasonable, discursive approach to the conventions for grammar and punctuation in standard written English, and thus neither becomes preoccupied with the fears about metaphor that I go on to document in this chapter.

6. See, for example, Willard, *Rhetoric* 166; and Jamieson, *A Grammar of Rhetoric and Polite Literature* 144.

7. One of the early figures in the teaching of college composition to condemn such an approach to metaphor was Gertrude Buck, whose dissertation views metaphor as an aspect not of rhetorical persuasion but of psychological development. For Buck, the inherent flaw in traditional views of metaphor lies in their assumption that figures serve as devices for pleasing or convincing the reader. As Buck recognizes, this assumption holds certain consequences for readers themselves, who learn to be skeptical of metaphor and its supposedly manipulative character:

> Acquiescing in the theory of rhetoric that the metaphor is an expression not necessarily of the speaker's own vision of things, but of his desire to make other people see them in a certain way, the "practical man" is straightway seized with a distrust of the figure, amounting almost to a fear. He regards metaphors much as the old saints regarded women—as charming snares, in which he may too easily be entangled. Tell a jury that your opponent's most telling argument is "only a beautiful metaphor," and you have at once wholly discredited it. (qtd. in Jo Ann Campbell, ed., *Toward a Feminist Rhetoric* 39)

The composition textbooks I consider in this chapter suggest that not only the "practical man" but also teachers of writing themselves share "a distrust of the figure, amounting almost to a fear."

Buck provides a serious reconsideration of metaphor that is especially acute in its examination of why the metaphors in student texts often seem so superficial. Yet because her alternative approach to metaphor has received considerable, albeit infrequent, praise (see, for instance, Albert Kitzhaber, *Rhetoric in American Colleges*), I want to briefly mention my discomfort with her categories of analysis. As the above passage indicates, Buck relies on a distinction between metaphors that spring from "the speaker's own vision of things" and those that derive from the "desire to make other people see them in a certain way." While the latter, from Buck's perspective, leads to artificiality, the former leads to what she calls "genuine poetic metaphor" (37). Genuine or authentic metaphors—"those fresh and vital figures which need no external witness to their spontaneous origin" (37) are thus produced by a kind of *non*rhetorical motive, one in which the speaker or writer's relationship to audience is beside the point. Though radical in certain respects, Buck's theory of metaphor depends upon a distinction between the artificial and the natural that creates as many problems as it resolves.

8. One book—though unfortunately not a textbook—that both usefully and playfully overturns such injunctions against mixed metaphor is Jeremy Lawrence, *Mix Me a Metaphor*. Practicing what he preaches, Lawrence contends: "Truly our lives without the mixed metaphor . . . would be sour grapes and ashes" (10).

9. For an important discussion of the ways in which the teaching of writing has been aligned with the teaching of manners, see Susan Miller, *Textual Carnivals*. Miller suggests that composition, as it came into its institutional existence in departments of English, "focused on . . . correct written vernacular language, as a matter of politeness and good breeding" (55).

10. For arguments that metaphor should not be considered an elliptical simile, see Mark Johnson, "Metaphor in the Philosophical Tradition"; and Cooper, *Metaphor* 56–58, 142–46. For further discussion of the relationship between metaphor and simile, see chapter 3.

11. For an essay that includes a reading similar to the one I am offering of Richards's conception of metaphor, see Kameen, "Metaphor and the Order of Things."

12. See Berthoff, ed., *Reclaiming the Imagination,* especially the preface. For evidence that I. A. Richards's notion of "interaction" remains influential in recent theories of metaphor, see Roger M. White, *The Structure of Metaphor* and Hausman, *Metaphor and Art.*

13. See Eagleton, *Literary Theory;* Culler, "Imagining Changes"; and Mailloux, *Rhetorical Power.*

14. Not that seamlessness as a goal for student texts has not been challenged by certain composition scholars. See, for example, Bartholomae, "What Is Composition"; Faigley, *Fragments of Rationality* 132–62, 200–24; Junker, "Writing (with) Cixous"; and Spellmeyer, *Common Ground* 67–92.

15. Another example of this uncertainty about the consequences a new conception of metaphor might hold for English studies can be found in McLaughlin, "Figurative Language." After devoting most of his essay to an explanation of how figures like metaphor are at work through language and culture, McLaughlin concludes with the question of what difference it makes to be

aware that figurative language is ubiquitous. As with Miller's remarks, it is difficult to see how McLaughlin's final lines suggest anything we don't already know: "If figures tell us anything, it's that meaning is up for grabs, that the world can be shaped in an endless variety of forms, that language is a battle-ground of value systems. The challenge of figures is to make sure we are aware of their presence in discourse and their effects on our thought—but also to engage in the production of figures ourselves, in service of our own values" (90).

16. Other examples of fill-in-the-blank exercises with metaphor are Quackenbos, *First Lessons in Composition* 174–75; Harper, *Practical Composition* 156–57; and Williams, *Composition and Rhetoric by Practice* 174.

17. Other textbooks that include exercises of this sort are Lunsford and Connors, *The St. Martin's Handbook;* and Fowler and Aaron, *The Little, Brown Handbook*. In addition to identifying the figures in the sentences provided, the *St. Martin's* exercise asks that students "decide how each [figure] contributes to your understanding of the passage it appears in" (430), while the *Little, Brown* exercise asks that students "analyze how [the figure] contributes to the writer's meaning" (471). I would suggest that the term *contributes* in each of these instances implies that figures provide auxiliary assistance to meaning, not that they make meaning possible in the first place.

18. A handful of textbooks since the mid-nineteenth century that include conversion exercises are Quackenbos, *First Lessons in Composition* 175–76; Kerl, *Elements of Composition and Rhetoric* 234–36; Harper, *Practical Composition* 156–58 (in which metaphors are converted to similes and similes to metaphors); Kellogg, *A Text-Book on Rhetoric* 116–17; Huntington, *Elements of English Composition* 199; Flesch, *The Art of Plain Talk* 108; Barzun, *Simple and Direct* 141–42; and McCrimmon et al., *Writing with a Purpose* 178–79.

19. The challenge of determining just what instruction in metaphor has to offer undergraduates is not reserved for the authors of composition textbooks; this challenge confronts literature textbooks as well. Consider, for instance, the attempt by Waller, McCormick, and Fowler in *The Lexington Introduction to Literature*—a refreshingly perceptive understanding of recent theoretical material on the subject—to explain the uses of a broader conception of metaphor:

> So you can at least try to become increasingly attuned to the metaphors that are used today. You may then recognize, first, that many of your opinions are based on conventional, historically conditioned assumptions and values rather than on permanent, unchanging truths; and, second, that metaphors are not obscure figures of speech used only in poetry but rather that they pervade every aspect of our language. (1104)

As with Corbett's textbook, it is far from clear what good comes from recognizing such things. So students acknowledge that their opinions are cultural rather than universal and that metaphors are everywhere: what then? The authors go on to counsel only that students become more conscious of their interpretive activities as readers—though what this consciousness has to do with metaphor they neglect to say. Indeed, in the closing paragraphs of their section "The Pervasiveness of Metaphor," metaphor completely drops from view, as the authors turn to other concerns (1105).

20. See, for example, Bump, "Metaphor, Creativity, and Technical Writing"; Couser, "Seeing Through Metaphor"; Krupa, "Invention and Metaphor"; Linda Peterson, "Repetition and Metaphor"; Louise Smith, "Enigma Variations"; and Tobin, "Bridging Gaps."

21. Donald McQuade is not alone with his contention that metaphor *produces* similarities. For similar arguments, see Black, "Metaphor" 284–85; and Lakoff and Johnson, *Metaphors We Live By* 147–55.

22. This last term is taken from Berlin, *Rhetoric and Reality* 16.

23. The debate began as an exchange between Erika Lindemann, "Freshman Composition," and Gary Tate, "A Place for Literature in Freshman Composition," in 1993. In 1995 *College English* published a symposium that included Michael Gamer, "Fictionalizing the Disciplines"; Jane Peterson, "Through the Looking-Glass"; Erwin R. Steinberg, "Imaginative Literature in Composition Classrooms?"; along with Lindemann's and Tate's essays. Yet this debate by and large is limited to the issue of whether students should read— not write—"imaginative literature" in the first-year composition course.

Chapter 2. Higher Learning

1. What follows is the text of the study guide I handed out in class:

Please discuss and take notes on the following:

1. What is the "plot" of the poem your group has been assigned? What story of the past, present, and/or future does the speaker tell, and what appears to be his attitudes toward the people or events in this story?

2. What do you find valuable and/or troubling in the speaker's attitudes? (Be sure to identify particular lines that display those attitudes.)

3. Imagine that the speaker is *not* Frost himself. What do you think Frost, as the poet, is attempting to say about the speaker and his situation? (Be sure to identify particular lines that seem to indicate *Frost's*—not the speaker's— views.)

2. Except, that is, for W. Ross Winterowd, who in *The Contemporary Writer* outlines Perrine's discussion of metaphor and refers to his essay as "an extremely interesting discussion" of the subject (427).

3. Roger M. White observes, "The poverty of so many treatments of the na-

ture of metaphor . . . stems directly from the extent to which writers have been content to conduct their discussions in terms of a very few simple metaphors, and to use these examples to illustrate, rather than to test or to refine, their theoretical statements" (*The Structure of Metaphor* 118). White's study is useful not only because he points to this problem but because he is determined to avoid it himself—for his book is saturated with examples of fascinating and complicated metaphors from various works of literature, which enrich his discussion considerably.

4. Not only poetry but also prose can cause interpretive difficulties of the kind that Laurence Perrine addresses. On any number of occasions, I have asked students in my freshman composition courses to read and discuss Ernest Hemingway's "Hills Like White Elephants"—whereupon I'm always surprised to find that over 90 percent of them do not recognize that the two characters in the story are discussing an abortion. Since what Perrine would call the "literal term" is never named (for the characters speak of it euphemistically), students have only the "figurative terms" ("operation," "it," and so on) on which to rely, and many of them fail to catch the contextual cues that aid interpretation. But the problem doesn't end with my pointing out these cues, for cues are themselves metaphors, and students read them in any number of ways, not all of which support the argument that the "operation" is an abortion.

5. For another discussion of literature in which the metaphor of "conjuring" is prominent, see Marjorie Pryse and Hortense Spillers, *Conjuring.* While I am contending that readers conjure the metaphors they are presumed to "find" in the text, Pryse and Spillers concentrate on the conjurings of *writers* —specifically, female African-American writers: "In the 1970s and 1980s, black women novelists have become metaphorical conjure women, 'mediums' like Alice Walker who make it possible for their readers and for each other to recognize their common literary ancestors" (5).

6. Cleanth Brooks and Robert Penn Warren are among the few commentators on metaphor who share I. A. Richards's recognition that metaphor represents the dissimilarities as well as the similarities between its terms: "We think of metaphors (and related figurative expressions) as 'comparisons,' and yet it is plain that we might as accurately refer to them as 'contrasts.' For the elements of dissimilarity between the terms of a metaphor may be of just as much importance as the elements of likeness. One can go further still: In an effective metaphor there must be a *considerable degree of contrast*" (*Modern Rhetoric* 344).

7. In the fourth edition of *Understanding Poetry,* the discussion of "After Apple-Picking" has been dropped, though the poem still remains in the "Supplemental Poems" section of a chapter on "Theme, Meaning, and Dramatic Structure." Interestingly, one of the appendices that Brooks and Warren have

added to this edition is entitled "Metaphor and Symbol Compared and Contrasted," wherein they again note that "the metaphor derives its strength from contrast—very often from the very unlikeness of the things compared" (578).

8. I have encountered two other critics who say much the same about the rewards of a literal reading of "After Apple-Picking." In *The Major Themes of Robert Frost*, Radcliffe Squires remarks, "Though most good poems have symbolic extensions, halos, I feel rather stubbornly that this poem loses brilliance the moment the reader tries to make it other than a literal harvest or even other than an apple harvest" (57–58). And in *The Poems of Robert Frost: An Explication*, Mordecai Marcus offers a refreshingly literal interpretation of the poem that he concludes as follows: "The poem's title suggests humanity expelled from Eden but treats the aftermath of almost-tragic knowledge so gently that the biblical allusion is muted. Other allegorical interpretations are possible, and many have been made, but the speaker does not seem to be an old man on the verge of death or someone thinking more about the writing of poems than about life's fulfillments, as is sometimes suggested" (53).

9. Another critic that seizes on this line is Ruben Brower, who, in *The Poetry of Robert Frost*, contends that "essence of winter sleep" serves as "the central metaphor of the poem" (25).

10. About a third of the way into their reading of "After Apple-Picking," Brooks and Warren "go back and take a fresh start with the poem" (365). At this stage they note that the ladder is pointing not merely upward, "but toward *heaven*, the place of man's rewards, the home of his aspirations, the deposit of perfection and ideal values" (365)—and thus begins their interpretation that Frost is metaphorically presenting a set of contrasts between the real and the ideal. Whereupon they immediately turn back to a literal reading, recognizing the potential objection that, rather than representing an ideal, "the dream seems to be a bad dream, a nightmare of the day's labor" (365). And so on: Brooks and Warren move through the poem dialogically, testing the literal against the metaphorical, and vice versa.

None of which is to say that I endorse *Understanding Poetry* as a pedagogical instrument. Rather, I wish only to contend that Brooks and Warren demonstrate a form of reading alert to the productive interplay of the metaphorical and literal dimensions of language. Whether such demonstrations do much in teaching students themselves to read with similar attention to metaphor and literalism is another question altogether, one that depends as much on the educational context as on the merits of the display.

11. The essays my class read were White's "Once More to the Lake," Orwell's "Shooting an Elephant," Baldwin's "Stranger in the Village," and Kingston's "No Name Woman."

12. The combination of these two attitudes toward language has been astutely described by Catherine Belsey as "expressive realism." In *Critical Practice,* Belsey contends that expressive realism "is the theory that reflects the *reality* of experience as it is perceived by one (especially gifted) individual, who *expresses* it in a discourse which enables other individuals to recognize it as true" (7).

13. While Robert Pattison does not emphasize the relationship between metaphorical and literal discourse in his treatment of "the questions posed by language," he does observe that the figure of the vaudeville clown—such as Gracie Allen—enacts a certain kind of illiteracy, one that cannot distinguish between the literal and the metaphorical. After quoting part of a Burns and Allen routine in his book *On Literacy,* Pattison comments: "The clown is programmed to understand language only in its most literal form. He cannot adjust for context, tone, or nuance" (14). In other words, Gracie Allen's clown cannot "adjust for" metaphor, which is often signaled by "context, tone, or nuance."

Chapter 3. Literal Fictions

1. An otherwise excellent collection of essays entitled *Metaphor and Thought,* ed. Andrew Ortony, illustrates the problem to which I refer, wherein speech and writing are often presumed equivalent. For a prominent example in Ortony's volume of an essay that mentions only the "speaker" and "hearer" of metaphor, see Searle, "Metaphor." For an essay that alternates its terms between *speaker/hearer* and *writer/reader,* see Levin, "Language, Concepts, and Worlds."

2. See Derrida, *Of Grammatology* 6–26.

3. Pratt, "Linguistic" 51. Interestingly, one of the theories of discourse Pratt rejects in her essay is speech act theory, which she herself had formerly promoted in *Toward a Speech Act Theory of Literary Discourse.* In "Linguistic Utopias," Pratt perceives that one of the problems with speech act theory lies in its assumption that speakers hold a "shared understanding about who wants or needs to say what" (51).

4. I am thinking, for instance, of the kind of study Shirley Brice Heath performed in *Ways with Words,* which vividly documents the difference between teacher and student conceptions and uses of speech, reading, and writing in the Carolina Piedmonts.

5. Max Black's essay reappears as the third chapter in his *Models and Metaphors.* In "Metaphor and the Cultivation of Intimacy," Ted Cohen remarks, "The pivotal text, I think, is Max Black's 'Metaphor.' It has been an extremely influential and provocative piece and it continues to hold a central

position in contemporary discussions" (3). Similarly, Paul Ricoeur observes in *The Rule of Metaphor:* "Max Black's article 'Metaphor' . . . has become a classic in its field on the west side of the Atlantic. And justly so" (83). But Ricoeur gives more credit to I. A. Richards for taking the initial step: "This brief essay does not eclipse Richards' work, despite the tentativeness and a certain lack of technical development in the latter. For Richards made the breakthrough; after him, Max Black and others occupy and organize the terrain" (83–84).

6. Though Davidson certainly deserves credit as the first to fully expound the literalist approach, it is interesting to note a precursor in the teaching of writing—namely, David Lord, whose *The Characteristics and Laws of Figurative Language* contains the following passage on metaphor: "The terms . . . that are used by this figure *always carry with them their literal sense, not a different or modified meaning.* Thus when the valleys are said to laugh, and the floods to clap hands, it is laughing that is affirmed of the valleys, and clapping hands that is ascribed to the floods, not anything else" (37; emphasis added).

7. For Black's response to Davidson's critique, see Black, "How Metaphors Work."

8. Fogelin perceptively notes, for instance, how each quatrain in Shakespeare's sonnet offers "a rather routine comparison of something with the beginning of old age. Then, within each quatrain, a second metaphor is introduced that relates the initial metaphor to death" (109)—so that the metaphors that open each quatrain are all complicated by the metaphors that follow and interact with them.

9. In "Logic and Conversation," Grice cites four sets of "maxims" (concerning quantity, quality, relation, and manner) that constitute what he calls the "Cooperative Principle"—a general principle that in Grice's view structures the behavior of participants in speech situations. For a discussion of Grice's maxims, see Pratt, *Toward a Speech Act Theory of Literary Discourse* 125–51.

10. In "A Developmental Analysis of Metaphoric Competence and Reading," James D. Pickens, Marilyn R. Pollio, and Howard R. Pollio note that if we read first for literal understanding, figurative understanding should be more time-consuming. But "the empirical evidence concerned with figurative comprehension demonstrates that readers do not wait until a literal meaning has been discarded before processing metaphoric meaning" (486). Consequently, the authors conclude that "figurative understanding does not require a comprehension process different from either literal or cliched usage" (486).

11. This problem is likewise evident in one of the most knowledgeable books on the subject—and one much influenced by Davidson's literalist position—David Cooper's *Metaphor.* Like Davidson, Cooper rejects the notion that "maverick utterances" such as metaphor contain propositions; rather, he argues that

metaphor should be "taken out of the orbit occupied by the information-giving devices of language and brought into, or close to, the one occupied by songs, poems, myths, allegories, and the like" (108). While Cooper apparently means to celebrate metaphor by aligning it with "the evocation of moods or the stimulation of imagery" (108), he overlooks the ways in which this alignment keeps metaphor tied to "literary" discourse and its contradictory social status.

12. Another intriguing discussion of metaphor can be found in John S. Hart's *A Manual of Composition and Rhetoric:* "In metaphor, the comparison, if made at all, is not formally expressed in words. . . . If the metaphor expressses, or even suggests comparison, that metaphor is faulty. Not that a metaphor may not be taken to pieces, and be shown to owe its existence to comparison; but it should not, at first sight, suggest comparison. The figure should be so involved in the subject you can hardly pull the two apart" (155). The visceral metaphors here are fascinating: at first the figure should be so intertwined one "can hardly pull the two apart," though when one finally succeeds in taking the metaphor "to pieces," comparison is discovered as the very reason for its existence.

13. On the one hand, Davidson rejects the notion that metaphor is an elliptical simile: "Both the elliptical simile theory of metaphor and its more sophisticated variant, which equates the figurative meaning of the metaphor with the literal meaning of a simile, share a fatal defect. They make the hidden meaning of the metaphor all too obvious and accessible" ("What Metaphors Mean" 37). On the other hand, he keeps metaphor linked to simile through the common goal of comparison: "Metaphor and simile are merely two among endless devices that serve to alert us to aspects of the world by inviting us to make comparisons" (38).

14. In *Metaphoric Worlds,* Levin makes much of the difference between "conceiving" and "conceiving *of.*" Conceiving, according to Levin, leads to "concepts," which are "clear and distinct representations"—whereas conceiving *of* leads to "conceptions," which are more loosely designed "mental schemas" (6). For Levin, metaphors produce conceptions, not concepts.

15. Theorists of metaphor tend to make claims about metaphor in general on the basis of their insight into a particular *kind* of metaphorical expression. From this perspective, it is not that either interactionist or literalist theories are "wrong" but that they attempt to map a broader terrain than they have actually taken the time to survey. Robert J. Fogelin's theory of figurative comparisons, for instance, works just fine provided the metaphor in question is of the comparative kind—by which I mean the type of metaphor which suffers little when stated as a simile, with the omitted "like" or "as" replaced. Similarly, Max

Black's interactionist theory, explained at greater length in *Models and Metaphors*, gains credence (as Fogelin himself observes [*Figuratively Speaking* 105]) when applied to extended analogies in which the subject is seen through the "lens," so to speak, of the metaphorical term(s). In *The Philosophy of Rhetoric*, Richards anticipates by over forty years the now well-known position of George Lakoff and Mark Johnson, who contend in *Metaphors We Live By* that we organize not only language but thought itself through "conceptual" metaphors of which we are typically unconscious—yet another kind of metaphor that is not necessarily representative of metaphor writ large. And finally, Davidson and Levin provide intriguing theories not of all or even most metaphors but of what Cooper, a fellow literalist, calls "maverick" metaphors—metaphors whose novelty and freshness are endlessly evocative, stirring us to contemplation of the sort provoked by unconventional works of art.

16. For a valuable discussion of the enabling function of figurative language, see Olmsted, "The Uses of Rhetoric." Olmsted counters the deconstructionist claim that "to reveal the ambiguity of a word or the figurality of a definition is to undermine it" with the view that "meanings of words, distinctions, arguments and figures are partly determinate and partly open. This partial definition facilitates thought" (2).

17. For a complex discussion of, among other things, the inescapable presence of metaphor in even the most rigorous attempts to elude it, see Derrida, "White Mythology."

18. In "Signature Event Context," Derrida calls this necessary repeatability of writing its "iterability" (315–16).

19. For all of his engagement in the quandaries of language, Italo Calvino rejects in his final book, *Six Memos for the Next Millennium*, the notion of "writing as a model for every process of reality . . . indeed the only reality we can know, indeed the only reality *tout court*. . . . No, I will not travel such roads as these, for they would carry me too far from the use of words as I understand it—that is, words as a perpetual pursuit of things, as a perpetual adjustment to their infinite variety" (26; ellipses in original).

20. For further discussion of the "play" granted by "distance," see Barbara Herrnstein Smith, *On the Margins of Discourse* (esp. chap. 5, "Licensing the Unspeakable," 107–32).

21. John Gatt-Rutter, for instance, claims that "the wealth of realistic detail which Calvino very skillfully weaves into his narratives remains merely a *spectacle*" ("Calvino Ludens," 322) and that Calvino "imprisons himself in an elegant, but essentially monodic, style" (331).

22. Instructively, Meryl Altman cites her former attraction to the metaphor of "teaching composition [as] the housework of the English department"—

until she recalled that there are "people who actually do clean the toilets in the English department," people whose working conditions tend to be forgotten in the course of their appropriation by metaphors like this one (501).

23. The texts assigned in this class were Achebe's *Things Fall Apart,* Davidson's *Tracks,* Brown's *Rubyfruit Jungle,* Baldwin's "Stranger in the Village," Gordimer's "Town and Country Lovers," Mukherjee's "Jasmine," and Leavitt's "Territory." The film was Nair's *Mississippi Masala.*

24. The importance of moving from the issue of what *metaphors* do as figures to the issues of what *readers* do with metaphors accounts for my resistance to what is otherwise a very elegant approach to metaphor and figurative language—namely, the approach taken by Paul de Man in *Allegories of Reading.* In his chapter on metaphor, de Man contends: "Metaphor is error because it believes or feigns to believe in its own referential meaning. . . . Metaphor overlooks the fictional, textual element in the nature of the entity it connotes" (151). Initially, my own theory of metaphor can be said to draw upon such a view, for I claim that metaphor necessarily commits the "error" of the fictional equivalence it posits. But unlike de Man, I would argue that it is also the *reader,* not just the metaphor, that "believes or feigns to believe" the equivalence, and it is therefore possible for the reader to resist the fiction composed by the metaphor in favor of alternative metaphoric fictions.

25. For a discussion of the dialogic quality of participation and spectatorship as they pertain to student writing, see Summerfield and Summerfield, *Texts and Contexts* (123–84).

26. For further discussion of Bakhtin's different uses of dialogue, see Morson, "Dialogue, Monologue, and the Social."

Chapter 4. "Other Formulations"

1. See, for example, Salvatori, "Italo Calvino's *If on a Winter's Night a Traveler.*"

2. Note, for instance, Calvino's remarks in an interview with Francine du Plessix Gray shortly after the publication of *If on a Winter's Night:*

> And of course there is always something sadistic in the relationship between writer and reader. In this new novel . . . I may be a more sadistic lover than ever. I constantly play cat and mouse with the reader, letting the reader briefly enjoy the illusion that he's free for a little while, that he's in control. And then I quickly take the rug out from under him; he realizes with a shock that he's *not* in control, that it is always I, Calvino, who is in total control of the situation." ("Visiting Italo Calvino" 23)

While these comments do not directly bear on the subject of fragmentation, they illustrate Calvino's sense that *If on a Winter's Night* serves as an illustration of authorial power and control. (Of course, it might also be said that here Calvino himself "enjoy[s] the illusion . . . that he's in control," ignoring the ways in which, from the moment of publication, his book is taken over by its readers.)

3. Admonitions to avoid fragmentary prose remain ever-present in mainstream composition textbooks. See, for example, Kennedy, Kennedy, and Holladay, *The Bedford Guide for College Writers*, H-88–93 (on sentence fragments) and 380–84 (on "achieving coherence").

4. Another feature of the teacher's relationship to student texts that should be mentioned here is the way in which these texts are read within institutional contexts primarily for the purpose of locating their flaws. Thus, as C. H. Knoblauch and Lil Brannon report in *Rhetorical Traditions and the Teaching of Writing*, when texts by a writer like D. H. Lawrence are distributed to teachers as if they were texts written by students, teachers "will tend without hesitation to cite any idiosyncrasy of form, technique, idea or style, any authorial choice that challenges their personal preferences as an 'error'" (161). Student writing, then, is positioned in such a way that the very strategies that might be advantageous to other texts are perceived as erroneous when employed by students.

5. In one of his interviews, Barthes offers succinct definitions of the terms *writer* and *author:* "The writer is someone who thinks that language is a pure instrument of thought, who sees only a tool in language. For the author, on the contrary, language is a dialectical space where things are made and unmade, where the author's own subjectivity is immersed and dissolved" (*Grain* 105). A little later in the interview, Barthes adds, "I would like to be an author" (105). For further discussion of these terms, see "Authors and Writers" in Barthes's *Critical Essays* (143–50).

6. See, for example, Barthes, *Roland Barthes:* "Transposed to the level of discourse, even a just victory becomes a bad value of language, an *Arrogance:* the word, encountered in Bataille, who somewhere mentions the arrogance of science, has been extended to all triumphant discourse. Hence I suffer three arrogances: that of Science, that of the *Doxa,* that of the Militant" (47).

7. For an important essay that closely considers the language of reader-text relations (and speaker-hearer relations as well), see Reddy, "The Conduit Metaphor." Reddy observes that the English language "has a preferred framework for conceptualizing communication" (165)—a framework in which language moves through a conduit from the producer to the recipient. As Reddy suggests, this frame is so ubiquitous and habitual that it becomes all but impossible to discuss communication without recourse to it; and I would add that the

prevalence of the conduit metaphor makes discussions of alternative rhetorics such as fragmentation extremely difficult to describe.

8. Both feminist and psychoanalytic criticism would surely have something to say about the "staff" as Barthes's metaphor for the critic's means of interpretation!

9. Jonathan Culler, among others, has noticed this feature of Barthes's conception of reading: "A striking feature of Barthes's accounts of literature since *S/Z* is how easily reader and text switch places in the stories he tells: the story of the reader structuring a text flips over into a story of the text manipulating the reader" (*Roland Barthes* 118).

10. Yet Barthes also undermines this distinction between readerly and writerly texts through his own practices as a critic. In *S/Z,* for example, the story under scrutiny, Balzac's *Sarrasine,* ostensibly represents a readerly text—and yet as Terrence Hawkes has observed, "The exercise Barthes performs on Balzac's short story has the effect of turning a 'readerly' text into a 'writerly' one" (118). After all, the five codes—hermeneutic, semic, symbolic, proairetic, and referential—through which Barthes conceives the act of reading ultimately demonstrate how a particularly astute reader (in this case, Barthes himself) imaginatively creates a text of his own on the ruins of what supposedly allows only for "consumption."

For a nuanced discussion of the relationship between reader, text, and issues of coherence, see Phelps, *Composition as a Human Science,* chap. 7, "Dialectics of Coherence," 160–82. Phelps offers the valuable metaphor that "a text functions like a play script to evoke performances from its readers that are both bound and free, receptive and interpretive" (166).

11. In *The Pleasure of the Text,* for example, Barthes claims that "the reader of the text at the moment he takes his pleasure" is "someone . . . who abolishes within himself all barriers, all classes, all exclusions . . . who silently accepts every charge of illogicality, or incongruity" (3). Citing this tendency toward hyperbole, Geoffrey Strickland notes Barthes's "fondness for the legislative 'all' or 'never'" and "his ostensible precision" through the use of terms like "exactly" (130–31).

12. A similar pattern can be found in Muriel Harris's "Mending the Fragmented Free Modifier," which takes an otherwise unusually tolerant attitude toward the fragment. Though Harris complicates this discussion by examining modifiers that have been separated by periods from the sentences to which they supposedly belong, she nevertheless contends that fragmented free modifiers represent language to be "mended" because of the challenge they pose to readers. Relying on Linda Flower's distinction between "Writer-Based" and "Reader-Based" prose (which in some ways is analogous to Barthes's "writerly"

and "readerly" texts—except that Flower, unlike Barthes, values the latter over the former), Harris comments: "Seen from this perspective, such fragments are but one more characteristic of Writer-Based prose which does not take the needs of the reader into consideration, and could then be dealt with when examining ways to turn Writer-Based prose into Reader-Based prose" (181). Yet it remains uncertain why so-called "Writer-Based" prose should be converted into a reader-friendly text to begin with, as if the only rhetoric that readers can appreciate is that which does all the work for them in advance.

13. For another valuable discussion of a so-called "error" in student writing that might be reconsidered from the perspective of its power in the work of experienced writers, see Schor, "Reclaiming Digression."

14. Though I find much to praise in this textbook, I believe its subtitle—*An Introduction to Literary Language*—is somewhat regrettable, for while much of the book works to eliminate the divide between composition and literature, the identification of its subject as *literary* language affirms rather than subverts the idea that English studies concerns itself with a "special" discourse, one set apart from the "ordinary."

15. Not that I wish to discount the significance of placing challenging reading material before students in introductory courses. As Mariolina Salvatori has indicated from her own experience as a teacher of writing, "the improvement in writers' ability to manipulate syntactic structures—their maturity as writers—is the result, rather than the cause, of their increased ability to engage in, and to be reflexive about, the reading of highly complex texts" ("Reading" 659).

16. In one of his interviews, Barthes notes that alphabetizing his fragments allows him "to preserve the radical discontinuity of the linguistic torment unfolding in the lover's head" and "to break up the construction of any story" (*Grain* 286).

17. Another interesting set of assignments can be found in an earlier chapter devoted to metaphor. As part of a section that examines what the authors call "surrealist metaphor"—whereby the writer "can suggest new realities by metaphorically linking unusual or incompatible things" (64)—Scholes, Comley, and Ulmer ask students to do the following exercise:

> Go back to the poem by Robert Herrick ["Delight in Disorder"]. . . . Starting with the title, make a few changes in every line so as to turn "Delight in Disorder" into a surrealist poem. Try to produce something in the spirit of Breton. Don't worry if the lines lose their rhythm or rhyme. In class, exchange poems and discuss the most interesting poems or lines with their authors. The point of this exercise is to confront the problems of interpretation and the problems of composition together. (68)

What makes this assignment unusual and potentially exciting is the way in which it displaces reverential concern for sound and sense with a more impious concern for the ways in which apparent "nonsense" can stimulate the making of meaning.

18. For an extensive discussion of the inevitable "gaps" in texts—and of the reader's constructive response to such gaps—see Wolfgang Iser, *The Act of Reading*. Iser argues that "if all linguistic acts were explicit, then the only threat to communication would be acoustic. . . . Indeed, there would never be any dyadic interaction if the speech act did not give rise to indeterminacies that needed to be resolved" (59).

19. See, for example, Mas'ud Zavarzadeh, "Theory as Resistance." Zavarzadeh constructs a simplistic binary opposition between the "familiarizing classroom" on the one hand and the "defamiliarizing classroom" on the other. For him, the "classroom of pleasure" is aligned with the former, while the latter "is the classroom that aims at making itself opaque, 'strange,' 'different' from the world outside" (41). Relying on this opposition through his essay, Zavarzadeh rather predictably regards the classroom of pleasure as an attempt to escape politics, history, and reflexive attention to its cultural context.

20. For further discussion of Barthes's contribution to the teaching of writing, see Patricia Donahue, "Teaching Common Sense" and Joseph Harris, "The Plural Text/The Plural Self."

Chapter 5. Performing Selves

1. Courses in style are almost always offered under the rubric of "advanced composition" or within the upper-division English studies curriculum. At the university where I teach, for instance, there is a course entitled "Advanced Writing: Prose Style," taken primarily by juniors and seniors who have already completed their introductory composition course and now seek to engage in supposedly more complex endeavors. For further discussion of how style might be reconceived so as to indicate its relevance to *all* composition and rhetoric, see Flannery, *The Emperor's New Clothes;* Lanham, *Literacy and the Survival of Humanism* (esp. chap. 5); Gage, "Philosophies of Style and Their Implications for Composition"; Rankin, "Revitalizing Style"; and Schuster, "Mikhail Bakhtin as Rhetorical Theorist."

2. See also Gibson's earlier and more substantial book, *Tough, Sweet, and Stuffy.*

3. For a further collection of role-play assignments, see the Summerfields's *Frames of Mind.* For a perceptive essay on the value of conceiving the struggle of discourses (and of student writers) as a drama, see Bialostosky, "Liberal Education, Writing, and the Dialogic Self."

4. Though this claim can be regarded as impressionistic, it is based on the following evidence: (1) the Summerfields are hardly ever cited in composition books and journals; (2) neither role-play nor persona form major subjects of discussion at the annual convention of the Conference on College Composition and Communication; and (3) role-play assignments have made no more than a minor appearance in recent composition or literature textbooks.

5. Even the proponents of role-play can give this impression, as I believe Walker Gibson does in *Persona* by continually referring to his writing assignments as "exercises." Recognizing the denigration implicit in this term, Wayne Booth argues that role-oriented assignments must produce "instances" of writing rather than "exercises" in writing ("LITCOMP" 61).

6. For a perceptive collection of essays that attempt to provide alternative conceptions of argument and its postmodern elements, see Baumlin and Baumlin, eds., *Ethos.*

7. In *Persona,* Walker Gibson anticipates the charge that role-play might advocate "little more than a kind of technical facility" (76–77), and he goes on to argue that role-play helps to further "self-discovery" (77). While I agree that an investigation of the self constitutes one of the benefits of role-play assignments, I don't think that this goal sufficiently responds to the questions that concern me here—questions, that is, about the ideological dimensions of writing.

8. In *Texts and Contexts,* the Summerfields provide a sequence of assignments in which students adopt the roles of the prisoner in solitary confinement and of the psychiatrist who evaluates the prisoner's mental health (208–20). In the final pages of the book, the Summerfields also include a student text in which the writer plays the role of her mother, a Holocaust survivor, recalling the day she watched a Nazi officer slowly kill a fellow prisoner (292–93)—though it is not clear from the discussion that surrounds this text just what the assignment was that provoked it.

9. A refreshing exception to the typical textbook approach to fiction can be found in Bartholomae and Petrosky, *Ways of Reading*—a collection that includes, along with its selection of essays, works of fiction by Lewis Nordan and Joyce Carol Oates, and a long poem by James Schuyler. Following the Nordan stories, Bartholomae and Petrosky invite students to write "a Nordan-like story" (468); and following the Schuyler poem, students are asked to compose "a poem of [their] own based on Schuyler's" (615).

10. For discussion of another course designed to help students work on their writing by asking them to compose prose fiction, see Charles Moran, "Teaching Writing/Teaching Literature." In this essay, Moran describes a literature course in which he gave students writing assignments structured on

predicaments similar to those faced by the novelists they read. When the course came to Willa Cather's *Death Comes to the Archbishop,* for instance, Moran asked students to describe a place and then attempt to recount its history, much as Cather does with her New Mexican landscapes (22). But what makes Moran's assignment especially interesting is that he gave it to students *before* they read Cather's book or were told anything about her. Thus, as a result of their writing assignment, students went on to read the book with a better understanding of its lack of "character" and "action": "They saw that [Cather] was writing what she herself had called *legend,* and that, as she had said, 'In this kind of writing the mood is the thing—all the little figures and stories are mere improvisations that come out of it'" (23).

11. Currie does not overlook the problematic nature of "metafiction" as a critical term. Given the wide range of methods by which texts can be said to dramatize the boundary between fiction and criticism, Currie suggests that "metafiction might be better understood not as a generic category but, in the words of Patricia Waugh, as 'a function inherent in all novels'" (5). Thus, "metafiction is less a property of the primary text than a function of reading" (5).

12. Some of the language of this assignment comes from an assignment that I had co-written with my colleague Nicholas Coles the previous year—though in that instance the assignment was part of a different sequence of readings and did not serve as the opening tale in a multichapter "book."

13. For further discussion of the problematic role given to the writing of narrative in the English studies curriculum, see Judith Summerfield, "Is There a Life in This Text" and "Principles for Propagation."

14. Each week, students were given copies of one or two of their classmates' texts—with names removed—so that by the end of the term all twenty students had had their work placed at the center of class discussion at least once. Students were also placed in small writing groups that exchanged and responded to each others' texts every week.

15. I should add to this list of problems one noted by Jean Ferguson Carr in conversation—that the female students in my class were in the position of reading a very male-dominated book in a course taught by a man who assigned them to spend the semester writing a "war story."

16. See Austin, *How to Do Things with Words,* and Searle, *Speech Acts.* As I observe in chapter 3, Mary Louise Pratt, "Linguistic Utopias," criticizes speech act theory and other discourse theories for their failure to acknowledge the conflict that often structures various contexts for speech and writing.

17. What makes Richard Rodriguez's *Hunger of Memory* so interesting—to my mind, at least—is not the fact that a Mexican-American would object to bilingual education but that his performance is both complicated and under-

cut by a "voice" he cannot seem to suppress. Rodriguez works very hard to tell a certain story—how he became an assimilated member of the middle class—but ends up revealing another story altogether—how he became a very sad and lonely man who has dearly paid the price of assimilation. Thus, simultaneously, both the Left and the Right hear exactly what they want to hear from Rodriguez, and thereby miss the poignant intricacies of his performance as a writer. For further discussion of the complications in Rodriguez's book, see Staten, "Ethnic Authenticity, Class, and Autobiography."

18. In *Fragments of Rationality,* Lester Faigley observes: "The notion of subjectivity itself . . . is far too complex to be 'read off' from texts. It is a more complex notion than that of 'roles' because it is a conglomeration of temporary positions rather than a coherent identity . . . and it resists deterministic explanations because a subject always exceeds a momentary subject position" (110).

19. See Tompkins, "Pedagogy of the Distressed." For an insightful and critical reply to Tompkins's essay, see Carroll, "A Comment on 'Pedagogy of the Distressed.'"

20. For a perceptive reading of Plato's *Phaedrus*—and of Derrida's reading of Plato—see Jasper Neel, *Plato, Derrida, and Writing.* Neel argues that while Derrida offers a corrective to Plato, Plato also offers a corrective to Derrida.

Epilogue

1. I am aware that these terms, all of which I borrow from Mikhail Bakhtin, should not be endorsed without reservation. "Carnivalesque," for instance, is particularly problematic, in part because, as many have observed, carnivals are licensed events that in some contexts may do no more than ensure that potentially serious social and political resistance is kept in check. On the other hand, as Stallybrass and White contend in *The Politics and Poetics of Transgression,* carnival may in other contexts "act as *catalyst* and *site of actual and symbolic struggle*" (14). The ambiguity of the term leads me to attach it to metaphor, which likewise offers the possibility of transgression but can also serve the interests of the status quo.

2. While my survey should be considered informal, it was nevertheless fairly extensive. With the help of Juli Parrish, a Ph.D. candidate at the University of Pittsburgh who served as my research assistant during the summer of 1997, I sought information on a wide range of colleges and universities that offer undergraduate majors in nonfictive forms of writing. In other words, I wanted to investigate how "writing"—apart from programs in "creative" writing, many of which run smoothly alongside programs in literature—has been conceived in the latest versions of the college English curriculum. Much of my informa-

tion came from the Internet, where numerous catalogue descriptions of programs and graduation requirements can be found. But I also received data from *The College Blue Book, Cass and Birnbaum's Guide to American Colleges,* the *Chronicle Four-Year College Databook,* and several program directors who were kind enough to respond to my inquiries. Additionally, I learned much from an essay by Donald Stewart entitled "What Is an English Major, and What Should It Be?," which reported on a more formal survey conducted in 1987. Though I don't find Stewart's suggestions for change as substantial as I would prefer, my survey echoes his to the extent that both reveal the curricular separation of composition, literature, and creative writing in English departments across the country.

3. An interesting exception to this curricular rule separating the study of writing from the study of literature turned up in my survey: the degree in "Writing and Literature" at Southampton College of Long Island University. According to Southampton's site on the World Wide Web, the requirements for this degree include three core courses (two of which are in creative writing); four courses in various forms of professional writing (journalism, script writing, research writing, technical writing, and so on); and seven courses in literature. My point is that such a degree, unlike most others, assumes that the study of English *necessarily,* not optionally, includes both writing and literature.

4. Master's degree candidates in the English department at the University of Pittsburgh are required to complete, in lieu of an M.A. examination, four core courses in English—three of which represent major programs in the department ("Institutions of Literature"—the literature program; "Seminar in Rhetoric and Literacy"—the composition program; and "Film History/Theory" —the film studies program) and one of which ("Practices and Texts") represents no one program in particular. As I supported this move from a written examination to a core curriculum, my comments are not meant to overlook its benefits. But I think it evident that, in the absence of structural conditions that ensure the integration of these courses, their contents are bound to move, whether slowly or quickly, toward the isolated interests of the different programs that support them.

5. See Graff, *Beyond the Culture Wars.* In questioning the value of "conflict" for a revised curriculum, I echo the concerns of numerous others. See, for instance, Foley, "What's at Stake in the Culture Wars?" Foley notes Graff's "tendency to idealize the university as the site for negotiations" (473), and she argues that his vision of productive conflict within the university seems "vastly to underestimate the extent to which academics working in capitalist universities are less disinterested seekers of the truth than petty bourgeois entrepreneurs who gain status, honoraria, book contracts, and salary increments by

investing their modest assets in a portfolio—sometimes diverse, sometimes concentrated—of critical enterprises. While their ideas take on exchange value in the intellectual marketplace, this marketplace fosters not so much debate as territoriality and profiteering" (473).

6. For a classic discussion of the ways in which metaphor lies at the roots of myth, see Cassirer, *Language and Myth* (esp. chap. 6, "The Power of Metaphor," 83–99).

7. See Graff and Looby, "Gender and the Politics of Conflict-Pedagogy." Responding to Looby's concern that "a conflictual or agonistic model will inadvertently reinforce some old gendered hierarchies" (447), Graff replies: "what is the alternative? . . . does *avoiding* public discussion of our differences somehow discourage the emergence of crudely binary and polarized positions?" (447). Here, as elsewhere, Graff presents the situation as if there were only two choices for the curriculum—teaching the conflicts or keeping things as they are.

8. Obviously, a crucial text on the ways in which language instruction can empower students to produce and take responsibility for knowledge is Freire, *Pedagogy of the Oppressed*. But see also Bartholomae, "Writing Assignments": "There is . . . a way of studying psychology by learning to report on textbook accounts or classroom lectures on the works of psychologists. But there is also a way of learning psychology by learning to write and, thereby, learning to compose the world as a psychologist. In his four years of college education, a student gets plenty of the former but precious little of the latter. He writes many reports but carries out few projects" (306).

9. See Graff, *Beyond the Culture Wars:* "To combat the deadly syndrome in which teachers talk only to other teachers and students remain passive spectators, students could be assigned various roles in such a [transcourse] conference, ranging from writing papers about it afterward (it becomes easier to write about ideas when one is describing an actual event rather than abstractions in a void) to giving some of the papers and responses in it to eventually organizing and running the event themselves" (190). While I appreciate Graff's interest in giving students more active roles in his multicourse fora, I find his conception of student writing—which consists of "writing about ideas"— somewhat desultory when compared with the kinds of assignments that seek engagement with a variety of discursive forms.

10. As the widespread popularity of "peer response" in composition courses suggests, student texts are generally presented for the purpose of evaluating the extent of their "success" in the eyes of individual readers—not for purpose of exploring the issues of *language* they address or evade. There are, however, any number of exceptions to this rule: see, for example, Coles, *The Plural I.* See also Donahue and Quandahl, *Reclaiming Pedagogy.*

11. I am grateful to Evelyn Tribble of Temple University for reminding me of the productive aspects of specialization when I presented a paper there in April 1998.

12. For Pattison's own suggestions for the teaching of English, see *On Literacy* (165–69). In short, Pattison argues for three changes: "First, standard English should be taught as a practical tool of social advantage, never as a moral or aesthetic norm. . . . Second, standard English should be treated as a second language, not as the correct form of the language the student already speaks and writes. . . . Third, students should be encouraged to think, speak, and write according to their own conceptions of literacy" (168). If this sounds like a rather permissive vision of language instruction, consider that Pattison goes on to suggest that all students be taught Greek and Latin so that they might read ancient writers in their original languages. Indeed, his argument is that "the liberation of the vernacular would also be the liberation of the classics, as it was in the Renaissance" (211).

WORKS CITED

Achebe, Chinua. *Things Fall Apart.* 1959. New York: Ballantine, 1983.

Altman, Meryl. "How Not to Do Things with Metaphors We Live By." *College English* 52 (1990): 495–507.

Aristotle. *Poetics.* Trans. Ingram Bywater. New York: Modern Library, 1954.

———. *Rhetoric.* Trans. W. Rhys Roberts. New York: Modern Library, 1954.

Atkins, G. Douglas, and Michael L. Johnson, eds. *Writing and Reading Differently: Deconstruction and the Teaching of Composition and Literature.* Lawrence: University of Kansas Press, 1985.

Austin, J. L. *How to Do Things with Words.* 2nd ed. Cambridge, Mass.: Harvard University Press, 1975.

Axelrod, Rise B., and Charles R. Cooper. *The St. Martin's Guide to Writing.* 5th ed. New York: St. Martin's Press, 1997.

Bain, Alexander. *English Composition and Rhetoric: A Manual.* 1866. American ed., revised. New York: A. Appleton, 1873.

Bakhtin, Mikhail M. "Discourse in the Novel." In *The Dialogic Imagination,* trans. Caryl Emerson and Michael Holquist, 259–422. Austin: University of Texas Press, 1981.

Baldwin, Charles Sears. *Writing and Speaking: A Text-Book of Rhetoric.* New York: Longmans, Green, 1909.

Baldwin, James. "Stranger in the Village." *Notes of a Native Son,* 159–75. Boston: Beacon Press, 1955.

Barthes, Roland. *Critical Essays.* Trans. Richard Howard. Evanston: Northwestern University Press, 1972.

———. *Criticism and Truth.* Trans. Katherine Pilcher Keuneman. Minneapolis: University of Minnesota Press, 1987.

———. *Empire of Signs.* Trans. Richard Howard. New York: Hill and Wang, 1982.

———. *The Grain of the Voice.* Trans. Linda Coverdale. New York: Farrar, Straus and Giroux, 1985.

———. *A Lover's Discourse.* Trans. Richard Howard. New York: Hill and Wang, 1978.

————. "On Reading." *The Rustle of Language*. Trans. Richard Howard. Berkeley: University of California Press, 1989.

————. *The Pleasure of the Text*. Trans. Richard Miller. New York: Hill and Wang, 1975.

————. *Roland Barthes*. Trans. Richard Howard. New York: Noonday Press, 1977.

————. *S/Z*. Trans. Richard Miller. New York: Noonday Press, 1974.

Bartholomae, David. "Freshman English, Composition, and CCCC." *College Composition and Communication* 40 (1989): 38–50.

————. "What Is Composition and (If You Know What That Is) Why Do We Teach It?" In *Composition in the Twenty-First Century: Crisis and Change,* ed. Lynn Z. Bloom, Donald A. Daiker, and Edward M. White, 11–28. Carbondale, Ill.: Southern Illinois University Press, 1996.

————. "Writing Assignments: Where Writing Begins." In *Forum: Essays on Theory and Practice in the Teaching of Writing,* ed. Patricia L. Stock. Upper Montclair, N.J.: Boynton/Cook, 1983.

Bartholomae, David, and Anthony Petrosky. *Facts, Artifacts, and Counterfacts: Theory and Method for a Reading and Writing Course*. Portsmouth, N.H.: Boynton/Cook, 1986.

————. *Ways of Reading: An Anthology for Writers*. 4th ed. Boston: Bedford, 1996.

Barzun, Jacques. *Simple and Direct: A Rhetoric for Writers*. New York: Harper and Row, 1975.

Baumlin, James S., and Tita French Baumlin, eds. *Ethos: New Essays in Rhetorical and Critical Theory*. Dallas: Southern Methodist University Press, 1994.

Beacham, Walton. "Robert Frost." In *Critical Survey of Poetry: English Language Series,* vol. 3, ed. Frank N. Magill, 1171–82. Pasadena, Calif.: Salem Press, 1992.

Belanoff, Pat, Betsy Rorschach, Mia Oberlink. *The Right Handbook: Grammar and Usage in Context*. 2nd ed. Portsmouth, N.H.: Boynton/Cook, 1992.

Belsey, Catherine. *Critical Practice*. London: Methuen, 1980.

Berlin, James A. *Rhetoric and Reality: Writing Instruction in American Colleges, 1900–1985*. Carbondale, Ill.: Southern Illinois University Press, 1987.

Berthoff, Ann, ed. *Reclaiming the Imagination: Philosophical Perspectives for Writers and Teachers of Writing*. Upper Montclair, N.J.: Boynton/Cook, 1984.

Bialostosky, Don H. "Liberal Education, Writing, and the Dialogic Self." In

Contending with Words: Composition and Rhetoric in a Postmodern Age, ed. Patricia Harkin and John Schilb, 11–22. New York: Modern Language Association, 1991.

Bizzell, Patricia. "On the Possibility of a Unified Theory of Composition and Literature." *Rhetoric Review* 4 (1986): 174–79.

Black, Max. "How Metaphors Work: A Reply to Donald Davidson." In *On Metaphor,* ed. Sheldon Sacks, 181–92. Chicago: University of Chicago Press, 1979.

————. "Metaphor." *Proceedings of the Aristotelian Society* 55 (1954–55): 273–94.

————. *Models and Metaphors.* Ithaca, N.Y.: Cornell University Press, 1962.

Blair, Hugh. *Lectures on Rhetoric and Belles Lettres,* ed. Harold F. Harding. 1783; Carbondale, Ill.: Southern Illinois University Press, 1965.

Bloom, Harold. *Wallace Stevens: The Poems of Our Climate.* Ithaca, N.Y.: Cornell University Press, 1976.

Booth, Wayne. "'LITCOMP': Some Rhetoric Addressed to Cryptorhetoricians about a Rhetorical Solution to a Rhetorical Problem." In *Composition and Literature: Bridging the Gap,* ed. Winifred Bryan Horner, 57–80. Chicago: University of Chicago Press, 1983.

————. *The Rhetoric of Fiction.* Chicago: University of Chicago Press, 1961.

Boyd, James R. *Elements of Rhetoric and Literary Criticism.* 8th ed. New York: Harper, 1844.

Bradford, Curtis, and Hazel Moritz. *The Communication of Ideas.* Boston: D. C. Heath, 1951.

Brandt, Deborah. *Literacy as Involvement: The Acts of Writers, Readers, and Texts.* Carbondale, Ill.: Southern Illinois University Press, 1990.

Brooks, Cleanth, and Robert Penn Warren. *Modern Rhetoric.* 2nd ed. New York: Harcourt Brace, 1958.

————. *Understanding Poetry.* 3rd ed. New York: Holt, Rinehart and Winston, 1960.

————. *Understanding Poetry.* 4th ed. Fort Worth, Tex.: Harcourt Brace Jovanovich, 1976.

Brower, Ruben A. *The Poetry of Robert Frost: Constellations of Intention.* New York: Oxford University Press, 1963.

Brown, Andrew. *Roland Barthes: The Figures of Writing.* Oxford: Clarendon Press, 1992.

Brown, Rita Mae. *Rubyfruit Jungle.* 1973. New York: Bantam, 1977.

Brown, Stuart C., Paul R. Meyer, and Theresa Enos. "Doctoral Programs in

Rhetoric and Composition: A Catalogue of the Profession." *Rhetoric Review* 12 (1994): 240–389.

Bump, Jerome. "Metaphor, Creativity, and Technical Writing." *College Composition and Communication* 36 (1985): 444–53.

Burke, Kenneth. *Permanence and Change*. New York: New Republic, 1935.

———. *A Rhetoric of Motives*. New York: Prentice-Hall, 1952.

Calvino, Italo. *Cosmicomics*. Trans. William Weaver. San Diego: Harcourt Brace Jovanovich, 1968.

———. *If on a Winter's Night a Traveler*. Trans. William Weaver. San Diego: Harcourt Brace Jovanovich, 1981.

———. *Six Memos for the Next Millennium*. Trans. Patrick Creagh. Cambridge: Harvard University Press, 1988.

Cambell, George. *The Philosophy of Rhetoric*. 1776. London: William Tegg, 1850.

Campbell, Jo Ann, ed. *Toward a Feminist Rhetoric: The Writing of Gertrude Buck*. Pittsburgh: University of Pittsburgh Press, 1996.

Canby, Henry S., and John B. Opdycke. *The Elements of Composition*. 1913. Rev. ed. New York: Macmillan, 1927.

Carroll, Michael. "A Comment on 'Pedagogy of the Distressed.'" *College English* 53 (1991): 599–601.

Cass, Melissa, and Julia Cass-Liepmann, eds. *Cass and Birnbaum's Guide to American Colleges*. 16th ed. New York: Harper Perennial, 1994.

Cassirer, Ernst. *Language and Myth*. Trans. Susan K. Langer. New York: Dover, 1946.

Cather, Willa. *Death Comes for the Archbishop*. 1926. Boston: Houghton Mifflin, 1938.

Chronicle Four-Year College Databook (for 1993–94 School Year). Moravia, N.Y.: Chronicle Guidance Publications, 1993.

Cleaver, Eldridge. *Soul on Ice*. New York: McGraw-Hill, 1968.

Cohen, Ted. "Metaphor and the Cultivation of Intimacy." In *On Metaphor*, ed. Sheldon Sacks, 1–10. Chicago: University of Chicago Press, 1979.

The College Blue Book: Degrees Offered by College and Subject. 24th ed. New York: Macmillan, 1993.

Coles, William E., Jr. "The Literacy Crisis: A Challenge How?" In *Forum: Essays on Theory and Practice in the Teaching of Writing*, ed. Patricia L. Stock, 15–23. Upper Montclair, N.J.: Boynton/Cook, 1983.

———. *The Plural I—and After*. Portsmouth, N.H.: Boynton/Cook, 1988.

Connors, Robert J. *Composition-Rhetoric: Backgrounds, Theory, and Pedagogy*. Pittsburgh: University of Pittsburgh Press, 1997.

Cooper, David. *Metaphor*. Oxford: Basil Blackwell, 1986.

Corbett, Edward P. J. *Classical Rhetoric for the Modern Student*. 3rd ed. New York: Oxford University Press, 1990.

Couser, G. Thomas. "Seeing Through Metaphor: Teaching Figurative Literacy." *Rhetoric Society Quarterly* 19 (1989): 143–53.

Culler, Jonathan. "Imagining Changes." In *The Future of Doctoral Studies in English,* ed. Andrea Lunsford, Helene Moglen, and James F. Slevin, 79–83. New York: Modern Language Association, 1989.

———. *Roland Barthes*. New York: Oxford University Press, 1983.

Currie, Mark, ed. *Metafiction*. London: Longman, 1995.

Davidson, Donald. "What Metaphors Mean." In *On Metaphor,* ed. Sheldon Sacks, 29–45. Chicago: University of Chicago Press, 1979.

Davidson, Robyn. *Tracks*. New York: Pantheon, 1980.

de Man, Paul. *Allegories of Reading*. New Haven: Yale University Press, 1979.

———. "The Epistemology of Metaphor." In *On Metaphor,* ed. Sheldon Sacks, 11–28. Chicago: University of Chicago Press, 1979.

Derrida, Jacques. *Of Grammatology*. Trans. Gayatri Chakravorty Spivak. Baltimore: Johns Hopkins University Press, 1976.

———. "Signaure Event Context." In *Margins of Philosophy,* trans. Alan Bass, 307–30. Chicago: University of Chicago Press, 1982.

———. "White Mythology: Metaphor in the Text of Philosophy." In *Margins of Philosophy,* trans. Alan Bass, 207–71. Chicago: University of Chicago Press, 1982.

Donahue, Patricia. "Teaching Common Sense: Barthes and the Rhetoric of Culture." In *Reclaiming Pedagogy: The Rhetoric of the Classroom,* ed. Patricia Donahue and Ellen Quandahl, eds., 72–82. Carbondale, Ill.: Southern Illinois University Press, 1989.

Donahue, Patricia, and Ellen Quandahl, eds. *Reclaiming Pedagogy: The Rhetoric of the Classroom*. Carbondale, Ill.: Southern Illinois University Press, 1989.

Donne, John. "A Valediction: Forbidding Mourning." In *The Complete Poetry of John Donne,* ed. John T. Shawcross, 87–88. Garden City, N.J.: Doubleday, 1967.

Donoghue, Dennis. *Ferocious Alphabets*. New York: Columbia University Press, 1984.

Doreski, William. "Meta-Meditation in Robert Frost's 'The Wood-Pile,' 'After Apple-Picking,' and 'Directive.'" *ARIEL: A Review of International English Literature* 23 (1992): 35–49.

Eagleton, Terry. *Literary Theory: An Introduction*. Minneapolis: University of Minnesota Press, 1983.

Faigley, Lester. *Fragments of Rationality: Postmodernity and the Subject of Composition*. Pittsburgh: University of Pittsburgh Press, 1992.

Flannery, Kathryn T. *The Emperor's New Clothes: Literature, Literacy, and the Ideology of Style*. Pittsburgh: University of Pittsburgh Press, 1995.

Fleissner, Robert F. *Frost's Road Taken*. New York: Peter Lang, 1996.

Flesch, Rudolph. *The Art of Plain Talk*. New York: Harper, 1946.

Fogelin, Robert J. *Figuratively Speaking*. New Haven: Yale University Press, 1988.

Foley, Barbara. "What's at Stake in the Culture Wars." *The New England Quarterly* 68 (1995): 458–79.

Fowler, H. Ramsey, and Jane E. Aaron. *The Little, Brown Handbook*. 7th ed. New York: Longman, 1998.

Freire, Paulo. *Pedagogy of the Oppressed*. New York: Herder and Herder, 1970.

Frost, Robert. "After Apple-Picking." *Collected Poems, Prose, and Plays*. New York: Library of America, 1995.

———. "Education by Poetry: A Meditative Monologue." *Collected Poems, Prose, and Plays*. New York: Library of America, 1995.

Frye, Northrop. *Anatomy of Criticism*. Princeton: Princeton University Press, 1957.

Gage, John T. "Philosophies of Style and Their Implications for Composition." *College English* 41 (1980): 615–22.

Gamer, Michael. "Fictionalizing the Disciplines: Literature and the Boundaries of Knowledge." *College English* 57 (1995): 281–86.

Gatt-Rutter, John. "Calvino Ludens: Literary Play and Its Political Implications." *Journal of European Studies* 5 (1975): 319–40.

Genung, John F. *The Practical Elements of Rhetoric*. 1886. Boston: Ginn, 1894.

Gibson, Walker. *Persona: A Style Study for Readers and Writers*. New York: Random House, 1969.

———. *Tough, Sweet, and Stuffy: An Essay on Modern American Prose Styles*. Bloomington: Indiana University Press, 1966.

Goffman, Erving. *The Presentation of Self in Everyday Life*. Garden City, N.J.: Doubleday, 1959.

Gordimer, Nadine. "Town and Country Lovers." *A Soldier's Embrace*, 73–93. London: Jonathan Cape, 1980.

Graff, Gerald. *Beyond the Culture Wars: How Teaching the Conflicts Can Revitalize American Education*. New York: Norton, 1992.

———. "Other Voices, Other Rooms: Organizing and Teaching the Humanities Conflict." *New Literary History* 21(1990): 817–39.

Graff, Gerald, and Christopher Looby. "Gender and the Politics of Conflict-Pedagogy: A Dialogue." *American Literary History* 6 (1994): 434–52.

Gray, Francine du Plessix. "Visiting Italo Calvino." *New York Times Book Review* 21 June, 1981: 1, 23.

Grice, H. P. "Logic and Conversation." In *Syntax and Semantics*. Vol. 3, *Speech Acts*, ed. Peter Cole and Jerry L. Morgan, 41–58. New York: Academic Press, 1975.

Guth, Hans P. *Words and Ideas*. 3rd ed. Belmont, Calif.: Wadsworth, 1969.

Hall, Dorothy Judd. *Robert Frost: Contours of Belief*. Athens, Ohio: Ohio University Press, 1984.

Harper, Mary J. *Practical Composition*. New York: Charles Scribner, 1870.

Harris, Joseph. "The Plural Text/The Plural Self: Roland Barthes and William Coles," *College English* 49 (1987): 158–70.

Harris, Muriel. "Mending the Fragmented Free Modifier." *College Composition and Communication* 32 (1981): 175–82.

Hart, John S. *A Manual of Composition and Rhetoric*. 1870. Philadelphia: Eldredge and Brother, 1871.

Hausman, Carl R. *Metaphor and Art: Interactionism and Reference in the Verbal and Nonverbal Arts*. Cambridge: Cambridge University Press, 1989.

Hawkes, Terrence. *Structuralism and Semiotics*. Berkeley: University of California Press, 1977.

Heath, Shirley Brice. *Ways with Words: Language, Life and Work in Communities and Classrooms*. Cambridge: Cambridge University Press, 1983.

Hemingway, Ernest. "Hills Like White Elephants." *The Short Stories of Ernest Hemingway*, 273–78. New York: Simon and Schuster, 1995.

Hepburn, A. D. *Manual of English Rhetoric*. Cincinnati: Van Antwerp, Brace, 1875.

Hill, Adams S. *Beginnings of Rhetoric and Composition*. New York: American Book Company, 1902.

Hill, David J. *The Science of Rhetoric: An Introduction to the Laws of Effective Discourse*. 1877. New York: Sheldon, 1883.

Hirschkop, Ken. "A Response to the Forum on Mikhail Bakhtin." *Critical Inquiry* 11 (1985): 672–78.

Hjortshoj, Keith. "The Marginality of the Left-Hand Castes (A Parable for Writing Teachers)." *College Composition and Communication* 46 (1995): 491–505.

Horner, Winifred Bryan. *Composition and Literature: Bridging the Gap*. Chicago: University of Chicago Press, 1983.

Huntington, Tuley Francis. *Elements of English Composition*. New York: Macmillan, 1905.

Iser, Wolfgang. *The Act of Reading: A Theory of Aesthetic Response*. Baltimore: Johns Hopkins University Press, 1978.

Jamieson, Alexander. *A Grammar of Rhetoric and Polite Literature*. New Haven, Conn.: A. L. Malthy, 1831.

Johnson, Mark. "Metaphor in the Philosophical Tradition." In *Philosophical Perspectives on Metaphor*, ed. Mark Johnson, 3–47. Minneapolis: University of Minnesota Press, 1981.

Johnson, Nan. "Rhetoric and Literature: Politics, Theory, and the Future of English Studies." *ADE Bulletin* 77 (1984): 22–25.

Johnson, Samuel. *Lives of the English Poets,* ed. George Birkneck Hill. 1779. New York: Octagon, 1967.

Junker, Clara. "Writing (with) Cixous." *College English* 50 (1988): 424–36.

Kameen, Paul. "Metaphor and the Order of Things." In *Audits of Meaning: A Festschrift in Honor of Ann E. Berthoff,* ed. Louise Smith, 125–37. Portsmouth, N.H.: Boynton/Cook, 1988.

Kane, Thomas S. *The Oxford Guide to Writing*. New York: Oxford University Press, 1983.

Kavana, Rose M., and Arthur Beatty. *Composition and Rhetoric Based on Literary Models*. Chicago: Rand, McNally, 1902.

Keith, Philip M. "How to Write Like Gertrude Stein." In *Audits of Meaning: A Festschrift in Honor of Ann E. Berthoff,* ed. Louise Smith, 229–37. Portsmouth, N.H.: Boynton/Cook, 1986.

Kellogg, Brainerd. *A Text-Book on Rhetoric*. New York: Clark and Maynard, 1880.

Kennedy, X. J., Dorothy M. Kennedy, and Sylvia A. Holladay. *The Bedford Guide for College Writers*. 4th ed. Boston: Bedford, 1996.

Kerl, Simon. *Elements of Composition and Rhetoric*. New York: Ivison, Blakeman, Taylor, 1869.

Kingston, Maxine Hong. "No Name Woman." *The Woman Warrior: Memoirs of a Girlhood Among Ghosts,* 1–16. New York: Vintage, 1976.

Kirszner, Laurie G., and Stephen R. Mandell. *The Holt Handbook*. 3rd ed. Fort Worth, Tex.: Harcourt Brace Jovanovich, 1992.

Kitzhaber, Albert R. *Rhetoric in American Colleges, 1850–1900*. Dallas: Southern Methodist University Press, 1990.

Kline, Charles R. Jr., and W. Dean Memering. "Formal Fragments: The English Minor Sentence." *Research in the Teaching of English* 11 (1977): 97–110.

Knoblauch, C. H., and Lil Brannon. *Rhetorical Traditions and the Teaching of Writing*. Upper Montclair, N.J.: Boynton/Cook, 1984.

Krupa, Gene. "Invention and Metaphor." *Journal of Advanced Composition* 3 (1982): 79–83.

Lakoff, George, and Mark Johnson. *Metaphors We Live By*. Chicago: University of Chicago Press, 1980.

Lanham, Richard. *Literacy and the Survival of Humanism*. New Haven: Yale University Press, 1983.

———. *Style: An Anti-Textbook*. New Haven: Yale University Press, 1974.

Lavers, Annette. *Roland Barthes: Structuralism and After*. Cambridge, Mass.: Harvard University Press, 1982.

Lawrence, Jeremy. *Mix Me a Metaphor*. London: Gentry Books, 1972.

Leavitt, David. "Territory." *Family Dancing*, 3–27. New York: Knopf, 1984.

Lentricchia, Frank. *After the New Criticism*. Chicago: University of Chicago Press, 1980.

———. "Last Will and Testament of an Ex-Literary Critic." *Lingua Franca* (Sept.–Oct. 1996): 59–67.

Levin, Samuel R. "Language, Concepts, and Worlds: Three Domains of Metaphor." In *Metaphor and Thought,* ed. Andrew Ortony, 112–23. 2nd ed. Cambridge: Cambridge University Press, 1993.

———. *Metaphoric Worlds*. New Haven: Yale University Press, 1988.

Lindemann, Erika. "Three Views of English 101." *College English* 57 (1995): 287–302.

———. "Freshman Composition: No Place for Literature." *College English* 55 (1993): 311–16.

Lord, David N. *The Characteristics and Laws of Figurative Language*. 1854. New York: Franklin Knight, 1857.

Lunsford, Andrea, and Robert Connors. *The St. Martin's Handbook*. 3rd ed. New York: St. Martin's Press, 1995.

Lunsford, Andrea A., and Lisa Ede. "Representing Audience: 'Successful' Discourse and Disciplinary Critique." *College Composition and Communication* 47 (1996): 167–79.

Mailloux, Steven. *Rhetorical Power*. Ithaca, N.Y.: Cornell University Press, 1989.

Marcus, Mordecai. *The Poems of Robert Frost: An Explication*. Boston: G. K. Hall, 1991.

Márquez, Gabriel García. *Love in the Time of Cholera*. Trans. Edith Grossman. New York: Penguin, 1988.

McCrimmon, James M., with Susan Miller and Webb Salmon. *Writing with a Purpose*. 1950. 7th ed. Boston: Houghton Mifflin, 1980.

McLaughlin, Thomas. "Figurative Language." In *Critical Terms for Literary Study,* ed. Frank Lentricchia and Thomas McLaughlin, 80–90. Chicago: University of Chicago Press, 1990.

McQuade, Donald. "Metaphor, Thinking, and the Composing Process." In *The Writer's Mind: Writing as a Mode of Thinking,* ed. Janice N. Hays, Phyllis A. Roth, Jon R. Ramsey, and Robert D. Foulke, 221–30. Urbana, Ill.: NCTE, 1983.

Meyers, Jeffrey. *Robert Frost: A Biography*. Boston: Houghton Mifflin, 1996.

Miller, Arthur. *Death of a Salesman*. New York: Penguin, 1949.

Miller, J. Hillis. "Composition and Decomposition." In *Composition and Literature: Bridging the Gap,* ed. Winifred Bryan Horner, 38–56. Chicago: University of Chicago Press, 1983.

———. "The Two Rhetorics: George Eliot's Bestiary." In *Writing and Reading Differently: Deconstruction and the Teaching of Composition and Literature,* G. Douglas Atkins and Michael L. Johnson, eds., 101–14. Lawrence, Kans.: University of Kansas Press, 1985.

Miller, Susan. *Rescuing the Subject: A Critical Introduction to Rhetoric and the Writer*. Carbondale, Ill.: Southern Illinois University Press, 1989.

———. *Textual Carnivals: The Politics of Composition*. Carbondale, Ill.: Southern Illinois University Press, 1991.

Moran, Charles. "Teaching Writing / Teaching Literature." *College Composition and Communication* 32 (1981): 21–29.

Moriarty, Michael. *Roland Barthes*. Stanford, Calif.: Stanford University Press, 1991.

Morson, Gary Saul. "Dialogue, Monologue, and the Social: A Reply to Ken Hirschkop." *Critical Inquiry* 11 (1985): 679–86.

Mukherjee, Bharati. "Jasmine." *The Middleman and Other Stories,* 123–35. New York: Ballantine, 1988.

Neel, Jasper. *Plato, Derrida, and Writing*. Carbondale, Ill.: Southern Illinois University Press, 1988.

Newcomer, Alphonso G., and Samuel S. Seward Jr. *Rhetoric in Practice*. 1905. 2nd ed. New York: Henry Holt, 1908.

Newman, Samuel P. *A Practical System of Rhetoric*. Portland, Maine: William Hyde, 1827.

Nietzsche, Friedrich. "On Truth and Falsity in Their Extramoral Sense." In *Essays on Metaphor,* ed. Warren Shibles, 1–13. Whitewater, Wis.: Language Press, 1972.

O'Brien, Tim. *The Things They Carried*. New York: Penguin, 1990.

Ohmann, Richard. "Literacy, Technology, and Monopoly Capital." *Politics of Letters*, 215–29. Middleton, Conn.: Wesleyan University Press, 1987.

Olmsted, Wendy Raudenbush. "The Uses of Rhetoric: Indeterminacy in Legal Reasoning, Practical Thinking and the Interpretation of Literary Figures." *Philosophy and Rhetoric* 24 (1991): 1–24.

Ong, Walter. "The Writer's Audience Is Always a Fiction." *PMLA* 90 (1975): 9–21.

Ortony, Andrew, ed. *Metaphor and Thought*. 2nd ed. Cambridge: Cambridge University Press, 1993.

Orwell, George. "Shooting an Elephant." *Shooting an Elephant and Other Essays*, 3–12. New York: Harcourt, Brace, 1950.

Oster, Judith. *Toward Robert Frost: The Reader and the Poet*. Athens, Ga.: University of Georgia Press, 1991.

Ozick, Cynthia. *Metaphor and Memory*. New York: Knopf, 1989.

Park, Douglas. "Analyzing Audiences." *College Composition and Communication* 37 (1986): 478–88.

Pattison, Robert. *On Literacy: The Politics of the Word from Homer to the Age of Rock*. New York: Oxford University Press, 1982.

Pavel, Thomas G. *Fictional Worlds*. Cambridge, Mass.: Harvard University Press, 1986.

Perrine, Laurence. "Four Forms of Metaphor." *College English* 33 (1971): 125–38.

Peterson, Jane. "Through the Looking-Glass: A Response." *College English* 57 (1995): 310–18.

Peterson, Linda. "Repetition and Metaphor in the Early Stages of Composing." *College Composition and Communication* 36 (1985): 429–43.

Phelps, Louise Wetherbee. *Composition as a Human Science: Contributions to the Self-Understanding of a Discipline*. New York: Oxford University Press, 1988.

Pickens, James D., Marilyn R. Pollio, and Howard R. Pollio. "A Developmental Analysis of Metaphoric Competence and Reading." In *The Ubiquity of Metaphor*, ed. Wolf Paprotte and Rene Dirven, 481–522. Amsterdam: J. Benjamins, 1985.

Plato. *Phaedrus*. Trans. Reginald Hackforth. Indianapolis: Bobbs-Merrill, 1952.

Poirier, Richard. *The Performing Self*. New Brunswick, N.J.: Rutgers University Press, 1992.

———. *Poetry and Pragmatism*. Cambridge, Mass.: Harvard University Press, 1992.

————. *The Renewal of Literature: Emersonian Reflections.* New York: Random House, 1987.

————. *Robert Frost: The Work of Knowing.* New York: Oxford University Press, 1977.

Pratt, Mary Louise. "Linguistic Utopias." In *The Linguistics of Writing: Arguments Between Language and Literature,* ed. Nigel Fabb, Derek Attridge, and Colin MacCabe, 48–66. New York: Methuen, 1987.

————. *Toward a Speech Act Theory of Literary Discourse.* Bloomington: Indiana University Press, 1977.

Pryse, Marjorie, and Hortense Spillers, eds. *Conjuring: Black Women, Fiction, and Literary Tradition.* Bloomington: Indiana University Press, 1985.

Quackenbos, George P. *Advanced Course of Composition and Rhetoric.* 1854. New York: D. Appleton, 1867.

————. *First Lessons in Composition.* 1851. New York: D. Appleton, 1859.

Queneau, Raymond. *Exercises in Style.* New York: New Directions, 1981.

Ramey, A. R. *Art and Principles of Writing.* Chicago: J. B. Lippincott, 1936.

Rankin, Elizabeth D. "Revitalizing Style: Toward a New Theory and Pedagogy." *Freshman English News* 14 (1985): 8–13.

Reddy, Michael J. "The Conduit Metaphor: A Case of Frame Conflict in Our Language About Language." In *Metaphor and Thought,* ed. Andrew Ortony, 164–201. 2nd ed. Cambridge: Cambridge University Press, 1993.

Rhetorica ad Herennium. In *Cicero in Twenty-Eight Volumes,* ed. and trans. Harry Caplan. Cambridge, Mass.: Harvard University Press, 1968.

Richards, I. A. *Interpretation in Teaching.* New York: Harcourt, Brace, 1938.

————. *The Philosophy of Rhetoric.* Oxford: Oxford University Press, 1936.

Ricks, Christopher. "The Pursuit of Metaphor." In *What's Happened to the Humanities?,* ed. Alvin Kernan, 179–97. Princeton, N.J.: Princeton University Press, 1997.

Ricoeur, Paul. "The Metaphorical Process as Cognition, Imagination, and Feeling." In *On Metaphor,* ed. Sheldon Sacks, 141–57. Chicago: University of Chicago Press, 1979.

————. *The Rule of Metaphor.* Trans. Robert Czerny, with Kathleen McLaughlin and John Costello, S.J. Toronto: University of Toronto Press, 1977.

Rodriguez, Richard. *Hunger of Memory.* New York: Bantam, 1982.

Roth, Robert. "The Evolving Audience: Alternatives to Audience Accommodation." *College Composition and Communication* 38 (1987): 47–55.

Rothwell, Kenneth S. *Questions of Rhetoric and Usage.* Boston: Little, Brown, 1971.

Salvatori, Mariolina. "Italo Calvino's *If on a Winter's Night a Traveler:* Writer's Authority, Reader's Autonomy." *Contemporary Literature* 27 (1986): 182–212.

———. "Reading and Writing a Text: Correlations Between Reading and Writing." *College English* 45 (1983): 657–66.

Scholes, Robert. *Textual Power: Literary Theory and the Teaching of English.* New Haven: Yale University Press, 1985.

Scholes, Robert, Nancy R. Comley, and Gregory L. Ulmer. *Text Book: An Introduction to Literary Language.* New York: St. Martin's Press, 1995.

Schor, Sandra. "Reclaiming Digression." In *Audits of Meaning: A Festschrift in Honor of Ann E. Berthoff,* ed. Louise Smith, 238–47. Portsmouth, N.H.: Boynton/Cook, 1988.

Schuster, Charles. "Mikhail Bakhtin as Rhetorical Theorist." *College English* 47 (1985): 594–607.

Searle, John R. "Metaphor." In *Metaphor and Thought,* ed. Andrew Ortony, 83–111. 2nd ed. Cambridge: Cambridge University Press, 1993.

———. *Speech Acts: An Essay in the Philosophy of Language.* Cambridge: Cambridge University Press, 1969.

Shapiro, Michael, and Marianne Shapiro. *Figuration in Verbal Art.* Princeton, N.J.: Princeton University Press, 1988.

Shibles, Warren. *Metaphor: An Annotated Bibliography and History.* Whitewater, Wis.: Language Press, 1971.

Silverman, Jay, Elaine Hughes, and Diana Roberts Wienbroer. *Rules of Thumb: A Guide for Writers.* New York: McGraw-Hill, 1990.

Slevin, James F. "Connecting English Studies." *College English* 48 (1986): 543–50.

———. "Genre Theory, Academic Discourse, and Writing Within Disciplines." In *Audits of Meaning: A Festschrift in Honor of Ann E. Berthoff,* ed. Louise Smith, 3–16. Portsmouth, N.H.: Boynton/Cook, 1988.

Smith, Barbara Herrnstein. *On the Margins of Discourse.* Chicago: University of Chicago Press, 1978.

Smith, Louise. "Enigma Variations: Reading and Writing Through Metaphor." In *Only Connect: Uniting Reading and Writing,* ed. Thomas Newkirk. Upper Montclair, N.J.: Boynton/Cook, 1986.

Sontag, Susan. "On Style." *Against Interpretation,* 15–36. New York: Dell, 1981.

Spellmeyer, Kurt. *Common Ground: Dialogue, Understanding, and the Teaching of Composition.* Englewood Cliffs, N.J.: Prentice Hall, 1993.

Squires, Radcliffe. *The Major Themes of Robert Frost.* Ann Arbor, Mich.: University of Michigan Press, 1963.

Stallybrass, Peter, and Allon White. *The Politics and Poetics of Transgression.* London: Methuen, 1986.

Staten, Harry. "Ethnic Authenticity, Class, and Autobiography: The Case of *Hunger of Memory.*" *PMLA* 113 (1998): 103–16.

Stein, William Bysshe. "'After Apple-Picking': Echoic Parody." *The University Review* 25 (1969): 301–05.

Steinberg, Erwin R. "Imaginative Literature in Composition Classrooms?" *College English* 57 (1995): 266–80.

Stevens, Wallace. "The Motive for Metaphor." *The Collected Poems,* 288. New York: Randon House, 1982.

Stewart, Donald. "What Is an English Major, and What Should It Be?" *College Composition and Communication* 40 (1989): 188–202.

Strickland, Geoffrey. *Structuralism or Criticism?* Cambridge: Cambridge University Press, 1981.

Stuckey, J. Elspeth. *The Violence of Literacy.* Portsmouth, N.H.: Boynton/ Cook, 1991.

Summerfield, Geoffrey. "Luminous Realms of Jupiter, or: When A Student Writes, Who Is Writing?" Unpublished essay.

Summerfield, Judith. "Is There a Life in This Text? Reimagining Narrative." In *Writing Theory and Critical Theory,* ed. John Clifford and John Schilb, 179–94. New York: Modern Language Association, 1994.

———. "Principles for Propagation: On Narrative and Argument." In *Argument Revisited; Argument Redefined: Negotiating Meaning in the Composition Classroom,* ed. Barbara Emmel, Paula Resch, and Deborah Tenney, 153–80. Thousand Oaks, Calif.: Sage Publications, 1996.

Summerfield, Judith, and Geoffrey Summerfield. *Frames of Mind: A Course in Composition.* New York: Random House, 1986.

———. *Texts and Contexts: A Contribution to the Theory and Practice of Teaching Composition.* New York: Random House, 1986.

Tate, Gary. "Notes on the Dying of a Conversation." *College English* 57 (1995): 303–09.

———. "A Place for Literature in Freshman Composition." *College English* 55 (1993): 317–21.

Tobin, Lad. "Bridging Gaps: Analyzing Our Students' Metaphors for Composing." *College Composition and Communication* 40 (1989): 444–58.

Tompkins, Jane. "Pedagogy of the Distressed." *College English* 52 (1990): 653–60.

Troyka, Lynn Quitman, with Judith A. Stanford, Ann B. Dobie, and Emily R. Gordon. *Simon and Schuster Handbook for Writers.* 4th ed. Upper Saddle River, N.J.: Prentice-Hall, 1996.

Van Noppen, J. P., S. de Knop, and R. Jongen. *Metaphor: A Bibliography of Post–1970 Publications*. Amsterdam: J. Benjamins, 1985.

Van Noppen, J. P., and Edith Hols. *Metaphor II: A Classified Bibliography of Publications 1985–1990*. Amsterdam: J. Benjamins, 1990.

Waller, Gary. "Polylogue: Reading, Writing, and the Structure of Doctoral Study." In *The Future of Doctoral Studies in English,* ed. Andrea Lunsford, Helene Moglin, and James F. Slevin, 111–20. New York: Modern Language Association, 1989.

Waller, Gary, Kathleen McCormick, and Lois Josephs Fowler. *The Lexington Introduction to Literature*. Lexington, Mass.: D. C. Heath, 1987.

Whately, Richard. *Elements of Rhetoric*. 1828. New York: Harper, 1852.

White, E. B. "Once More to the Lake." In *The Norton Reader,* ed. Arthur M. Eastman, 49–54. New York: Norton, 1977.

White, Roger M. *The Structure of Metaphor: The Way the Language of Metaphor Works*. London: Blackwell, 1996.

Whitman, Walt. "Song of Myself." *Leaves of Grass,* 188–247. 1855. New York: Vintage, 1992.

Willard, Samuel. *Rhetoric, or The Principles of Elocution and Rhetorical Composition*. Boston: Leonard C. Bowles, 1830.

Williams, William. *Composition and Rhetoric by Practice*. 1888. Boston: D. C. Heath, 1889.

Winterowd, W. Ross. *The Contemporary Writer: A Practical Rhetoric*. 2nd ed. New York: Harcourt Brace Jovanovich, 1981.

Young, Art. "Rebuilding Community in the English Department." *Profession 84,* 24–32.

Zavarzadeh, Mas'ud. "Theory as Resistance." In *Pedagogy Is Politics,* ed. Maria-Regina Kecht, 25–47. Urbana, Ill.: University of Illinois Press, 1991.

INDEX